ANALYZING ELECTORAL HISTORY

SAGE FOCUS EDITIONS

ANALYZING
ELECTORAL HISTORY
A Guide to the Study of
American Voter Behavior

edited by
JEROME M. CLUBB
WILLIAM H. FLANIGAN
NANCY H. ZINGALE

 SAGE PUBLICATIONS   Beverly Hills   London

To the memory of Angus Campbell

For information address:

SAGE Publications, Inc.
275 South Beverly Drive
Beverly Hills, California 90212

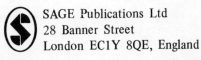

SAGE Publications Ltd
28 Banner Street
London EC1Y 8QE, England

Printed in the United States of America

Library of Congress Cataloging in Publication Data

Main entry under title:

Analyzing electoral history.

    (Sage focus editions ; 33)
    Includes bibliographical references and index.
    1. Voting research--United States--Addresses, essays, lectures. 2. Elections--United States--History--Addresses, essays, lectures. I. Clubb, Jerome M., 1928-
II. Flanigan, William H. III. Zingale, Nancy H.
IV. Series.
JK1967.A84   324.973092   81-9162
ISBN 0-8039-1673-6   AACR2
ISBN 0-8039-1674-4 (pbk.)

FIRST PRINTING

CONTENTS

INTRODUCTION

Since the late 1950s, interest has increased among historians, political scientists, and other social scientists in the systematic analysis of American elections past and present. On the one hand, historians have become increasingly concerned with the regularities that may exist in political behavior across the entire sweep of the American past and with the social science techniques that can be used to identify them and verify their existence. On the other hand, social scientists are increasingly interested in the dynamics of the phenomena they study and convinced of the utility of multiplying the available cases for analysis by employing historical instances. This collection of essays is not intended to argue for the desirability of this disciplinary convergence; admirable arguments to this effect are provided elsewhere, and we suppose that most readers of this volume will already be among the converted.[1] Rather, we have tried to provide a series of essays to serve as a reference guide and a source of information for scholars embarking upon or involved in research based upon historical aggregate election, social, economic, and demographic data. Our purpose in this introduction is to point out some of the assumptions and orientations which underlie our approach to research and analysis employing such data.

Systematic analysis of quantitative historical data has served a variety of scholarly purposes. For some, it is a more sophisticated means to pursue traditional goals of historiography—a more exact method for reconstructing past events, a means to avoid the biased perspectives that result from reliance upon traditional source materials for historical inquiry, or a way of providing greater detail in the description and interpretation of particular cases that are themselves unique but intrinsically interesting or important. For others, these data provide an opportunity to explore similarities and, rather than to document uniqueness, to identify regularities in the political behavior of elites and masses, to test hypotheses about general relationships among relevant variables, and to specify the conditions in time and space under which such generalizations hold. While both the ideographic and nomothetic approaches have produced valuable results, our orientation is decidedly toward the latter, toward the development of laws or generalizations aimed at describing, explaining, and predicting political behavior.

In this enterprise, historical quantitative data offer important benefits and opportunities. For the social scientist working with data from the contemporary era, critical variables are often unavailable for inclusion in analytical models simply because they are constant during the period under study. The results of research thus run the risk of being time-bound. Moreover, if the previously constant conditions begin to change, predictive anomalies may result that cannot be accounted for by the existing theory. Contextual factors—such as legal requirements governing the conduct of elections, societal educational levels, and the characteristics of the mass communications systems—are among those in which there is little or no variation in the contemporary United States. Hence, the effects of factors such as these cannot be adequately diagnosed if only data for the contemporary period are relied upon.

Historical analysis affords an opportunity to cope with these difficulties in much the same fashion as do cross-national comparisons. It enables the investigator to compare cases which have a range of characteristics in common, but which also differ in other crucial aspects. In a very real sense, theory can only be advanced to the degree that we develop generalizations about behavior that hold in varying contexts or, alternatively, that specify the conditions under which the contextual factors interact with and modify particular relationships that obtain in other situations. Viewed in these terms, historically oriented research, like other forms of comparative inquiry, is an integral part of the general social scientific enterprise and necessary to the development of sound theory.

This is not to say that all researchers who investigate behavioral processes and phenomena in historical contexts must constantly work at a high level of theoretical abstraction. Quite the contrary, studies of limited scope—even the oft-maligned case study—are valuable in offering the raw materials to be used in supporting or refuting theory or in developing inductively the hypotheses that may give rise to new theories. It is important to stress, however, that theory and theorizing are integral parts of all research whether historical or contemporary in immediate focus. We would also argue the need for erasing the dichotomy between past and present—or between historian and social scientist—and to recognize the opportunities provided by a mode of inquiry in which, to borrow Charles Tilly's phrase, "situations, persons, or events plucked from the past or the present serve as tests of general statements about social life."[2]

The focus of the essays included in this volume is, in certain respects, relatively narrow. They are concerned primarily with the research possibilities and problems presented by electoral, social, economic, and demographic data aggregated to the levels of geographic units—the nation, states, congressional districts, counties, or other smaller units. Little attention is devoted to the opportunities presented by data collected through sample surveys—or public opinion polls, to use a less accurate but perhaps more familiar term. These opportunities are indeed substantial for investigation of the contemporary period, and the theoretical interplay between research employing data from sample surveys and that based upon data of other forms is of major importance. Similarly, data at the individual level from such sources as poll books and directories are touched upon only in passing, although such data can sometimes be used to shed light on the electoral politics of even the distant past.

For the most part, however, the social scientist interested in any period before the 1950s, and certainly before the 1930s, or interested in testing generalizations about the full range of American electoral history, is compelled to place primary reliance upon aggregated data. Often this reliance is treated as a rather bad second choice. Bereft of data at the individual level, the analyst attempts to answer the same kind of research questions that might be asked of sample survey data. Witness to this are the techniques advertised as allowing inferences about individual behavior from aggregated data while avoiding the "ecological fallacy."

While a preference for individual data is often appropriate, this attitude ignores the opportunities for conceptualizations based upon aggregate units. The outcome of an election is itself an aggregate concept, not only determining the winners and the losers but also offering to victorious candidates their only firm mandate for governing, while administering a rebuke to their opponents. Thus, for any research concerned with the link between the popular will and the behavior of policy-making elites, the aggregate electorate is not only an acceptable unit of analysis but a preferable one. Electoral competitiveness is another concept that has meaning only as a property of an aggregate unit. Other concepts, such as voter turnout and the expected vote, can apply to either individuals or aggregate units, and in their aggregate form have clear applications as variables with the potential for explaining the behavior and performance of the political system.

The opportunities for research employing historical cases and the utility of aggregate concepts in electoral analysis point to a central concern underlying the selection of essays in this volume: the need for explicit conceptualization of the factors included in the analysis and the further and equally important need for care in operationalizing these concepts. Too often, analysts accept data at face value as meeting whatever substantive requirements they have in mind without examining and critically evaluating the linkage between available data and conceptualization.

These issues are of critical importance to the entire research process and require elaboration. Although often neglected, explicit conceptualization and theory are central to research in the social sciences, both as goals of inquiry and as tools of analysis. In any empirical research, a theory or conceptualization is employed which specifies the critical elements of the phenomenon under study and which describes the relationships among those elements. The theory or conceptualization is an abstraction, an intellectual construct, derived from intuition or from a broader theory or conceptual framework. The elements and relationships which it specifies are also nonempirical concepts, such as partisan identification, policy preference, social status, wealth, religious attitudes, and the like. These conceptualizations, or models, of reality can be manipulated in purely logical ways or, if they can be stated in sufficiently formal terms, they also can be manipulated through mathematical operations.

Logical and mathematical manipulation of conceptual formulations can serve as tests of their internal consistency and provide a means to derive their implications. To employ such formulations in empirical research designed to test their conformity to reality requires additional operations. A complex process of translation is required which explicitly defines these concepts in terms of particular data and particular arithmetic and statistical operations. In effect, an "analytic model" is created in which particular empirical data and operations are intended to correspond with the nonempirical concepts and relationships that are components of the conceptualization. Manipulation of the data then provides a basis for inferences about the phenomenon or process of concern and a means to test the adequacy of the conceptualization in terms of the presence or absence of hypothesized relationships. It is in this sense that Alfred Marshall described economic theory as "not a body of concrete truth, but an engine for the discovery of concrete truth,"[3] and the statement is equally applicable to conceptualizations and theories in the area of political behavior.

Problems encountered in translating nonempirical concepts into empirical data and arithmetic and statistical operations are of critical importance in all social scientific research and, indeed, in scientific research more generally. The process of translation itself is inevitably imperfect and the precision of correspondence between empirical data and nonempirical concepts can probably never be known with certainty. Blalock states this set of problems in the following way:

> *There appears to be an inherent gap between the languages of theory and research* which can never be bridged in a completely satisfactory way. One *thinks* in terms of a theoretical language that contains notions such as causes, forces, systems and properties. But one's

tests are made in terms of covariations, operations and pointer readings. Although a concept such as "mass" may be conceived theoretically or metaphysically as a property, it is only a pious opinion, in Eddington's words, that mass as a property is equivalent to mass as inferred from pointer readings [Emphasis in original].[4]

Viewed in these terms, the data and quantitative operations of social scientists—whether concerned with the past or the present—are at best indicators of concepts; their validity depends upon particular operational definitions of concepts; and their use requires explicit theories, conceptualizations, and theorizing about underlying reality. Without minimizing the value of exploratory data analysis, it is worth noting that from this perspective quantification can be seen as the end product of conceptualization and theorizing rather than its beginning.[5]

This perspective also allows us to cast the characteristics of historical source materials and the research problems which they present in a somewhat different light. Source materials for the study of historical voting behavior and its determinants are fragmentary and inadequate; critical conceptual variables are frequently unmeasured; the available units of analysis are often inappropriate to the substantive questions of interest; the analytic methods commonly employed are of questionable adequacy in terms of these characteristics; and the data are marred by random error and bias of unknown magnitude and direction. The list could be extended almost indefinitely.

These characteristics impinge directly upon and blur substantive questions. To what degree, for example, are the apparently high levels of voter participation in the latter nineteenth century merely the product of an inflated vote count produced by corruption? To what degree are they a reflection of systematic undercounts of the national population and hence underestimation of the size of the eligible electorate? Is the highly correlated nature of the partisan distribution of the vote from one election and office to the next in the nineteenth and much of the twentieth century to be taken as an indication of highly stable attitudinal identifications with the parties? Is it to be seen instead as only one more example of the ecological fallacy? Or is it to be seen as a product of institutional factors governing electoral participation?

For a number of purposes, it is useful to see these characteristics of historical source materials as reducing to matters of specification and measurement. Stated in general terms, the researcher concerned with historical processes often encounters difficulty in developing analytic models that involve units of analysis that are appropriate to the research questions of concern and which include reasonably accurate and valid empirical measures of all relevant conceptual variables. Viewed in these terms, difficulties encountered in quantitative historical research can be seen as integrally related to the specification and measurement problems encountered in all of the social sciences. Thus, in addressing these issues, a large methodological literature drawn from the various social sciences can be brought to bear.

Specification error arises when, either through neglect or because of lack of appropriate data, empirical measures of relevant conceptual variables are not brought directly into analytic models. The consequences are several: The effects of these missing variables are not estimated, the explanatory utility of the model is reduced, the effects of variables that are included in the model may be misestimated, and erroneous conclusions may result. One possible example of these difficulties is provided by what is often referred to as the ethnocultural interpretation of nineteenth century American electoral politics. This interpretation views the voting behavior of the nineteenth century electorate as strongly related to the ethnic and cultural (primarily religious) divisions and groups of the times. In general, however, data bearing upon the distribution of wealth, income, and property ownership in all of their various dimensions are difficult to find for much of the nineteenth century. Thus the question becomes whether these factors have been adequately specified in the analytic formulations that underlie the ethnocultural interpretation and whether, as a consequence, the effects of ethnocultural factors have been misestimated.[6]

As will be readily recognized, issues of this sort are virtually endemic in research into historical voting behavior, as well as most other areas of systematic, quantitative historical inquiry. Generally speaking, the more remote the time period, the greater the gravity of these issues. The most consistent and comprehensive source of data bearing upon the social and economic characteristics of the national population is the reports from the censuses of the United States. The earlier censuses collected only limited information, which was often not tabulated and reported in particularly elaborate ways. With the passage of time, the censuses became progressively more elaborate and the data which they provided more abundant. At best, however, data directly relevant to what now appear to be critical explanatory factors were often not collected or, in some cases, not tabulated and reported for the nineteenth century and, for that matter, the twentieth. The consequence is, of course, that the risk of misspecifying analytic models of historical processes is consistently high.

Fortunately, there are partial remedies for difficulties of this sort. There is a growing technical literature concerned with these issues. Moreover, while it is not possible to conduct new censuses or surveys of historical populations, the range of available data can be expanded. There are, for example, a substantial number of state censuses, often conducted between the decennial national censuses, which sometimes provide systematic information bearing upon characteristics of the population that were not included in the national censuses. As Burnham notes in Chapter 2 of this volume, a variety of other state, local, and, more occasionally, national sources yield important systematic information bearing upon the characteristics of the population. A signal advantage of the national censuses, however, is their comprehensive scope. As attention is shifted to state and local sources (which are often only occasional and not available for all areas of the nation), questions of representativeness inevitably arise.

The primary means to cope with specification issues of this sort is of a different order. These issues dictate careful and more subtle conceptualizations of historical processes. Without such conceptualizations, these problems cannot be identified, the need for additional data diagnosed, technical remedies invoked, or the conditional nature of research findings recognized.

Issues of specification such as these are, of course, part and parcel of the more general problem of measurement, which is common in one way or another to all of the social sciences. For present purposes, measurement problems can be divided into two forms. One form is theoretical in nature and arises when empirical indicators are employed which are not valid measures of the conceptual variables of concern. A second form involves inaccuracies in data which result from the introduction of erroneous values through misenumeration, mistabulation, falsification, inaccurate recording, and the like.

Obviously, historical source material—and virtually all data employed in the social sciences—are marred by measurement error of both forms. Because historical data are limited, empirical variables must be employed which are at best highly imperfect measures of conceptual or theoretical variables. Data on the religious affiliations of the nineteenth century population illustrate the point. The available data are frequently based upon counts of seats in churches or the reports of ministers or other religious officials rather than upon direct enumeration of the population. Such data for obvious reasons do not differentiate between church attendance, church membership, or nominal affiliation.[7] In other words, these data taken alone do not provide valid measures of religious practices or of the strength and intensity of religious convictions and identifications. Hence, they do not provide a valid indication of the likelihood that religious views, tenets and group relations would influence attitudes and practices in other areas of life.

Data on economic status are similarly limited. For the nineteenth century and into the twentieth, the most commonly and comprehensively available economic data concern the size and value of property holdings, for the most part in the form of farms. Information on income from wages, liquid assets, and property of other forms is less common. Thus, the most generally available data provide at best a highly imperfect measure of the economic conditions of the population.

Voting returns, in many respects the most basic data for research into historical electoral processes, provide a further illustration of these issues. Data from this source are frequently employed in research into partisan attitudes, policy preferences, and reactions to candidates and public issues of individuals and groups in past elections. However, these data cannot be seen as analogues to the data provided by contemporary sample surveys, which are designed to diagnose the political orientations, preferences, interests, and attitudes that underlie and determine individual decisions to vote for one party or candidate or another. Voting returns, in contrast, record the end product of this individual decision-making process, the actual vote cast. To employ these data to diagnose voter attitudes, preferences, and interests involves a complex inferential process. That process must draw upon information in addition to the voting returns themselves and, of greater importance, upon assumptions, conceptual frameworks, or theories about the nature of the decision-making process that underlies actual voting behavior.

The partial remedies for this situation are for the most part obvious. Additional data from diverse sources can be collected. Tax and court records, for example, often provide information on property holdings and other assets, and other sources sometimes provide a basis for estimating income from wages. However, such sources are usually not comprehensive, and questions of representativeness will often arise. Here again, conceptualization is of central importance. The underlying question concerns the ways in which available empirical variables relate to conceptual variables of concern. In effect, "auxiliary theories" are involved which describe the nature of these relationships and the degree to which empirical variables do or do not constitute valid measures of conceptual variables.[8] As is discussed in Chapter 7, this conceptualizing and theorizing process can provide a basis for the construction of indices which reduce measurement error of this form.

For present purposes, the second form of measurement error can also be divided into two categories. One of these is simple random error introduced by misrecording, miscounting, and other forms of inaccuracy. In this case, recorded values are equally likely to be higher or lower than the true values. In contrast, error can introduce bias into data and in this case, recorded values tend to be systematically higher (or lower) than the true values. While historical data are likely to be marred by both of these types of error, the analytic consequences are quite different. Random error works to mask and reduce the strength of statistical relations between empirical variables. If one knew or could reasonably assume that only random error was present in data, one could also conclude that the true relation between variables was likely to be stronger than those observed through statistical analysis. Put somewhat differently, less strenuous levels of significance could be employed in assessing observed statistical relationships.

The effect of bias, in contrast, is likely to lead to observation of statistical relationships that are spurious. That is, the systematic nature of this type of error in a variable can itself create a statistical relationship with other variables. Obviously if one knows that bias is present and can reasonably assume its direction, compensatory steps can be taken, if only by discounting particular observed statistical relationships. If both the direction and magnitude of bias are known or can be reasonably assumed, then at least partial corrective steps can be taken. An example of the latter case is discussed by Shortridge in Chapter 5.

The essays included in this volume are concerned with methodological and conceptual issues and problems such as these. Thus, an initial section deals with sources of data relevant to the study of historical voting behavior, with the essays commenting on the strengths and limitations of the data which these sources provide. A second section focuses on what might be called problems of interpretation. Here the essays consider the possible distorting effects of past political corruption on the data provided by historical voting records; certain categories of error characteristic of data from historical censuses of the United States; the characteristics of the various subunits into which the United States has been divided historically and for which voting returns and social and economic data have been most consistently recorded; and patterns of population change and their consequences for research into historical voting behavior. Two chapters in the final section address quantitative analytic methods for the study of historical voting behavior. The third is concerned with the problems of employing aggregated data to infer individual-level relations.

We do not pretend that this volume addresses in comprehensive fashion all of the many difficulties confronted in systematic quantitative investigation of historical voting behavior and its correlates. Even less do we, or the contributing authors, pretend to provide categorical solutions for the problems that are addressed. Rather, the volume attempts to call attention to the nature and dimensions of some of the many perils and pitfalls in the study of electoral history and to suggest some possible routes to partial solutions.

If pressed, we would be forced to concede that many of the problems confronted in research into historical voting behavior, including many of those explored in this volume, are not subject to complete and final solution. In the most basic sense, the fundamental problem is that historical sources are fragmentary and partial. There is no opportunity to interview the dead or to return and observe long past situations. Information that was never recorded cannot be created, and information that was once recorded but since destroyed cannot be recreated. The researcher must make do with the sources that exist.

However, our conclusions are not pessimistic. It may be that the aspirations of researchers must be more modest. There are certainly research questions that cannot be answered. Even so, problems confronted in the conduct of historical research can be reduced through improved methodological training and methodological innovation. More and better data can be collected. Research into the nature of historical records to assess error rates and to identify bias can also reduce difficulties or at least contribute to better diagnoses of their consequences. If difficulties such as those considered in this volume are not subject to total solution, they can be partially circumvented by adherence to sound principles of research design and analysis. And certainly these difficulties can be recognized; they will not go away simply because they are ignored.

Above all, in our opinion, investigation of historical phenomena requires strong theory and the use of explicit and controlled assumptions. Contrary to an opinion often asserted by many historians, inquiry into the past cannot be atheoretical. In our view, historical inquiry must in the long run be the most theoretical of the social sciences.

NOTES

1. Lee Benson, "Research Problems in American Political Historiography," in Mirra Komarovsky, *Common Frontiers of the Social Sciences* (Glencoe, IL: The Free Press, 1957); Richard Jensen, "American Election Analysis: A Case History of Methodological Diffusion," and "History and the Political Scientist," in Seymour Martin Lipset (ed.) *Politics and the Social Sciences* (New York: Oxford University Press, 1969); Jerome M. Clubb and Allan G. Bogue, "History, Quantification, and the Social Sciences," and Bogue et al., "The New Political History," *American Behavioral Scientist*, 21 (November/December 1977); and Joel H. Silbey, Allan G. Bogue, and William H. Flanigan (eds.) *The History of American Electoral Behavior* (Princeton: Princeton University Press, 1978).

2. Charles Tilly, "Quantification in History As Seen from France," in Val R. Lorwin and Jacob M. Price (eds.) *The Dimensions of the Past: Materials, Problems, and Opportunities for Quantitative Work in History* (New Haven: Yale University Press, 1972), 108.

3. Quoted in Peter D. McClelland, *Causal Explanation and Model Building in History, Economics and the New Economic History* (Ithaca, NY: Cornell University Press, 1975), 105.

4. Hubert M. Blalock, Jr., *Causal Inferences in Nonexperimental Research* (Chapel Hill, NC: University of North Carolina Press, 1961), 5-6.

5. See in this respect Arthur L. Stinchcombe, *Theoretical Methods in Social History* (New York: Academic Press, 1978), 4-7.

6. James E. Wright, "The Ethnocultural Model of Voting," *American Behavioral Scientist* 16 (May/June 1973), passim.

7. *Ibid.*

8. Hubert M. Blalock, Jr., "The Measurement Problems: A Gap Between the Language of Theory and Research," in Hubert M. Blalock, Jr. and Ann B. Blalock (eds.) *Methodology in Social Research* (New York: McGraw-Hill, 1968), passim.

PART I
FINDING DATA ON AMERICAN ELECTIONS

The two chapters in this section are concerned with sources of data for the study of popular voting behavior in historical contexts. Very extensive collections of voting returns and social and economic data are available in highly usable form. Numerous compendia have been published and are to be found in most libraries. Large collections of relevant data are also available in readily usable computer-readable form. These compendia and collections of voting returns tend to concentrate, however, on elections to national and major state offices, and they constitute only a small proportion of the data available in other published and unpublished sources. Returns for elections to numerous other offices, often at low levels of aggregation, can be found in a variety of scattered sources, although locating these sources often requires considerable effort.

The initial chapter in this section is primarily concerned with the extensive computer-readable data holdings of the Inter-university Consortium for Political and Social Research (ICPSR). In this discussion, emphasis is placed upon ICPSR collections of historical voting returns as well as historical social, economic, and related political data. These collections are the product of a large-scale and continuing collaborative and multidisciplinary effort which has now extended for over a decade and a half. In this chapter, somewhat more limited attention is also given to the extensive bodies of data from sample surveys held and disseminated by the ICPSR, the Roper Center for Public Opinion Research, and the Louis Harris Data Center. Data of this sort are available for the years since the 1930s and in more sophisticated form for the years since the early 1950s. These data constitute a rich and increasingly valuable resource for the study of recent electoral history.

Despite their extent and accessibility, ICPSR historical data holdings constitute only a small portion of the historical data that are available for the study of popular voting behavior and processes, as Burnham makes clear in Chapter 2. This chapter provides an extended list of published sources of election returns and, to a lesser extent, sources of data bearing upon the social, economic, and demographic characteristics of the population. The sources which Burnham lists have the advantage of providing data for elections to numerous offices in addition to national and major state offices. Data provided by these sources also are often available for a variety of subunits in addition to states, counties and congressional districts. As Burnham makes clear, the list of sources which he provides is not comprehensive. Newspapers, archival, and other unpublished materials constitute further, extensive sources of relevant data. It would, however, be impossible to provide a comprehensive list of such sources in anything approaching brief space.

Neither chapter in this section attempts to provide an extended treatment of sources of data bearing upon the social and economic characteristics of the population. To do so would require space much beyond the present volume. Three readily available sources of information on these materials can be mentioned here. Henry J. Dubester has provided a comprehensive catalog of the publications of the United States Bureau of the Census and its predecessor agencies from 1790 through 1945 and a similar catalog of state census publications.[1] *The Historical Statistics of the United States* constitutes not only an important source of relevant data, but its various introductory essays also provide a wide range of information bearing upon sources of relevant social, economic, and demographic data.[2] Finally, the numerous working papers and special studies published through the years by the Bureau of the Census and its predecessor agencies provide a wealth of information bearing upon the conduct of national censuses and the strengths and limitations of the data which they provide.

NOTES

1. Henry J. Dubester, *Catalog of United States Census Publications, 1790-1945* (Washington, DC: Government Printing Office, 1950); and *State Censuses: An Annotated Bibliography of Censuses of Population Taken After the Year 1790 by States and Territories of the United States* (Washington, DC: Government Printing Office, 1948).

2. Bureau of the Census, *Historical Statistics of the United States: Colonial Times to 1970* (Washington, DC: Government Printing Office, 1975).

1

COMPUTER-READABLE DATA SOURCES

Michael W. Traugott
Jerome M. Clubb
Erik W. Austin

This chapter describes in summary terms data resources for the study of American electoral behavior and related political processes that are available in computer-readable form. An initial section is concerned with data in this form that span much of the sweep of American history. A second and briefer section describes data that are pertinent to more recent years. Taken together, these resources reflect significant change in the technology of political research and, indeed, of social research more generally. Their availability reflects, moreover, the development of more cooperative and cumulative approaches to research.

It is commonplace to observe that the advent of computer technology has led to radical change in the conduct of research in the social sciences. Research into mass political behavior in historical and contemporary contexts is no exception to this generalization. It is now possible to routinely manipulate massive bodies of data using highly complex statistical procedures in a manner that would be virtually unimaginable if human labor alone could be employed. Hence, individual researchers can now carry out research of a scope, magnitude, and complexity that would have been impossible a few short decades ago.

The impact of computer technology upon research in the social sciences, moreover, is continuing. Steady and continuing decline in the costs of computational equipment is rapidly increasing the number of researchers who have effective access to these resources. This cost decline has also reduced the premium that was once placed upon machine efficiency. The consequence is that a substantially broadened and more diverse range of applications has become feasible. These same considerations make it feasible to emphasize ease of human use at the cost of machine efficiency. Computer systems can now be designed that allow researchers to make effective use of computational resources without the heavy investment in technical training that was once required. Here again, the result is to bring computational facilities within the reach of increasing numbers of researchers for increasingly diverse applications.

Computer technology has contributed in still other ways to change in the style of work and, indeed, the ethics of social research. While computers allow manipulation and analysis of very large collections of complex research data, the costs of data collection and of preparing data for machine analysis remain high. Beginning particularly in the 1960s it was increasingly recognized that the research value of substantial collections of computer-readable data was rarely if ever exhausted by a single researcher or research group. The cumulative value of data collections was also recognized. That is, it was recognized that extant data collections gain added value as new data collections are created; comparisons become possible and the combination of data collections serves research values beyond those contemplated by original data collectors.

Recognition of the importance of "secondary analysis" and of the scientific values of replication and verification of research findings has led to the gradual development of an ethic of data sharing. Rather than hoarding data collections against all comers, increasing emphasis has been placed upon providing generalized access by other scholars to data collections which individual scholars and research groups had created in the course of their research. This changing emphasis has led to a variety of large-scale collaborative data collection efforts. It has led as well to the development of a number of data repositories, often referred to as social science data archives, which function to preserve and provide access to collections of computer-readable data for research in the various disciplines of the social sciences.

This chapter focuses upon the holdings of three repositories of computer-readable research data, the Inter-university Consortium for Political and Social Research (ICPSR), the Roper Center for Public Opinion Research, and the Louis Harris Data Center. While all three repositories are sources of data pertinent to research in diverse areas of the social sciences, they are also major resources for the study of American electoral behavior and related political processes. The data holdings of both the Roper Center and the Louis Harris Center are primarily pertinent to the contemporary period; those of ICPSR include materials pertinent to the full sweep of the history of the nation. Thus, primary emphasis is placed upon the latter organization.

HISTORICAL DATA AT ICPSR

Beginning in the mid 1960s, the confluence of several disciplinary interests resulted in a major project, under the auspices of the ICPSR, to collect and convert to readily usable computer-readable form basic data for quantitative research in American political history. Three categories of data constituted the core focus of the project. The first of these was historical voting returns for elections to major offices beginning in 1824. The second data category was matching social and economic data drawn primarily from the published reports of the 1790 and subsequent censuses of the United States. The third was comprehensive roll call voting records for the United States Congress, beginning with the First Congress which convened in 1789.[1]

Since the completion of the initial work of collecting and processing the historical materials, the ICPSR has maintained the several collections by adding current data. Several additional collections of computer-readable historical data have also been added to the ICPSR repository, and through a subsequent project, the collection of historical election returns was extended to include data for elections prior to 1824. As a consequence, the ICPSR "Historical Archive" now includes extensive arrays of basic data for the study of American political processes from the founding of the nation to the present.

The ICPSR holdings of historical data, along with numerous and diverse additional data collections, are publicly available for research and instructional applications.[2] Data can be supplied either as subsets or as entire data collections in readily usable computer-readable form suitable to the technical requirements of diverse computational systems. The ICPSR is, however, a membership organization with its headquarters and central staff located in the Institute for Social Research of The University of Michigan. The current membership includes some 240 colleges and universities in the United States and a dozen other nations. Data and related services and resources are supplied to member institutions without charge, beyond an annual institutional membership fee. A charge is assessed, however, in supplying data to individuals at institutions not affiliated with the ICPSR.

HISTORICAL ELECTION RETURNS

The core collection of popular voting data includes returns from elections to the offices of President, Governor, Senator (after the institution of direct election), and Representative in Congress. As originally conceived, the collection was to include returns for these offices for elections, general as well as special interim elections, from 1824 through the most recent elections. In 1968 and continuing thereafter, returns for a second major state office (usually Secretary of State or Attorney General) were systematically included in the collection as were comprehensive returns for statewide referenda, initiatives, and other forms for expression of popular preferences on public policy issues. As noted above, the collection was also extended to include voting returns for presidential, gubernatorial, and congressional elections prior to 1824. As a consequence, the collection now spans the entire period of the history of the nation from its founding to the present, with additional elections included for the most recent period. ICPSR plans are to maintain the collection on a continuing basis, and at this writing returns for the 1980 general elections are being added.[3]

Since the United States lacks a centralized repository or recording office for election returns, recovery of these materials required a major effort by numerous archivists, historians, and political scientists, who worked voluntarily in each of the various states to identify and provide the most accurate and complete returns that could be found.[4] For the years beginning in the latter nineteenth century, state manuals, bluebooks, legislative reports, and other similar state publications, many of which are listed in Chapter 2, were the most common sources for these materials. For the earlier years, however, the returns were significantly more fugitive, and much more diverse sources were drawn upon, including unpublished archival sources, legislative proceedings, newspapers, almanacs, and other unofficial sources. Here again, the following chapter exemplifies the kinds of sources relied upon.

Through this effort, returns for approximately 90 percent of the targeted elections were recovered. Elections for which returns were not found tend, as might be expected, to be concentrated in the earlier years, and, as also might be expected, returns for uncontested elections and for special elections tend to be more fragmentary than returns for contested general elections. In converting the data to computer-readable form, extended series of procedures were routinely carried out. These procedures were designed to identify and correct errors made in the process of conversion to computer-readable form and to identify errors and inconsistencies in the original sources themselves. When errors and inconsistencies of the latter sort were identified, an effort was made to locate superior sources.[5] Subsequent use of the data has identified additional errors and has also led to recovery of superior returns, and occasionally returns for elections that had not been located. As identified, errors have been corrected and new or superior returns added to the collection. As it now stands, the collection is probably as error-free and complete as can reasonably be expected.

The collection is of considerable magnitude, amounting at present to approximately 80 million characters of computer-readable data. It is organized in terms of three geographical units of analysis—states, congressional districts, and counties. However, counties and county equivalents, which number something in excess of 3,000 at present, constitute the basic units of analysis for the collection. Several considerations underlie the selection of the county as the basic unit. Counties are the smallest geographical and jurisdictional units for which election returns have been most consistently recorded and preserved. Historically, voting returns have been much less consistently recorded for smaller units such as wards, precincts, and townships. The task of recovering even fragmentary returns for such smaller units would have been monumental and resulted in a substantially less comprehensive collection. Counties have also been significantly more stable over time in terms of boundaries than have units such as wards and precincts. As a consequence, the task of creating longitudinal files of electoral data for equivalent units is greatly facilitated. Finally, matching social and economic data are much more abundantly and comprehensively available for counties than for other, smaller units. Both censuses of the United States and other sources of such data more consistently employed the county as a basic reporting unit, as is discussed in Chapter 3.

The collection is also marked by considerable complexity reflecting the complex nature of American electoral processes and the data processing strategies required to accommodate these complexities. One such element has to do with changes in county boundaries, which is also discussed in Chapter 3. Generally, most changes in county boundaries occurred early in the histories of the various states. In many, but by no means all, cases, the occurrence of boundary changes is known and documented. Frequently, however, information needed to estimate the population change produced by boundary changes is unavailable. The timing of historical elections creates further complexity. Prior to the latter decades of the nineteenth century, the timing of elections varied widely from state to state. Congressional elections, for example, frequently did not coincide with presidential elections, and the dates of the former were not consistent from one state to the next. Gubernatorial elections were characterized by similar and even greater variation. Unfortunately, the exact dates of many historical elections are unknown. While increased standardization of the timing of elections occurred in the latter decades of the nineteenth century, standardization was never perfect and, as is well known, the dates of gubernatorial elections are still not uniform from one state to the other, nor do they always coincide with elections to national offices. As a consequence, the researcher employing the collection cannot assume temporal consistency, particularly for the earlier years, in the dates of elections.

A further and in some respects less troublesome source of complexity derives from the manner in which the earlier presidential elections were held and the voting returns recorded. Extending well into the nineteenth century, the vote was cast in many states for presidential electors, all of whom were listed on the ballot, rather than for individual presidential candidates. In converting these data to computer-readable form, the vote cast for the first elector for each party and candidate was treated as the presidential vote. While there was in most cases some variation in the vote cast from one elector to the next, usually involving decline in the size of the vote across the ballot, the use of the first elector does not seriously distort the voting returns.

The nature of the American party system constitutes a source of much more serious complexity. The United States is usually thought of as characterized by a relatively consistent two-party system throughout its history. In fact, numerous minor parties in addition to the major parties have been on the ballot during relatively extended time periods, and a significantly larger number of such parties have appeared in particular elections and areas only to disappear a few years later. In addition, there are many elections, particularly those of the nineteenth century, where individual candidates appeared on the ballot in many states without any party identification. In converting election returns to computer-readable form, the decision was made to preserve, to the degree possible, the full detail of candidate labeling and party affiliation characteristic of the original sources. Thus rather than simply aggregating the vote for minor party candidates to an "other" vote, the individuality of the vote for these parties and of the vote for candidates without partisan affiliations was maintained.

The consequence is that the basic collection records the votes cast for more than 1,100 individual candidates, not to mention the vote for unidentified candidates and the "scattering" vote, which was apparently primarily a write-in vote.[6] With a few exceptions, the minor party vote, and certainly the vote for candidates without partisan identification, constituted only a miniscule proportion of the total national vote. On the other hand, from the perspective of particular congressional constituencies, states, or even regions, the vote for minor party candidates was often of considerable magnitude and sometimes constituted the margin of difference that tipped the balance in favor of the candidate of one major party or the other. Hence, the detailed nature of the collection in this respect holds significant analytic value.

Complexities of this sort can often be readily overcome in a way that satisfies the vast majority of the most common analytical needs and interests. Several specialized and simplified subcollections of returns derived from the basic collection are available. One of these, for example, records the vote for major party candidates and for the more important of the minor parties with the vote for minor parties of lesser importance aggregated to an "other" category. Similarly, a specialized file of returns aggregated to the level of the state is also available, and in supplying data the ICPSR is usually able to subset the larger collection and to supply data pertinent to particular areas or states and to particular time periods. In general, however, considerable attention to details of specific party identifications of candidates and the timing of elections is needed in designing research applications employing the collection.

DEMOGRAPHIC, ECONOMIC, AND SOCIAL DATA

The second major ICPSR historical collection concerns the demographic, economic, and social characteristics of the national population and is designed to support analysis of the correlates of popular voting behavior and estimation of the size and characteristics of the eligible electorate.[7] The primary source for the collection is the censuses of the United States, beginning with the census of 1790 and including a variety of interim censuses and enumerations, although various other sources were also employed. Like the historical voting returns, this collection is also continuing in nature. Materials for the 1970s have been added to the collection, and it is anticipated that additional relevant data, most notably from the 1980 census of housing and population, will be added as they become available.

In technical terms, this collection is significantly more straightforward than the collection of election returns. Its complexities are largely substantive in nature and descend from the nature of the original sources on which it is based. Counties and states constitute the organizing units for the collection, and the same numerical identification codes are employed for these units as are employed in the collection of election returns. Thus data from the two collections can be readily combined for analytic purposes. The Bureau of the Census has rarely reported data for congressional districts, and then only for selected years in the 1960s and 1970s. The county data included in this collection can be aggregated to the district level insofar as congressional districts were composed of whole counties or combinations of whole counties, and to the degree that the boundaries of the districts are known. Without substantial additional information, the collection cannot be employed to create matching data for congressional districts that cross county boundaries or which were composed of parts of counties, as in the case of districts in major cities.

The content of the historical core of the collection is strictly limited by the historical sources employed and by the monetary support that was available at the time of its development. As in the case of the historical voting returns, a premium was placed upon comprehensive, comparable, and systematic data for the entire nation. This premium in turn dictated heavy reliance upon national census materials as the best and most reliable source of such data. As a consequence, the collection reflects both the strengths and the weaknesses of that source. The earlier censuses collected and reported little more than data on the size of the total population and its age, sexual, and racial distribution. In the case of these censuses, effectively all data provided by the published reports at the county and state level were converted to computer-readable form and included in the collection.

Beginning in the mid-nineteenth century, the national censuses become progressively more elaborate and the data which they provide more abundant. Thus, the data available for the later years are substantially more rich. At the same time, because of the limitations of monetary support and the extensive nature of the data which the later censuses provide, selectivity was required in converting data to computer-readable form for inclusion in the collection. The data included in the collection for the years from 1790 through 1970 amount to something in excess of 200 million characters.

It would be impractical to attempt to describe the content of the collection in detail here.[8] In general, the collection includes data on total population, age, race, and sex for each decennial beginning in 1790. To the degree available, economic data bearing upon income, property ownership, occupation, wealth, and the proportion of the population employed in various pursuits and sectors of economic activity are also included. Also, to the degree available in the census reports and in certain other comprehensive sources, the collection includes information on the urban/rural distribution of the population, religious affiliations, school attendance, and ethnicity.

As noted above, complexities in the use of the collection are largely those that derive from the nature of the original sources themselves. A number of these issues are discussed in the Introduction to Part II, in Chapter 5 and, less systematically, in other chapters. Some of the more grievous of these issues concern changes from one census or enumeration to the next in the classifications and definitions that were employed, incomplete or otherwise inaccurate enumerations and tabulations, failure to collect information relevant to characteristics of the population, and, as in the case of the historical election returns, boundary changes that sometimes render data incomparable from one time period to the other. The best sources of information for issues of this sort are the published census reports and the numerous published and unpublished working and analytic papers prepared by the Bureau of the Census and its predecessor agencies. Researchers who make use of the collection are advised to consult these sources.

HISTORICAL LEGISLATIVE DATA

ICPSR computer-readable data holdings also include a number of additional collections that are directly relevant to the study of popular voting behavior and its correlates in historical contexts. These collections, however, bear on particular time periods and areas and cannot be discussed here.[9] Three additional data collections do require brief discussion. Although they are not directly pertinent to mass voting behavior, they are of considerable intrinsic interest and provide a basis for exploration of the relation between mass voting behavior and legislative and governmental processes.

The first of these collections is composed of comprehensive voting records for the Senate and House of Representatives from the First Congress through the most recent, including votes cast in executive as well as open sessions. In preparing this collection, the ICPSR drew upon materials originally organized and tabulated by a WPA project conducted in the latter 1930s under the direction of Clifford Lord. These materials were also verified employing the *Congressional Record,* the House and Senate *Journals,* and the *Congressional Globe.*[10] The *Record* and the *Journals* were employed in converting data for subsequent Congresses to computer-readable form. As in the case of the other collections of historical data, a variety of computer-aided error checking procedures were employed in converting data to computer-readable form in order to identify transcription error as well as errors and discrepancies characteristic of the original sources. All such errors were either corrected or documented.

The collection includes the responses for each Congress of members on all issues that reached a record vote, including procedural matters. The responses are coded to reflect all possible voting options and organized in a form readily suited to analysis. A textual description of each vote is included, also in computer-readable form, which gives bill or resolution number (where relevant), the member who initiated the vote, a brief description of the issue to which the vote was relevant, and references to the location of the vote in the original source. The descriptions provide a comprehensive record of the legislative action of both chambers of Congress, insofar as these actions involved a record vote.

The voting records of the U.S. Congress are supplemented by the records of other national legislative bodies. ICPSR computer-readable data holdings in the legislative area also include comprehensive voting records for the Continental Congresses and the Congresses of the Confederation. In addition, the holdings include the voting records of the Confederate Congresses, originally provided by Thomas B. Alexander and Richard E. Beringer.[11] In total, this combined collection provides an extended record of legislative behavior at the national level from the founding of the nation to the present.

A related computer-readable data collection bears upon individuals who served in the First through the current Congresses. These data were originally drawn from the *Biographical Directory of the American Congress, 1961*[12] and record selected biographical characteristics of each member. These characteristics include dates of birth and congressional service, prior occupation and political experience, education and military experience, and relation to other members of Congress, as well as other information. The historical core of the collection was provided by Carroll R. McKibbin. Drawing upon revised editions of the *Biographical Directory* and current *Congressional Directories*, the data were subsequently extended by the ICPSR to include recent Congresses. These data are, of course, strictly limited by the content of the original sources employed and by the ambiguities characteristic of those sources. However, they provide a basic resource for examination of the congressional elite in historical depth.

The final legislative data collection to be discussed focuses on the various states. This collection records the partisan composition of each chamber of each state legislature from 1834 to the present. The data collection was originally provided by Walter Dean Burnham, and its currency has subsequently been maintained by the ICPSR. While the collection does not record the popular vote for state legislators (collection of such data would be a monumental task and probably impossible for some states and time periods), it does provide an analytic perspective on the partisan complexion of each state during the time period in question.

We have stressed the historical nature of the several computer-readable data collections that have been described, although these collections also span the contemporary period up to the present. These collections allow examination of the political life of the nation from diverse perspectives across the entire period of national existence. Each of the collections described is very large physically, and some are marked by considerable technical and substantive complexity. However, the data can be supplied in diverse technical forms to meet the requirements of particular computational systems, and they can also be combined in a variety of ways to serve diverse research goals.

DATA FROM POLITICAL SURVEYS

This volume is primarily concerned with investigation of electoral behavior over diverse and extended time periods. Thus, the preceding section was concerned with available data collections which facilitate such investigations. Consequently, the section also focused upon data that were originally produced by social bookkeeping systems, such as the national censuses, and by ongoing political processes such as elections and legislative proceedings. These are data, in other words, that were not originally collected, recorded, and preserved with the goals of researchers in mind. With very few exceptions, only data of this sort are available for the study of political behavior during most of the course of American history.

During the past several decades, sample surveys have come to constitute a primary method of data collection for investigation of electoral and, for that matter, other political processes. In contrast to the categories of data discussed in the preceding section, data produced by sample surveys are specifically designed to serve research goals. These data are the product of systematic interviews of scientifically selected samples of the national population, or of segments of that population, such as a particular social or economic group or the inhabitants of a particular constituency, state, or other unit. On the basis of information obtained from questions addressed to the sample, inferences can be drawn to the larger population which the sample is designed to represent. In the case of scientifically designed samples, the likely margin of difference between the information obtained from the sample and the information that would have been obtained had the entire population been interviewed ("sampling error") can be calculated on the basis of the method of sampling, the size of the sample, and, of much less significance, the size of the population which the sample is designed to represent.

Sample surveys concerned with electoral behavior and with political phenomena more generally are typically designed to provide information bearing upon such matters as individual social and economic characteristics, attitudes toward governmental institutions and processes including political parties, reactions to particular political issues and personalities, and forms of political behavior and participation which include recollections of past voting decisions and expressions of voting intentions. On the basis of this survey information, inferences can be drawn to individual attitudes or behavior in the larger population with a known, probable error margin. Thus, the survey method constitutes a substantially more flexible and direct method of collection than that available to researchers concerned with the political phenomena of the more remote past, and the data provided by surveys are not prone to many of the inferential difficulties that characterized data sources such as those discussed in the preceding section.

Data bearing upon mass electoral behavior and attitudes produced by a large number of sample surveys are currently available to researchers from a variety of sources. While these data span only a limited temporal era in relation to the full sweep of American history, they are usually quite extensive in their topical coverage and provide virtually limitless possibilities for tabulation and analysis. Furthermore, available data of this sort now span an extended and significant time period which is steadily lengthening. Moreover, the interplay between survey data and aggregated data of the sort discussed in the preceding section is often highly fruitful, as relationships uncovered in one category often elucidate analysis of the other. Survey data can also suggest relationships and hypotheses which illuminate earlier political processes, just as the reverse is also the case. It would be impossible to describe in detail the full range of sample survey data bearing upon electoral behavior that is currently available. It is only possible here to briefly indicate the rich resources of sample survey data for the United States that are available from three major social science data archives—the ICPSR, the Roper Center for Public Opinion Research, and the Louis Harris Data Center—and the variations in the uses to which they are usually put.

ICPSR HOLDINGS

The ICPSR holdings include extensive data of direct relevance to the investigation of electoral behavior and attitudes from which the basic models of American political behavior were developed. In the main, these surveys were conducted by academic researchers and organizations, although a limited number were conducted by commercial survey organizations. Foremost among the academic surveys are the American "National Election Studies" carried out by the Survey Research Center and the Center for Political Studies at The University of Michigan. These surveys have been conducted biennially at the time of each national election from 1952 to the present. In addition to the intrinsic research value of these data, this survey collection is of interest in other respects. In many ways, the series reflects the progress and development of the survey method for the last thirty years, essentially beginning with conversion from quota to probability sampling methods for respondent selection. The data collection method has involved personal interviews usually lasting at least one hour. In the presidential election years, independent cross-sectional samples have usually been drawn, and the respondents were interviewed both during the campaign and after the election. In the series including 1956, 1958, and 1960, as well as 1972, 1974, and 1976, true panel designs were employed in which the same respondents were interviewed for successive elections.

In general, the samples employed across the period have become progressively larger and more complex, the questionnaires employed have become progressively lengthier and more elaborate, and interviewing techniques have steadily improved. The data which the series provides include both comparable information collected across the entire period as well as data bearing upon more specific and topical issues. Thus, the series constitutes an increasingly rich research resource that spans an extended period of recent history.

In addition to the National Election Studies series, the ICPSR archive also includes data relevant to political behavior produced by a variety of other surveys. These include the seminal area studies conducted in Erie County in 1940 and Elmira in 1948 by Lazarsfeld and his colleagues at Columbia University. Other surveys of important historical value are the series conducted by the National Opinion Research Center (NORC) at the University of Chicago in 1944, 1947, and 1948. NORC is also represented in the archival holdings by a major national study, directed by Sidney Verba and Norman Nie in 1967, which focused on several dimensions of political participation in America. Since 1976, the ICPSR has also been preserving most of the survey data collected by CBS News and The New York *Times*. More than 20 surveys in this series covering the 1980 presidential campaign have just been released by the archive.[13]

While most of these surveys have focused upon the political behavior of the adult, voting age population of the United States, there are other studies available concerned with the acquisition of political information and the socialization of political norms and values. Most important of these are the Easton and Hess study of elementary school-children and the Jennings study of high school seniors.

Although the preponderance of archival data relates to mass behavior and attitudes, there are also studies which focus upon political elites. In the area of electoral politics, these include surveys of delegates to the nominating conventions of the two major parties in 1976 as well as surveys of congressional candidates and their campaign managers conducted in the same year for the Federal Election Commission.

With few exceptions, the data from these and numerous other surveys can be supplied for research and instructional applications in error-free and fully documented form suitable for use on diverse computational systems. The documentation provided when supplying the data normally includes descriptions of the design of the survey, an explanation of the sampling procedures, the text of the questionnaires employed, and other information describing the characteristics of each resulting variable. Thus, the researcher who receives data is informed of the nature, strengths, and weaknesses of the data collection procedures that were employed, as well as the extent of subsequent data processing and its results.

ROPER CENTER HOLDINGS

A second major repository of data from sample surveys is the Roper Center for Public Opinion Research maintained by the University of Connecticut, Yale University, and Williams College. In contrast to ICPSR, Roper Center holdings are largely derived from surveys conducted by commercial organizations such as the Gallup Organization, the Roper Organization, and Yankelovich, Skelly, and White, Inc. The political data included in the Roper Center collection are widely varied, but the emphasis is clearly upon public opinion at the time each survey was conducted. In contrast to the typical academic survey, which focuses upon a general topic in some depth, many of these surveys include a few questions of topical political interest. As a result, these data are particularly useful for supporting comparative inquiry over time. Among the holdings are data resulting from surveys of the national electorate as well as studies of the electorate in states or constituencies. In many cases, these are surveys that were commissioned by organizations of the news media or by candidates for office, political parties, or other partisan organizations. Many of the organizations that provided these data were concerned with assessing voter intentions or electoral reactions to specific issues and candidates. The diversity of these surveys and of the purposes for which they were conducted are of particular interest. Not only do the data provide a rich resource for the study of the electorate and electoral processes, they also provide an indirect indication of the goals, strategies, and interests of the individuals and organizations that commissioned them.

The Roper Center holdings of survey data are especially important for their temporal reach. The collection contains some of the earliest systematic surveys of national scope conducted in the United States, including Gallup surveys beginning with the election of 1936 and continuing to the present. Between 15 and 25 Gallup Polls are added to the Roper Center collection each year. Thus, they provide a rare opportunity to examine at the individual level the complex electoral processes that accompanied the Great Depression and the New Deal, and their aftermath.

Roper Center holdings have advantages over the data produced by academic survey organizations beyond their temporal reach. The surveys are conducted with greater frequency and are therefore more abundant. On the other hand, these data also have disadvantages. In general, the range and focus of questions that were included is often relatively limited, samples tend to be small, and, particularly for the earlier years, the surveys employed less satisfactory sampling methods and interviewing procedures than in the case of more recent academic surveys. Because of the sheer number of surveys included in its holdings, moreover, the Roper Center is often unable to supply these data in a technical form that is suitable to immediate analysis. Hence, the researcher who receives these data must sometimes invest significant additional effort in preparing the data for use. But whatever these difficulties and limitations, Roper Center data constitute a research resource of considerable value.

HARRIS DATA CENTER HOLDINGS

A final repository of data from sample surveys can also be mentioned here. The Louis Harris Data Center at the University of North Carolina is, like the Roper Center, primarily a repository of data produced by commercially conducted surveys, in this case conducted by Louis Harris and Associates, Inc. The surveys that produced these data span the period from the early 1960s through the present, and are marked by many of the same characteristics as those that produced Roper Center holdings. They include both national surveys and surveys of more limited geographical areas such as states and cities, most of which were originally carried out to serve the same general purposes as those of the Roper Center. In addition to their other values, these data have the advantage of being collected by the same organization under relatively constant methodological conditions.

Because of the Harris organization's involvement in presidential campaigns in the 1960s and its association with ABC News in the late 1970s, many of these surveys utilize statewide samples of the electorate. The content of the surveys is focused upon candidate evaluation, campaign events, and vote intention. There are also many studies which are related to statewide races for governor and U.S. Senator, data which are not frequently found in other archival holdings.

We are unable in this short space to do justice to the magnitude and diversity of the survey data resources that are available from these three repositories. Catalogues and guides to the holdings of these organizations are available and can be obtained upon request.[14] There are also other sources of sample survey data relevant to electoral behavior and other political processes. These three organizations, however, are the largest and most important sources of such material.

SUMMARY

Very large and valuable collections of computer-readable data are available for the study of electoral behavior and related political processes in historical and contemporary contexts. The availability of these resources does not, of course, diminish the importance of original data collection for many research purposes. On the other hand, these and related computer-readable data collections that have not been described here provide a basis for extensive original research through extended analysis of archived data. Moreover, they also reflect the development of an ethic of data sharing and a more general cooperative and cumulative approach to research.

NOTES

1. For the genesis and development of these projects, see Allan G. Bogue, "The Historian and Social Science Data Archives in the United States," in Richard I. Hofferbert and Jerome M. Clubb (eds.) *Social Science Data Archives: Applications and Potential* (Beverly Hills: Sage Publications, 1977), 45-68. These projects were undertaken in large part due to the efforts of political scientist Warren E. Miller and historian Lee Benson, whose commitments to systematic inquiry of past politics and efforts to obtain funding were instrumental in initiating these activities.

2. Information about ICPSR data holdings can be found in the *Guide to Resources and Services* published annually by ICPSR. Copies of the current *Guide* can be obtained by writing to ICPSR, P.O. Box 1248, Ann Arbor, MI 48106.

3. An award from the Social Science Research Council supported initial development of the collection. A series of awards from the National Science Foundation supported completion of the work of data collection and the processing of data for elections from 1824 through the late 1960s. Collection and processing of data for elections prior to 1824 was supported by the National Endowment for the Humanities. Maintenance, continuation, and dissemination of the collection has been supported by the ICPSR.

4. Returns for elections prior to 1824 were collected by Gene Male of the State Historical Society of Wisconsin.

5. The data collection effort was initiated by Walter Dean Burnham and completed by Howard W. Allen. Organization, preparation, and conversion of the data to computer-readable form was also carried out under Allen's direction with the assistance of Erik W. Austin, Janice S. Plotkin, and Charlotte A. Goodman. Gregory A. Marks was responsible for developing the computational capabilities required for the

processing, management, and dissemination of this and other historical data collections.

6. *Congressional Quarterly's Guide to U.S. Elections* (Washington, DC: Congressional Quarterly Inc., 1975) provides an indication of the diversity of the minor party vote. The data appearing in this volume were provided from the ICPSR historical election data collection.

7. Development of this collection was supported by awards from the National Science Foundation. Organization and conversion of the collection to computer-readable form was carried out under the direction of Jerome M. Clubb and Erik W. Austin. A national advisory group composed of social scientists from diverse disciplines aided in the selection of data for inclusion in the collection. See Allan G. Bogue, "The Historian and Social Science Data Archives."

8. The collection and the sources on which it is based are described in "Historical Demographic, Economic and Social Data: The United States, 1790-1970" (published documentation for ICPSR collection 0001), available from the ICPSR.

9. See, however, the annual *Guide to Resources and Services.*

10. Organization and processing of these materials was supported by an award from the Ford Foundation and carried out under the direction of Jerome M. Clubb and Santa A. Traugott. Conversion of data for subsequent Congresses to computer-readable form was supported by the ICPSR.

11. See Thomas B. Alexander and Richard E. Beringer, *The Anatomy of the Confederate Congress* (Nashville: Vanderbilt University Press, 1972).

12. *Biographical Directory of the American Congress, 1774-1961* (Washington, DC: Government Printing Office, 1961).

13. A grant from the Russell Sage Foundation supported the processing of these data.

14. These materials can be obtained from the Louis Harris Data Center, Institute for Research in Social Science, 026A Manning Hall, University of North Carolina, Chapel Hill, NC 27514, and the Roper Center, Box U-164R, University of Connecticut, Storrs, CT 06268.

2

PRINTED SOURCES

Walter Dean Burnham

INTRODUCTION

Students of American electoral politics find very early on that they are dealing with data which are extraordinarily complex and fragmented. This arises in large part from the electoral consequences of federalism and separation of powers. The complexity has been further amplified by the continuous extension of popular election (and the legitimacy which accompanies it) to more and more political offices, from the time of Jackson through the Progressive Era. This proliferation, culminating in the conversion of Senatorial elections to popular elections in 1913, has been most extensive at the state and local levels. To take a reasonably typical case, the voters of Missouri were asked in 1976 to make choices for President, U.S. Senator, Governor, Lieutenant Governor, Secretary of State, State Treasurer, State Attorney General, U.S. Representative, State Senator (in half the districts), State Representative, State Appeals Court Judge, State Circuit Court Judge, and three statewide constitutional amendments.

In a parliamentary regime, the voter is asked to choose a single candidate or party list. Typically this is all, except that where federal or regional systems have come into being (as in Canada or Italy), the same process is repeated for those legislative bodies and candidates. Compilation of electoral data in such a system is relatively a much simpler matter. Thus, F.W.S. Craig has compiled the complete series of British parliamentary-election data from 1832 through 1979 in five volumes of handbook size, with very ample margins and large type.[1]

Unfortunately, the task of American election analysts is much more complicated. For in addition to the plethora of elective offices and referenda, the problem of retrieval is deepened by the fact that the reporting of election returns in this country has always been primarily a state responsibility. The variation in the quality, extensiveness, and general availability of such official reporting has been enormous throughout American political history, and remains so to the present day. Moreover, mass electoral politics in the United States goes back to a much earlier time than in any other major nation—indeed, to a time in which social statistics were in their infancy. Particularly before about 1840, reporting of the most essential political data was correspondingly primitive in vast parts of the country—though even so, it remains true that, from their beginning, election data are among the best and "hardest" in existence.

It is little wonder that, as Erwin Scheuch points out, the postwar history of electoral research showed a vast development of survey instruments in the United States, while aggregate-data analyses were much more common and rigorous in Europe than they were here.[2] There can be no question that the immense problem of accessibility—not to mention those of cost and comparability—seriously discouraged extensive development of aggregate-data work on this side of the water. It was not until 1955 that the basic county-level presidential data became available to scholars, in a central and accessible source, for the whole period from 1836 onwards;[3] and at that, scholars were left only with the raw data itself. Establishment of the Inter-university Consortium for Political and Social Research, and the creation of its computerized electoral and census data archives after 1965, was of crucial importance in overcoming the many barriers to effective use of this material.

Since this archive now does exist, it may be wondered why further presentation of source materials is called for here. The answer to this question is twofold. In the first place, a very large part of the potentially available data is not included in the ICPSR archive, and much of it may never be included in the foreseeable future, for cost and other reasons. Thus, a full incorporation of minor civil division returns seems of remote likelihood. This material is remarkably abundant, and is of obvious importance for the detailed study of electoral coalitions in the times and places where it exists. It is especially valuable where—as in New York, Massachusetts, or Iowa, for example—it is directly linked at the same analytic level with first-rate state census materials. Those interested in working with

such data will most probably have to turn elsewhere. Similar considerations apply to the likelihood that a machine-readable file of American
state legislature elections will soon be constructed, though the partisan
outcomes of such elections are in the ICPSR archive.

Secondly, it is trite but true that researchers organize data in terms of
the substantive issues involved in their individual work, and the research
design developed to do it. There will no doubt be a number of cases in
which specialists will employ both the archive's materials and other data
which it does not contain as they develop these research designs. Moreover, even those who opt for exclusive use of ICPSR county-level data may
well wish to review the published materials which relate to the period or
the geographical area which is under analysis. For such purposes, a bibliography of source materials has its uses.

Three points should be emphasized about the limits of the inventory
which follows. In the first place, it is *not* a documentation as such of the
original sources on which the ICPSR archive's holdings are based, though
of course a good deal of it is in fact based on the published materials cited
below. Second, this listing cannot be regarded as either comprehensive or
definitive. While a great deal of effort has gone into preparing it, the
dispersed and fugitive character of even the published data—especially in
the early years—is so marked that some printed primary sources are certain
to have escaped our attention. Third, no effort is made to include manuscript materials which may exist in state historical archives or elsewhere,
though brief exemplary mention is made below to indicate the possibilities.

A further discussion of the last two of these points seems to be in
order. With regard to the complexities of retrieval, we should note that a
major and still largely untapped source of political and ecological information during the nineteenth century is the state legislative journal, and in
particular—where it exists—its appendix. At some point around or soon
after the Civil War, we often find the emergence of separate reports from
Secretaries of State and other state officials. This followed the increasing
division of labor which accompanied industrialization and the parallel
growth of governmental functions. Few if any such documents can be
traced back before about 1860 or so.

The converse of this is that in a presently unknown number of cases,
data which would later appear in such separate agency documents are to be
found as appendices to legislative journals during the first half of the
nineteenth century. Thus, we very frequently find official county returns
of elections in these journals. But much more than this information may
be found, two examples of which should suffice. The Missouri state
censuses of 1844 and 1852, including enumeration of males (white) 21

and over, are contained in the state's *Senate Journal.* Similar lists of
"taxables" (i.e., males over 20 who were entitled to vote) can be found in
Pennsylvania for at least 1814, 1821, and 1828 in both the legislative
journals and *Hazard's Register.* There is almost certainly more information
to be retrieved from such sources. Much the same can be said of congressional hearings and reports on affairs in the Southern states from about
1868 through 1881, as well as the quite numerous contested congressional
election hearings down through about 1901. In such hearings, or appended
to them, can be found such unusual data as precinct returns for the 1876
election in South Carolina; the Louisiana state census of 1875, as well as
the only known printed returns for Louisiana state treasurer in the 1874
election; and pollbooks for the 1876 election in Florida which, for several
counties, gives us information *on the individual level* as to race and party
affiliation.

Regarding manuscript election returns, only a few remarks are called
for. As any historian knows, large files of such information exist—very
often at micro-unit levels and in periods for which no published data are
available. Massachusetts, for example, has a splendidly preserved archive
which yields returns on the town level (in 1980 there were 351 towns) for
Governor, members of Congress, and other offices, and from 1780 to the
present. Connecticut has similarly well-preserved returns for the period
from 1818 on; and the election files in Maryland and Virginia are out-
standingly good and complete from federal times to the Civil War.[4] While
these sources lie beyond our scope, it seems appropriate to remind the
reader of their existence, extent, and importance.

This source listing is divided into several parts. The first section is
devoted to basic *national sources* of published election data. The second
comprises published *state* materials, which in most cases may be found in
university or state libraries. The third section enumerates sources and
types of *minor civil division* data for states which have published their
election statistics in that form. Finally, there is a section which includes a
brief sketch of sources of related *demographic* data—census data, maps,
and so on—which is designed to be only exemplary. Where not otherwise
specified, the materials in Sections I and II are published on the county
level.

PART I:
NATIONAL SOURCES OF ELECTION RETURNS

A. STATEWIDE AND CONGRESSIONAL-DISTRICT LEVELS

1824-1974: *Congressional Quarterly's Guide to U.S. Elections (CQ
Guide)* Washington. Congressional Quarterly, 1975. With supplements,

1976—. This extraordinary publication is the result of years of collabora-
tion between Congressional Quarterly and the staff of the ICPSR archive.
It constitutes published documentation of the archive's contents of American elections. The smallest unit of reporting is the state level for President,
U.S. Senator and Governor, and the congressional-district level for congressional (House) elections. The presidential data is reported (where relevant)
for the top four candidates, with a fifth residual column for "other" votes.
Senatorial, gubernatorial, and congressional data are reported only for
candidates winning 5 percent or more of the vote in any given election. All
data are given in raw form and in percentages of the total vote cast. The
data presentation is a marvel of compactness. Certain information is
necessarily lost—in particular, the total vote cast for each office in each
election, and the precise number of votes cast for any and all candidates
winning less than 5 percent of the total in senatorial, gubernatorial, and
congressional elections. This work is at an extremely high level of accuracy
and completeness (though not quite perfect in either respect) and contains
much narrative and other data in addition to the returns themselves. It
excludes the results of direct-primary elections.

1790-1978: Roy R. Glashan, *American Governors and Gubernatorial
Elections, 1775-1978* (Westport, CT: Meckler Books, 1979). Contains
complete lists of state governors with essential biographical information, as
well as general election data from the earliest times to the present.
State-level analysis, with four columns (Democratic, Republican/
Opposition, "Other Significant Vote," and scattered). One of this compilation's more valuable contributions is the listing of the precise month and
day of these elections. Primarily useful as a supplement to the *CQ Guide*
for the period after 1832, and as a source of state-level published information on gubernatorial elections from 1780 to 1832.

B. COUNTY-LEVEL DATA: PRESIDENTIAL ELECTIONS

Basic county data on presidential elections since 1824 exist in the
following published sources:

1828: *The United States Telegraph* (Washington: March 27-April 1,
1829), in the Library of Congress.

1832: Benjamin R. Matthias, *The Politician's Register* (Philadelphia:
1835) (also contains statewide and congressional races, county level,
1833-1834).

1836-1892: Walter Dean Burnham, *Presidential Ballots, 1836-1892*
(Baltimore: Johns Hopkins University Press, 1955; reissued by Arno Press,
New York, 1976). Raw figures only; four party columns.

1896-1932: Edgar E. Robinson, *The Presidential Vote: 1896-1932*
(Stanford: Stanford University Press, 1934, 1947). Raw figures only, three
party columns. The latter compression makes the data for the 1912

election largely useless, since the Roosevelt Progressive vote is lumped together with Socialist and other votes in the third ("other") column. To a much less extreme extent, the same applies to the 1924 election.

1920-1964: Richard M. Scammon, *America at the Polls* (Pittsburgh: University of Pittsburgh Press, 1965). Presidential vote by county, raw vote, and percentages. A three-column format (Democrat/Republican/ Other), which is particularly limiting in the multicandidate elections of 1924 and 1948. For the latter, county percentages of the three-party vote are provided (Dixiecrats in the South, Wallace Progressives elsewhere), along with totals, in an otherwise superseded work, George Gallup, *The Gallup Political Almanac* (New York: Forbes, 1952).

1952 to date: Richard M. Scammon, *America Votes* (New York: Macmillan; Pittsburgh: University of Pittsburgh Press; and Washington: Congressional Quarterly). Issued biennially. This is also the standard reference work for gubernatorial and senatorial elections at the county level from 1950 to the present. *America Votes* contains both raw figures and percentage computations for each party's share of the total vote and of the two-party vote. Reporting for the 1968 election (Volume 8) is in a four-column format with a separate place for Wallace (American Independent), with no computation for two-party presidential percentages.

An extremely important resource for third-party candidacies from 1900 onwards, as well as for a wide variety of gubernatorial and other non-presidential election data during the nineteenth century, exists in the major national political almanacs published since 1838. These include:

1838-1914: *The Tribune Almanac* (known as *The Whig Almanac and Politician's Register, 1838-1855*). This is an indispensable reference work. In addition to the county-level presidential coverage, it contains as well extensive reporting at this level for other offices, and also includes minor-civil-division data for New York state from 1858 through 1900. The extensiveness and quality of its reporting declines during the late 1890s.

1868-1876; 1886 to date: *The World Almanac*. This, the best-known of the political almanacs, is the only one still in existence today. After about 1900 it is to be preferred for extensiveness of reporting (especially votes for minor-party candidates) to the *Tribune Almanac*. Between about 1910 and 1922, the reporting becomes increasingly for President only, with no third-party votes reported after 1924 (except for 1968 and 1980).

1885-1938: *The Chicago Daily News Almanac*. This is fully as important a source as the two previously cited for the period it covers. Its reporting of third-party votes by county in presidential (and other) elections is extraordinarily detailed through 1912. This almanac is particularly useful for studies of Chicago and Illinois: It reports this city by wards and precincts, 1880-1928, and by wards only, 1932-1936; contains invaluable ethnic-composition data by ward for the 1888-1910 period; and reports the state of Illinois by minor civil divisions as well as counties for the 1880-1896 period.

1878-1889: *The American Almanac.* Very detailed for the brief period it covers, both for presidential and congressional elections.

A parenthetical note should be added regarding another early source:

1811-1849: *Niles' Register,* a semi-newspaper published in Baltimore and Philadelphia. A wide variety of valuable presidential and other election data is contained in scattered form in this publication, particularly from about 1828 onwards. Occasionally—especially before 1836—it will contain election data which are not available elsewhere.

PART II:
STATE PUBLICATIONS OF ELECTION RETURNS

NOTE. The dawn of the computer age in social science brought with it a number of state studies, patterned for the most part on the *America Votes* format. In most cases, they obviate the need for further research into the materials which they contain. See below under Arizona, California, Illinois, Indiana, Kansas, Kentucky, Maryland, Michigan, Minnesota, Montana, North Carolina, The South, South Dakota, West Virginia and Wisconsin. It should, however, be further noted that compilations of this type provide detailed information only for the topmost statewide offices (President, U.S. Senator, Governor and—sometimes—U.S. Representative). There are certain kinds of research situations where both state-level and county-level information on other statewide offices (e.g., Lieutenant Governor, Secretary of State) is needed. Here, only the state official publications or archives (and, to some extent, the almanacs between about 1850 and 1900) will be of help.

ALABAMA (see also The South)

Lewy Dorman, *Party Politics in Alabama from 1850 through 1860* (Montgomery: State Department of Archives and History, 1935). County returns for President, 1848-1860; Governor, 1853-1859; Congress, 1847-1859; and secession referendum, 1860. Accompanying maps. Some of the returns are official, many are from newspaper sources.

Department of Archives and History, *Alabama Official and Statistical Register,* 1903–. Biennial, 1903-1917; quadrennial, 1919–. Contains official returns for all state, general and primary elections, 1902–.

ALASKA

Secretary of State, *Official Abstract of the Vote,* 1958–. Contains official returns for all offices by election districts (Alaska's equivalent to the county), and by precincts.

ARIZONA

Bruce B. Mason, *Arizona General Election Results, 1911-1960.* (Tempe: Arizona State University, 1961). County returns for all statewide offices and congressional races since admission to the Union through 1960, as well as percentage computations.

ARKANSAS

Secretary of State, *Biennial Report,* 1878-1924. Contains county returns for general elections (1876-1924) and primaries (1908-1924). Since 1924, Arkansas has been the only state in the Union (with the possible exception of Texas) for which contemporary elections are not readily available in printed form.

CALIFORNIA

Secretary of State, *California Blue Book* (about 1880-1920). Contains returns for all statewide and congressional races. Publication of this volume has continued to the present, but without election returns.

––– *Statement of the Vote of California at the General Election,* 1904–. Contains returns for all statewide and congressional races, and by district for General Assembly. A similar pamphlet pertaining to primary elections has been issued since 1914. From 1962 to the present, reporting has been extended below the county level (cities, congressional districts, legislative districts), in *Supplement to Statement of the Vote.*

Eugene C. Lee, *California Votes, 1928-1960* (Berkeley: Institute of Governmental Studies, University of California, 1963). An extensive survey on the county level of presidential, gubernatorial, and senatorial returns, this work not only contains raw data and percentages, but also information concerning registration, political participation, and other material.

Eugene C. Lee and Bruce E. Keith, *California Votes, 1960-1972* (Berkeley: Institute of Governmental Studies, University of California, 1974); a continuation of the above in identical format.

COLORADO

Secretary of State, *Abstract of Votes Cast at the General Election,* 1884–. Similar abstract for primary elections after 1910, now bound together. Returns for all offices by county. Prior to about 1902, this material was appended to the biennial report of the Secretary of State.

CONNECTICUT

Secretary of State, *Connecticut Manual,* 1889—. Contains returns for all offices by towns and counties. The 1889 and 1890 editions also contain returns for President by towns, 1856-1888.

DELAWARE

Secretary of State, *Delaware State Manual,* 1929—. Contains returns for all statewide offices by county, 1928—; and by precinct (1976—).

FLORIDA (see also The South)

Secretary of State, *Report,* 1894—. In recent years, a specific document called *Statement of the Vote* exists; contains county returns for all statewide and legislative offices; and for primary and general elections.

Annie M. Hartsfield and Elston E. Roady, *Florida Votes, 1920-1970* rev. ed. (Tallahassee: Institute of Governmental Research, Florida State University, 1972). Contains primary and general election returns for Governor, U.S. Senator, and Railroad Commissioner.

GEORGIA (see also The South)

Department of Archives and History, *Georgia Official and Statistical Register,* 1923—. Issued quadrennially. Contains returns (including county-unit figures before 1964) for all offices, primary and general elections, 1922 to date.

Joseph L. Bernd, *Grass-Roots Politics in Georgia* (Atlanta: Emory University, 1960). Contains precinct returns for selected counties, Democratic gubernatorial primaries of 1946, 1948, 1950, and 1954, and the 1952 referendum on the county-unit rule, along with an extensive discussion and analysis.

HAWAII

Secretary of State, *Official Election Returns,* 1959—. The data are reported at the county and precinct levels.

Robert C. Schmitt, *Historical Statistics of Hawaii* (Honolulu: University Press of Hawaii, 1977). It is sometimes forgotten that this state has in turn been a Kingdom, a Republic, and an Organized Territory. Pages 593-608 of this work provide basic electoral information at the statewide level only for the period 1851-1976, information otherwise not readily obtainable. Included are a list of persons voting in general elections under the Kingdom and the Republic, 1851-1897; persons registered to vote, 1868-1897;

registered voters and votes cast in territorial/statewide general elections, 1900-1976; registered voters and votes cast in primary elections, 1930-1976; votes cast in major plebiscites, 1873-1959; votes cast for candidates in major elections, 1900-1976; and partisan composition of territorial and state legislatures, 1901-1977.

IDAHO

Secretary of State, *Abstract of Votes Cast . . .*, 1902–. Now appears as a printed broadside sheet.

Boyd Archer Martin, *Idaho Voting Trends: Party Realignment and Percentage of Votes for Candidates, Parties and Elections, 1890-1974.* (Moscow: Idaho Research Foundation, University of Idaho, 1975).

ILLINOIS

Theodore C. Pease, *Illinois Election Returns, 1818-1848* (Springfield: Illinois State Library, 1923). Contains county returns for all elective offices (including state legislature), as well as percentages rounded off to the nearest whole number.

Samuel K. Gove (ed.) *Illinois Votes: 1900-1958* (Urbana: Institute of Government and Public Affairs, University of Illinois, 1959, with biennial supplements). Contains vote for President, 1900-1956; Governor, 1900-1956; U.S. Senator, 1914-1956; and State Treasurer (the major official elected in off years until 1978), 1902-1958. This compilation closely follows the *America Votes* format, and includes a breakdown within Cook County between Chicago and its suburbs. Biennially updated, with pamphlet supplements.

Secretary of State, *Illinois Blue Book,* 1900-1942. General election and primary data, 1896-1940. The *Blue Book* is still published, but only with primary election data after 1940.

Secretary of State, *Official Vote of the State of Illinois,* 1918–, (pamphlet). Since 1952, provides not only the usual county-level information, but reports Cook County by wards (Chicago) and towns (suburbs).

INDIANA

Dorothy L. Riker, *Indiana Election Returns, 1816-1851* (Indianapolis: Indiana State Historical Society, 1960). Complete returns for all elective offices (including state legislature) during the period indicated.

Robert J. Pitchell, *Indiana Votes,* Vol. I (Bloomington: Bureau of Government Research, Indiana University, 1960). County returns and standard percentage computations, following the *America Votes* format, for Governor, 1852-1956, and U.S. Senator, 1914-1958.

W. L. Francis and S. E. Doerner, *Indiana Votes,* Vol. II. (Bloomington: Bureau of Government Research, Indiana University, 1962). Contains county returns and standard percentages for congressional elections and elections for both houses of the state General Assembly, 1922-1958.

Secretary of State, *Biennial Report,* 1877–. In recent years, a specific pamphlet, *General Election Report of Indiana,* has been issued by the Secretary. Returns by county for all elective offices.

IOWA

Secretary of State, *Iowa Official Register,* 1886–. Vote for all state-wide and congressional elections by county and minor civil division (townships, wards). The 1899 edition contains county returns for Governor, 1846-1897, and for Secretary of State, 1846-1896.

Iowa State Census. The 1873, 1875, and 1885 censuses, in addition to the usual census data, contain election returns for statewide offices and for the year of the census. The format and coverage is identical with that later used in the *Iowa Official Register.*

KANSAS

June G. Cabe and Charles A. Sullivant, *Kansas Votes: National Elections, 1859-1956* (Lawrence: Governmental Research Bureau, University of Kansas, 1957). Returns and standard percentages for President, U.S. Senator, and U.S. Representative since admission.

Clarence J. Hein and Charles A. Sullivant, *Kansas Votes: Gubernatorial Elections, 1859-1956* (Lawrence: Governmental Research Bureau, University of Kansas, 1958). Returns and standard percentages for gubernatorial elections.

Herman D. Lujan, *Kansas Votes, 1958-1968* (Lawrence, 1970). Continuation of the series.

Secretary of State, *Biennial Report,* 1877–. (Now under the title, *Election Statistics.*) Returns for all elective offices, general elections and primaries.

KENTUCKY

Jasper B. Shannon and Ruth McQuown, *Presidential Politics in Kentucky, 1824-1948* (Lexington: University of Kentucky Press, 1950). Contains vote for President by counties, and includes percentage computations of both the party vote and the estimated potential electorate actually voting.

Malcolm S. Jewell, *Kentucky Votes* (Lexington: University of Kentucky Press, 1963). In three parts: I. Presidential Elections, 1952-1960,

and Primary and General Election Returns for U.S. Senator, 1920-1960;
II. Gubernatorial Primaries and Elections, 1923-1959; III. Primary and
General Election Returns for U.S. Representative (contested elections
only), 1920-1960.

Kentucky State Library, *Kentucky Directory,* 1895–. Returns for
gubernatorial elections, 1895–.

LOUISIANA (see also The South)

Secretary of State, *Report,* 1880–. Complete primary and general
election returns for all elective offices. Precinct-level reporting for Governor in recent years, for President in 1964 and 1968.

MAINE

Maine Legislative Manual, 1855–. General election returns for Governor by county and town, 1854–; and for President, 1856–. Modern
editions also include votes by town for U.S. Senator and U.S. Representative.

MARYLAND

Hall of Records, *Maryland Manual,* 1900–. Contains county returns for
all statewide offices.

Evelyn L. Wentworth, *Election Statistics in Maryland, 1934-1958* (College Park: University of Maryland Press, 1959). Returns and standard
percentage computations for President, Governor, and U.S. Senator during
the period indicated. Also included are estimates of the eligible electorate
actually voting and registration data.

MASSACHUSETTS

Manual of the General Court, 1869-1969. Contains returns by town and
county for President, 1868-1968; Governor, 1874-1966; U.S. Representative, 1876-1966; and U.S. Senator, 1914-1964. Recent volumes no longer
include this material.

Secretary of State, *Assessed Polls, Registered Voters, etc.* (Now called
Massachusetts Election Statistics), Public Document No. 43, 1896–. Registration figures and election returns for all offices by town and county, for
state House of Representatives by precinct, ward, town, and district.

MICHIGAN

Secretary of State, *The Michigan Manual,* 1863–. Early editions of the
Manual vary widely as to the election material they contain; 1863 is the
first containing any. This edition contains county returns for Governor,
1856-1862. Thereafter, the *Manual* contains returns for President and

Governor by county through 1886, except for 1872 when both are also reported by minor civil division (MCD). From 1888 to the present, returns for Governor and Secretary of State are published by MCDs and by county, and for all other offices by county only. The 1913 edition contains presidential returns by county, 1836-1912.

John P. White, *Michigan Votes: Election Statistics, 1928-1956,* with 1958 and 1960 supplements (Ann Arbor: Institute of Public Administration, University of Michigan, 1958, 1959, 1961). This publication follows the *America Votes* format, with standard reporting by county for the four leading offices (including U.S. Representative) during the period covered.

MINNESOTA

Secretary of State, *Minnesota Blue Book,* 1885–. Returns for President, all statewide offices, and Congress by county and minor civil division, 1884–.

Secretary of State, *Report . . . to the Legislature of Minnesota,* 1861-1916. Contains county returns for all statewide offices.

Bruce M. White, *Minnesota Votes* (St. Paul: Minnesota Historical Society, 1977). Election returns by county for President, Senator, Governor, and U.S. Representative, 1857-1977.

MISSISSIPPI (see also The South)

Secretary of State, *Report,* 1871–. Published annually, 1871-1877, and biennially thereafter.

Department of Archives and History, *Official and Statistical Register,* 1904 to date. Issued quadrennially; returns for all offices, and for primary and general elections.

F. Glen Abney, *Mississippi Election Statistics, 1900-1967* (University: Bureau of Governmental Research, University of Mississippi, 1968). Contains returns for President, U.S. Senator, and all statewide offices, primary and general elections; as well as referenda on legalization of liquor (1952), right-to-work law (1960), and requirement of good moral character for voting (1960). Raw votes only.

MISSOURI

Missouri Senate Journal, 1844, 1848, 1852, 1857, 1860, 1864. County returns for Governor and Lieutenant Governor for years indicated. The 1844 and 1852 volumes also report the results of state censuses, which include the total number of eligible (potential) voters by county.

Secretary of State, *Missouri Manual,* 1879–. Returns for President and Governor by minor civil divisions and counties, and for U.S. Representative and minor statewise offices by county, 1880–. Since at least the mid-1960s, election material identical to that contained in the *Manual* has been published in a more conveniently sized publication, *Roster of State . . . Officers.*

MONTANA

Secretary of State, *Official Returns,* 1889–. Single broadside sheets reporting election returns for all offices and referenda.

Ellis Waldron, *Montana Politics Since 1864: An Atlas of Elections* (Missoula: Montana State University Press, 1958). Contains complete county returns for all territorial and state general elections and primaries through 1956, with accompanying maps for each election. Raw data only.

NEBRASKA

Legislative Reference Bureau, *Nebraska Blue Book (and Historical Register),* 1889–. The 1918 edition contains returns for territorial delegate, 1854-1865; Governor, 1866-1916; and President, 1868-1916. Subsequent volumes carry contemporary election returns for all elective offices. As is the case with a great many states, in recent years printed pamphlet county-level returns are available from the Secretary of State following each election.

NEVADA

Secretary of State, *Official Returns,* 1905– (general elections), 1910– (primary elections). These returns have been published on the precinct level since at least 1932.

NEW HAMPSHIRE

New Hampshire Manual, 1889–. Contains returns by county and town for all offices, 1888–. The 1889 edition also contains county returns for President, 1852-1888.

NEW JERSEY

Secretary of State, *Annual Returns of General Elections,* 1876-1884. In Volume II of *New Jersey Public Documents* for 1885.

Fitzgerald's Manual of the Legislature of New Jersey, 1883–. All offices are reported by county and minor civil division.

NEW MEXICO

Secretary of State, *The New Mexico Blue Book,* (or *Official Register*), 1912-1940.

――― *Official Returns of the . . . Elections,* 1942–. These sources include returns for all offices by county and precinct from the first state election in 1911 to the present.

NEW YORK

Secretary of State, *Manual for the Use of the Legislature,* 1873–. Editions of the *Manual* prior to 1873 contain no election returns. Gubernatorial returns are reported by county and minor civil division, 1872–; presidential returns by county and minor civil division, 1872 and 1880-1888, and by county only, 1876 and 1892– (in recent decades, presidential returns have also been reported by cities).

NORTH CAROLINA (see also The South)

Secretary of State, *Report,* 1868, 1869/70, 1870/71. Returns for all offices.

––– *North Carolina Manual,* 1913–. The 1913 edition (published by the North Carolina Historical Commission) contains returns for President, 1836-1912, and for Governor, 1835-1912, as well as votes on such significant questions as the secession referendum of February 1861. Unfortunately, these returns are not always entirely accurate and should be used with some caution. All editions of the *Manual* from 1913 to the present contain contemporary returns for all major offices, including U.S. Representative.

Donald R. Matthews, *North Carolina Votes* (Chapel Hill: University of North Carolina Press, 1962). Contains returns and standard percentage computations for President, 1868-1960; Governor, 1868-1960; and U.S. Senator, 1914-1960 (general elections only). This material is arranged county by county, rather than election by election (the *America Votes* norm).

NORTH DAKOTA

Secretary of State, *North Dakota Blue Book.* 1905–. The 1905 and 1907 editions contain historical returns for President, Governor, and U.S. Representative, 1889-1904. Subsequent volumes report elections contemporary to the date of publication, but they have been issued only at highly sporadic intervals.

Since 1904, the Secretary of State has also issued an *Official Abstract of the Votes Cast at the General Election* . . . , in broadside-sheet form, following each election, with a similar publication covering primary elections.

Boyd L. Wright, *North Dakota Election Statistics.* (Grand Forks: Election Research Division, Bureau of Governmental Affairs, University of North Dakota, 1977). Voting statistics for territorial delegate from 1878 to 1888 and for all national and statewide offices from 1889 to 1976.

OHIO

County returns for Governor, 1807-1865, are found in the relevant volumes of the *Ohio Senate Journal* and the *Ohio House Journal.* Returns by county and congressional district for U.S. Representative are in the same source, 1836-1950 (except 1842), and for all statewide offices, 1853-1865.

Secretary of State, *Annual Report,* 1868-1928. Contains election returns for all offices by county, and additionally by minor civil division for President, 1868-1904; for Governor and Secretary of State, 1905-1908, and 1916-1926. No minor civil division returns were published for any office between 1909 and 1915.

—— *Ohio Election Statistics,* 1928–. Contains returns for all offices by county, and for President and Governor by city also, 1928-1972. Reporting extends to the minor civil division level for Governor, 1928-1958, and for President, 1936-1956. Minor civil division reporting (except cities) ceased after 1958, and city reporting ceased after 1972.

OKLAHOMA

Oklahoma State Election Board, *Oklahoma Directory,* published biennially. Recent volumes contain county returns for Governor from 1907, and for President from 1912 (except for 1920, when for some reason the vote for U.S. Senator was substituted), and statewide totals for all offices and referendum outcomes.

Oklahoma State Election Board, *Election Results and Statistics,* 1920–. This pamphlet-sized publication gives complete reporting of all primary and general election results by county. It should be noted that since 1968, votes have not been tallied in unopposed elections. (This unfortunate practice has also been adopted by Arkansas, effective with the 1958 election, and Florida, effective with the 1970 election. One hopes that it will not spread further.)

Oliver Benson et al., *Oklahoma Votes, 1907-1962* (Norman: Bureau of Government Research, University of Oklahoma, 1964). An extensive and well-done statistical cartographic discussion of Oklahoma elections. Raw votes and percentages for President are reported, and both primary and general elections for Governor and U.S. Senator. Similar data for congressional elections is reported as well, but at the district level only.

—— *Oklahoma Votes for Congress, 1907-1964* (Norman: Bureau of Government Research, University of Oklahoma, 1965). More detailed reporting of congressional elections, paralleling first *Oklahoma Votes* format.

OREGON

Secretary of State, *Abstract of Votes,* 1864-1866/1872. Returns for all major offices.

––– *Report,* 1872–. Contains returns for all elective offices. In recent years, the title has become *Official Abstract of Votes,* published following each primary and general election.

––– *Blue Book and Official Directory of Oregon,* 1913–. Same material reported, 1912–.

PENNSYLVANIA

County returns for Governor, 1802-1872, can be found in the *Pennsylvania Senate Journal* (1802-1854), and in *Pennsylvania Legislative Documents* (1857-1872). Complete official returns for President by county and individual elector can be found for 1852 and 1856 in *Pennsylvania Legislative Documents,* 1857.

Edwin S. Bradley, *The Triumph of Militant Republicanism* (Philadelphia: University of Pennsylvania Press, 1964). The appendix to this volume contains returns for President and Governor by county, 1860-1872, including the otherwise fugitive data for the 1860 gubernatorial election (the latter taken from the sources listed above).

Smull's Legislative Hand Book, 1868-1921. Succeeded by *The Pennsylvania Manual,* 1922–, published biennially by the state's Department of Property and Supplies. These volumes contain returns for all elective offices by county, and additionally by minor civil division for President, 1868 and 1876–, and for Governor, 1866–. Congressional returns are included beginning with the 1872 edition.

RHODE ISLAND

Rhode Island Manual, 1876/77–. Contains presidential vote by towns and voting precincts, 1876-1908, and by towns only from 1912 to date; and gubernatorial returns by towns and voting precincts, 1876–. Returns for Congress are by gross district totals only.

State Board of Elections, *Official Count of the Ballots Cast . . .* (1900–). Complete reporting for all offices by town and precinct.

John O. Stitely, *Rhode Island Voting Patterns, 1940-1964.* (Kingston: Bureau of Governmental Research, University of Rhode Island, 1966).

THE SOUTH

Alexander Heard and Donald S. Strong, *Southern Primaries and Elections, 1920-1949* (University: University of Alabama Press, 1950). Contains complete returns for all significantly contested primary and general elections for Governor and U.S. Senator in the eleven ex-Confederate states, 1920-1949. Some of the races—those directly forming the data base for V. O. Key's *Southern Politics in State and Nation* (New York: Knopf, 1949)—include percentage computations. Major referenda and races of special historical interest prior to 1920, especially the Populist contests in the 1890s, are included.

Richard M. Scammon, *Southern Primaries 58* (Washington, DC: Governmental Affairs Institute, 1959). Following the *America Votes* format, this publication contains county returns and percentage computations for Southern gubernatorial and senatorial primaries, for the 1958 election only.

Numan V. Bartley and Hugh D. Graham, *Southern Elections: County and Precinct Data, 1950-1972* (Baton Rouge: Louisiana State University Press, 1978). This work is designed as a continuation of the Heard-Strong compilation, but fully computerized. Contains county returns for all significantly contested senatorial and gubernatorial primary elections, as well as significant referenda. This publication also provides county-level summaries by Geographic Class and by Demographic Class (Metro-Town-Rural). The 1972 Democratic presidential primaries for Florida and North Carolina are also included. Additionally, there is a second part which contains aggregations of precinct-level data for major cities in each of the Southern states. These data are stratified by social class among the white population (lower, lower-middle, upper-middle, upper) and by race, and they include significant general elections as well as primaries, especially the vote for President, 1952-1972. Percentage computations throughout.

SOUTH CAROLINA (see also The South)

Secretary of State, *Report,* 1868–. Many issues of this report are found in the bound South Carolina government publication, *Reports and Resolutions,* for the relevant years. In its more recent form, this report is entitled *Supplementary Report to the General Assembly of South Carolina,* and is issued as a separate pamphlet. Here as in many other states, the returns which are supplied on request immediately after an election (e.g., 1976) come as xerox copies of typescript returns, with everything reported at the county level, and entitled *Statement of the Whole Number of Votes Cast* . . .

SOUTH DAKOTA

Secretary of Finance, *Legislative Manual,* 1903–. Early numbers of this *Manual* (through the 1910 edition) contain complete county returns for President and statewide offices from the admission of the state in 1889.

Primary and general elections are included in relevant volumes down to the present.

Secretary of State, *Report*, 1889-1910/12. Returns for all offices. In recent years, the Secretary has issued a printed pamphlet, *Official Election Returns* . . . following each election.

Alan L. Clem, *South Dakota Political Almanac* (Vermillion: Governmental Research Bureau, State University of South Dakota, 1962). Contains the Republican percentage of the two-party vote by county for President, Governor, U.S. Senator, and U.S. Representative, 1928-1960, along with interpretive material and political maps. No raw figures are included, nor percentages of the total vote for either party.

—— *Precinct Voting* (Vermillion: Governmental Research Bureau, State University of South Dakota, 1964). Information at the precinct level for the state east of the Missouri River, 1940-1960.

—— *West River Voting Patterns* (Vermillion: Governmental Research Bureau, State University of South Dakota, 1964). Information at the precinct level for the state west of the Missouri River, 1940-1960.

TENNESSEE (see also The South)

Secretary of State, *Tennessee Directory and Official Vote*, 1905-1919; title changed to *Tennessee Blue Book*, 1920—. Contains returns for all major offices in general elections and, since 1922, in primary elections also.

TEXAS (see also The South)

Dallas Morning News, *The Texas Almanac*, has published a great deal of county information on Texas elections, both primary and general, from about 1922 to the present. There are now no officially printed sources of election returns (though xerox copies of typescript county-level returns for all offices are available from the Secretary of State's office following each primary and general election). In earlier decades (especially the 1880s and 1890s), gubernatorial returns can be found in the *Texas Senate Journal*. See the source bibliography in Heard and Strong, *op. cit.* (The South).

David M. Olson, et al., *Texas Votes, 1944-1963* (Austin: Institute of Public Affairs, the University of Texas, 1964). Contains returns by county for President, 1944-1960; Governor, 1962; U.S. Senate, 1961 (special election); U.S. Representative, 1962; and Poll Tax Amendment, 1963. One of a number of experimental computer-oriented data-retrieval efforts of the early 1960s. The motivation for the work is spelled out on p. v (introduction): "Students and politicians alike have suffered from a lack of available Texas election statistics. The state does not publish official returns of general elections and does not even have a record of returns in most party primaries." With the publication of Bartley and Graham, *op. cit.* (The South), this study is now completely superseded. But mentioning it makes a point: the quality, extensiveness, and availability of basic official data-reporting in the United States are arrayed in a wide continuum from excellent to abysmal. Texas and its neighbor Arkansas have by all odds been at the qualitative and quantitative bottom in official election reporting.

V. Lance Tarrance, Jr., *Texas Precinct Votes '66* (Austin: Politics, Inc., 1967). Reporting of precinct vote for Governor and U.S. Senator in 41 urban-metro counties, as well as statewide county vote for these offices. Raw votes, percentages, and precinct maps are included.

―― *Texas Precinct Votes '68, '70, '72* (Dallas: SMU Press, 1970; Austin: University of Texas Press, 1972, 1974). Same format as preceding.

(The latter publications are also useful in that they pinpoint a high level of error and incompetence—though probably not fraud—in the counting of the vote in Texas.)

Douglas S. Harlan, *TexaStats '74 and '76: County and Precinct Election Returns* (San Antonio: Trinity University Press, 1978). Complete county returns, primary and general elections, for President, Governor, U.S. Senator, and State Treasurer, as well as population and registration (1972-1977) data. Precinct returns for 53 counties and for these offices (general elections only). Most unfortunately, this publication does not contain precinct maps for cost reasons, and potential users are directed to county officials or the Secretary of State's office. As these units are constantly in flux, the advice should be promptly taken before the maps are discarded.

UTAH

Secretary of State, *Report,* 1897-1924. The *Report of the Board of State Canvassers* for the years 1916-1924 is to be found in the 11th through 14th volumes of the Secretary of State's *Reports.* Thereafter, and down to the present, Utah election statistics have been distributed in single broadsheet form following each election.

VERMONT

Vermont Legislative Directory, 1900–. Contains returns for all major offices by county and town, 1900–. Prior to 1900 the *Directory* does not contain any election data.

VIRGINIA (see also The South)

Secretary of the Commonwealth, *Annual Report.* 1903-1940. Since 1940 a pamphlet statement of the vote, with considerable variations in its precise title, has been published following each election by the State Board of Elections. Returns are reported for counties and independent cities.

Returns for gubernatorial elections, 1851 and 1873-1913, are found in the *Journal of the House of Delegates* for the year following the election.

WASHINGTON

Secretary of State, *Abstract of Votes Polled ...* , 1904–. Contains returns for every elective office and all referenda. The same information is also to be found in the Secretary's *Biennial Report,* 1914-1931. Since 1946 this official has also published a much more extensive abstract which reports returns at the precinct level.

WEST VIRGINIA

Clerk of the Senate, *West Virginia Blue Book,* 1913–. General election returns for all offices, 1912–.

Secretary of State, *Statement of the Vote ...* , 1922–. Separate pamphlet *SVs* for primary and general elections, merged into one in 1976. All elective offices reported, plus registration data.

William R. Ross, *The West Virginia Political Almanac,* (Morgantown: Bureau for Government Research, West Virginia University, 1956; *1960-Supplement, loc. cit.,* 1961). Contains vote for Governor by county, 1916-1952, with maps and party percentages. Supplement contains returns and percentages for Governor and U.S. Senator, 1956 and 1958 (material duplicated in Volumes 2 and 3 of *America Votes*) and for the 1960 presidential primary (Democratic).

WISCONSIN

Abstract of Votes Given for State Officers, 4 May 1848. Included in *Wisconsin Assembly Journal,* June 1848 (Appendix I).

Wisconsin Blue Book, 1862–. Issued annually, 1862-1883, and biennially thereafter. Contains returns by county for all offices, 1860–, and by minor civil division for President and Governor, 1860–.

James R. Donoghue, *How Wisconsin Voted: 1848-1960* (Madison: Bureau of Government, University Extension Division, University of Wisconsin, 1962). Contains county data for President, Governor, and U.S. Senator during the period indicated. This compilation contains percentages (Republican, usually of the two-party vote), but rounded off to the nearest whole number. A graver deficiency is the failure to report third-party votes, except for Socialists in Milwaukee County only.

WYOMING

Secretary of State, *Official Directory of Wyoming*, 1907–. Since at least 1918, in addition to the usual comprehensive county-level coverage, this *Directory* has reported the major offices (including U.S. Representative) by precinct.

PART III: ELECTIONS REPORTED BELOW THE COUNTY LEVEL

A. States

State	Years	Type of Unit	Offices	Sources
Alaska	1958-	precinct	all	*Official Abstract of the Vote*
California	1962-	cities, assembly districts	all	*Statement of Vote (Supplement)*
Connecticut	1888-	town	all	*Connecticut Manual; Statement of Vote* (Public Document No. 26)
Delaware	1834, 1863	hundred	Congress	*Politician's Register* (1835); *Tribune Almanac* (1864)
	1976	representative dist.	all	*Official Results of General Election*
Georgia	1942-1954	precinct	Governor	J. L. Bernd, *Grass-Roots Politics in Georgia*
Hawaii	1959-	representative dist.	all	*Official Statement of the Vote*
Illinois	1868, 1876,	township, ward	President	Legislative manuals, 1869, 1877; *Chicago Daily News Almanac*, 1885-1897
Indiana	1892	township, ward	President	*CDNA*, 1893
	1900, 1902	township, ward	all	*Abstract of Vote...*
Iowa	1873-1875, 1881, 1885	township, ward	all	*Census of Iowa*, 1873, 1875, 1881, 1885
	1886-	township, ward	all	*Iowa Official Register*, 1887-

PART III: ELECTIONS REPORTED BELOW THE COUNTY LEVEL (Continued)

A. States

State	Years	Type of Unit	Offices	Sources
Louisiana	1959-	police jury ward, precinct	Governor	*General Election Returns . . . ;* *Primary Election Returns . . .*
	1964-	police jury ward, precinct	President	*General Election Returns . . .*
Maine	1854	town	Governor, President, U.S. Senator, U.S. Representative	*Maine Legislative Manual.*
Maryland	1876-1910	election district	all	*Baltimore Sun Almanac,* 1876-1912
Massachusetts	1868/76-1968	town	all	*Manual of the General Court,* 1869/77-1969
	1896-	town, precinct (state rep.)	all	*Massachusetts Election Statistics,* Public Document No. 43, 1896-
Michigan	1872	township, ward	President, Governor	*Michigan Manual,* 1873
	1888-	township, ward, precinct	Governor, Sec. of State	*Michigan Manual,* 1889-
Minnesota	1884-	township, ward, precinct	all	*Minnesota Blue Book,* 1884-

PART III: ELECTIONS REPORTED BELOW THE COUNTY LEVEL (Continued)

A. States

State	Years	Type of Unit	Offices	Sources
Missouri	1880-	precinct	President, Governor, U.S. Senator (later all)	Missouri Manual, 1881-
Nevada	1932-	precinct	all	Official Returns
New Hampshire	1888-	town	all	New Hampshire Manual, 1889-
New Jersey	1868-1880	town, ward	President, Governor	Tribune Almanac, 1869-1881
	1882-	town, ward	all	Fitzgerald's Manual, 1883-
New Mexico	1911-	precinct	all	New Mexico Blue Book, 1912-1940; Official Returns, 1942-
New York	1858-1910	township, ward	President, Governor	Tribune Almanac, 1859-1911
	1872-	township, ward election dist. (NY city)	Governor	New York Legislative Manual, 1873-
Ohio	1868-1904	township, ward, precinct	President	Sec. of State, Annual Report
	1936-1956	township, ward, precinct	President	Ohio Election Statistics
	1905-1908	township, ward, precinct	Governor	Ibid.
	1916-1958	township, ward, precinct	Governor	Ibid.
	1928-1972	city	President, Governor	Ibid.

PART III: ELECTIONS REPORTED BELOW THE COUNTY LEVEL (Continued)

A. States

State	Years	Type of Unit	Offices	Sources
Pennsylvania	1868, 1876-1960	township, ward, precinct	President	Smull's (Pennsylvania) Manual, 1866-1961/62
	1866-1958	township, ward, precinct	Governor	Ibid.
	1964-	township, ward	President	Pennsylvania Manual, 1965/66-
	1962-	township, ward	Governor	Ibid., 1963/64
Rhode Island	1876-1908	town, voting precinct	President	Rhode Island Manual, 1877-1909
	1909-	town	President	Ibid., 1910-
	1876-	town, voting precinct	Governor	Ibid., 1877-
	1900-	town, voting precinct	all	Official Count of the Ballots Cast. .
South Dakota	1940-1960	precinct (R percentage only)	President	A. L. Clem, Precinct Voting; ___ West River Voting Patterns
	1960	precinct	President, Governor, Congress, Legislature	Ibid.
Texas	1966-	precinct (urbanized counties only)	President, Governor, U.S. Senator, Treasurer	V.L. Tarrance, Texas Precinct Votes, '66, '68, '70, '72 D. S. Harlan, TexaStats '74 & '76

PART III: ELECTIONS REPORTED BELOW THE COUNTY LEVEL (Continued)

A. States

State	Years	Type of Unit	Offices	Sources
Vermont	1900-	town	President, Governor, U.S. Senator	*Vermont Legislative Directory,* 1901-
Washington	1946-	precinct	all	Secretary of State, *Precinct Returns . . .*
Wisconsin	1860-	township, ward, precinct	President, Governor, U.S. Senator	*Wisconsin Blue Book,* 1862-
Wyoming	1918-	precinct	all	*Official Directory of Wyoming,* 1919-

PART III: ELECTIONS REPORTED BELOW THE COUNTY LEVEL (Continued)

B. Major Cities

Note: *America Votes* reports the usual offices in the usual format for cities of 500,000 and over, 1952-1970, provided that the cities in question have ward structures (this excludes, e.g., Houston). Apparently recognizing the declining electoral importance of the city, *America Votes* raised the minimum urban threshold to 1,000,000 beginning with the 1972 election (Volumn 10).

City	Years	Type of Unit	Offices	Sources
Baltimore	1824-	ward, sometimes precinct	all	*Baltimore Sun Almanac,* 1876-1912; city newspapers
Boston	1824- 1876-1922	ward ward, precinct	all all	city newspapers *Boston Municipal Register,* 1877-1923
	1898-	ward, precinct	all	*Report of City Board of Elections* (City Document No. 10 or No. 11)
Buffalo	1858-1910	ward	President, Governor	*Tribune Almanac,* 1859-1911
	1872-	ward	Governor	*New York Legislative Manual,* 1873-

PART III: ELECTIONS REPORTED BELOW THE COUNTY LEVEL (Continued)

B. Major Cities

Note: *America Votes* reports the usual offices in the usual format for cities of 500,000 and over, 1952-1970, provided that the cities in question have ward structures (this excludes, e.g., Houston). Apparently recognizing the declining electoral importance of the city, *America Votes* raised the minimum urban threshold to 1,000,000 beginning with the 1972 election (Volumn 10).

City	Years	Type of Unit	Offices	Sources
Chicago	1876	ward	President	*Tribune Almanac, 1877*
	1880-1936	ward, precinct, 1888-1928	all	*Chicago Daily News Almanac, 1885-1938*
	1952-	ward	all	*State of Illinois, Official Vote . . .*
Suburban Cook Co.	1952-	town	all	*Ibid.*
Cincinnati	1868-1904	ward, precinct	President, Governor	Sec. of State, *Annual Report*
	1905-1908	ward, precinct	Governor	*Ibid.*
	1916-1958	ward, precinct	President, Governor	
Cleveland	1868-1904	ward, precinct	President, Governor	Sec. of State, *Annual Report*
	1905-1908	ward, precinct	Governor	*Ibid.*
	1916-1958	ward, precinct	President, Governor	*Ibid.* (later, *Ohio Election Statistics*)

PART III: ELECTIONS REPORTED BELOW THE COUNTY LEVEL (Continued)

B. Major Cities

Note: *America Votes* reports the usual offices in the usual format for cities of 500,000 and over, 1952-1970, provided that the cities in question have ward structures (this excludes, e.g., Houston). Apparently recognizing the declining electoral importance of the city, *America Votes* raised the minimum urban threshold to 1,000,000 beginning with the 1972 election (Volumn 10).

City	Years	Type of Unit	Offices	Sources
Dallas: Houston	1966-1976	precinct	President, Governor, U.S. Senator	V. L. Tarrance, *Texas Precinct Votes*; D. S. Harlan, *TexaStats*, '74 & '76
Detroit	1872, 1888-	ward	Governor, Sec. of State	*Michigan Manual*, 1873, 1889-
Los Angeles Co.	1962-	assembly district, congressional district; supervisorial district	all	*Statement of Vote, Supplement*, 1962-
Milwaukee	1860-	ward (later precinct)	President, Governor, U.S. Senator	*Wisconsin Blue Book*, 1868-; *Biennial Report of Board of Election Commissioners*, 1911-
Minneapolis	1884-	ward, precinct	all	*Minnesota Blue Book*, 1885-

PART III: ELECTIONS REPORTED BELOW THE COUNTY LEVEL (Continued)

B. Major Cities

Note: *America Votes* reports the usual offices in the usual format for cities of 500,000 and over, 1952-1970, provided that the cities in question have ward structures (this excludes, e.g., Houston). Apparently recognizing the declining electoral importance of the city, *America Votes* raised the minimum urban threshold to 1,000,000 beginning with the 1972 election (Volumn 10).

City	Years	Type of Unit	Offices	Sources
New York	1834-1835	ward	Governor, Mayor	B. Matthias, *Politician's Register*
	1834-1868	ward	President, Governor, Mayor	*Valentin's Manual of the City of New York*, 1870 edition
	1840-1912	ward, assembly district (after 1871)	President, Governor, local	*Tribune Almanac*, 1841-1913
	1872-	ward, assembly district, election district	Governor	*New York Legislative Manual* 1873-
	1838-1882 1912-	ward, assembly district assembly district	Congress all	*Tribune Almanac*, 1839-1883 *Annual Report of City Board of Elections*, 1913-
Philadelphia	1824-1868	ward	all	*Hazard's Register* (1825-1835); city newspapers
	1866-	ward, division	President, Governor, U.S. Senator	*Smull's (Pennsylvania) Manual*, 1868-
	1866-1922	ward	Congress	*Ibid.* 1868-1923/24

PART III: ELECTIONS REPORTED BELOW THE COUNTY LEVEL (Continued)

B. Major Cities

Note: *America Votes* reports the usual offices in the usual format for cities of 500,000 and over, 1952-1970, provided that the cities in question have ward structures (this excludes, e.g., Houston). Apparently recognizing the declining electoral importance of the city, *America Votes* raised the minimum urban threshold to 1,000,000 beginning with the 1972 election (Volumn 10).

City	Years	Type of Unit	Offices	Sources
Philadelphia (cont.)	1866-1902	ward	all	*Philadelphia Inquirer Almanac,* 1887-1903
	1905-	ward, division	President, Governor, Mayor	*Annual Report of the Registration Commission for the City of Philadelphia*
	1900/10-	ward	*Ibid.*	*Philadelphia Bulletin Almanac*
Pittsburgh	1866-1962	ward, precinct	President, Governor, U.S. Senator	*Smull's (Pennsylvania) Manual,* 1868-1963/64
	1964-	ward	President, Governor, U.S. Senator	*Ibid.,* 1965/66—
San Francisco	1962-	assembly district, congressional district, supervisorial district	all	*Statement of Vote, Supplement,* 1962-
St. Louis	1880-	ward, precinct (usually)	President, Governor, U.S. Senator	*Missouri Manual,* 1881-

PART IV. DEMOGRAPHIC MATERIALS

Possible entries under this heading are so vast that a survey much more
extensive than this election data inventory would be required to do justice
to the subject. What follows, then, can be no more than the merest
suggestion of what is available.

The United States Census, 1790–. A substantial part of the census has
been incorporated into the historical archive of the Inter-university Consortium for Political and Social Research. The extent and contents of these
holdings are available on request from ICPSR, and their listing constitutes
a useful inventory of the extremely wide range of subjects reported by the
federal census. As is well known, the census grows more complex over
time; major increases in the volume and comprehensiveness of reporting
appear to occur around 1850, 1880, 1900, 1940 (with the general introduction of census tracting for metropolitan areas), and 1970 (the latter
mandated by the "new" public policy of the 1960s). One key demographic variable—religion—is covered in special censuses held in 1906,
1916, 1926, and 1936, with none held since the latter date.

State Censuses. These are often of greater detail and reliability for the
period they cover than the federal census. As we have suggested above,
there are important fragments of census data to be encountered in the
most unlikely places, particularly before the Civil War. Accessible and
well-known state censuses with a considerable time range include the
following:

Iowa, 1869-1915

Massachusetts, 1875-1915

Michigan, 1874-1904

New York, 1845-1905

Minnesota, 1885-1915

(In a number of cases, these censuses continue after the terminal dates
listed but with rapidly diminishing volume of information detail.) Of the
five cases listed, all but Michigan report extensively at the minor civil
division level as well as at the county level.

The Massachusetts and New York censuses are perhaps the most useful
of all to the researcher working on nineteenth- and early twentieth-century
problems. Massachusetts reports everything at the town level, and—among
other features—includes second-generation ethnic populations as well as
the foreign-born themselves. The New York census reports most of its
basic statistics on population, religious denominations, occupations, and so
forth on the township and city ward level. It includes, among other things,

a detailed and explicit statement of the citizen component of the adult male population.

Other Materials. Such data as tax rolls, assessments, and valuations of agricultural land for tax purposes should also not be overlooked. Ohio, for example, has a fairly complete publication of land assessments by county in its legislative journals, extending over the period 1807-1865. Very frequently, such economic data are found in the statistical publications of the Secretaries of State, often with a richness of detail which is lacking in federal censuses of the same period. Such states as Ohio and Indiana seem especially richly endowed in such materials from the end of the Civil War to the present.

Mapping. If aggregate correlates between materials in two separate data files are to be successfully organized, it is, of course, essential that the units in each file be substantially identical. This can often present surprisingly tricky problems of data management even at the county level, especially during the country's rapid growth during the nineteenth century. All that can be done here is to suggest certain sources which may help to close these gaps. So far as county-level information is concerned, a general verbal statement concerning the date of creation and the existing counties from which the new county was formed can be found for the period 1836-1932 in two standard references: Walter Dean Burnham, *Presidential Ballots, 1836-1892, op. cit.,* and Edgar E. Robinson, *The Presidential Vote: 1896-1932.* The great nineteenth-century American atlases, such as *Colton's* and *Johnson's,* provide usually highly accurate profiles of county boundaries at or around the date of publication of each of their various editions. They also normally include township lines and names for states having such subdivisions, and ward boundaries for the larger cities.

The most difficult research into historical electoral geography will probably involve these subcounty units, and particularly urban subdivisions. Situations like that existing in Philadelphia between 1854 and 1965 are relatively simple: during this entire period, ward reorganization was performed by the simple expedient of subdividing existing wards as population grew. Most cities, however, have thoroughly reshuffled their ward structures at frequent intervals. In a great many cases, city publications can be found which either describe ward boundaries verbally or reprint maps illustrating these boundaries, or both. Four examples are provided here.

Boston: *Boston Municipal Register,* 1850-1928. Precinct atlases for the period 1875-1925 also exist in the Massachusetts State Library.

Chicago: *Chicago Daily News Almanac* for the apportionments of 1901, 1911, 1921, and 1931.

New York: *Manual of the Common Council of the City of New York* (Valentine's Manual . . .), ca. 1840-1870. Excellent detailed maps.

Pittsburgh: *Centennial Volume of City Ordinances* (1908), which gives both maps and verbal descriptions of the city's ward boundaries from the first apportionment of 1804 to that of 1907-1908 (essentially that currently in use today).

Congressional District mapping can also present major complexities, particularly in urban districts. For the period from 1862-1864 to the present, generally accurate verbal descriptions of congressional districts can be found in the relevant volumes of the *Congressional Directory*. Work is underway to produce a comprehensive congressional-district historical atlas, which of course would be a most useful complement to the reporting of House elections now available in Congressional Quarterly's *Guide to U.S. Elections*.

NOTES

1. F.W.S. Craig, *British Parliamentary Election Results,* 4 vols. (1832-1880, 1885-1918, 1918-1949, 1950-1970) (Chichester: Political Reference Publications, 1969-1977); (n.a.), *Britain Votes 2* (Chichester: Parliamentary Research Services, 1980), for 1974-1979 period.

2. Erwin K. Scheuch, "Cross-National Comparisons Using Aggregate Data," in Richard L. Merritt and Stein Rokkan (eds.) *Comparing Nations* (New Haven: Yale University Press, 1966), pp. 131-168. The other reason which Scheuch advances for this set of differences in research strategies is the (then prevalent) absence of large historical macro-level issues affecting American voting behavior and their presence in the European context; but this line of analysis is outside our scope.

3. As early as 1934, the county-level presidential data from 1896 through 1932 were compiled in one convenient reference: Edgar E. Robinson, *The Presidential Vote: 1896-1932, infra*; but it was not until 21 years later that the cycle was completed back to the first election for which county returns were available for all states: Walter Dean Burnham, *Presidential Ballots, 1836-1892, infra.*

4. A work which particularly illuminates the utility of such archives in the period prior to the ICPSR archival holdings (1824)—as well as something of their range—is J. R. Pole, *Political Representation in England and the Origins of the American Republic* (New York: Macmillan, 1966), especially Appendix II, "Voting Statistics in America," pp. 543-564.

PART II
INTERPRETING ELECTORAL HISTORY

Investigations concerned with historical political phenomena confront many of the same problems as social research oriented toward the present. Historical investigations, however, involve additional problems of a different order. In general, historical sources are fragmentary and partial, and their relationship to past reality is often unknown. Of greater importance, there is no opportunity to add new information through direct observation or surveys, and the possibility of drawing upon the memories of participants in past events is, of course, strictly limited.

We are not concerned here with letters, diaries, memoirs, newspaper reports, or the other more complicated source materials of traditional political history. The essays in this section, as those in the other sections of the volume, are centrally concerned with two categories of source material that are substantially simpler and more straightforward than the sources of traditional political history: historical election returns, and more or less systematic social, economic, and demographic data. Taken together, these sources allow investigation of electoral processes and their correlates across an extended period of American history. As indicated in Part I, both of these categories of source materials exist in considerable abundance.

In many ways these sources are simpler and easier to use, interpret, and evaluate than the sources of traditional political history. With important exceptions, the timing of elections, particularly those for major offices, is known, and we also know the major geographical subunits and jurisdictions for which returns were customarily reported. Furthermore, much is known of the methods employed in censuses and other enumerations and of the purposes for which they were conducted. Since they were intended to be systematic and exhaustive, one source can be compared with another and with earlier and later enumerations. Thus, the capacity to assess accuracy and reliability is improved.

This is not to say, of course, that these source materials are without shortcomings and limitations. Election returns bear upon only one form of political participation. Both historical election returns and social and economic data are also characterized by error and distortion, presenting major problems of interpretation. The precise meaning to be assigned these data is sometimes unclear and in some cases changes over time.

An example of problems of the latter sort is provided by change and variation in the legal requirements and informal practices governing electoral participation and the conduct of historical elections. Four general areas of historical change of this sort can be particularly noted, and each area has important consequences for systematic research. One of these involves gradual extension of suffrage rights to new groups and to a larger and larger segment of the national population. A second involves change in residency and registration requirements for voting. A third involves change in ballot form; and the fourth, change in the timing of elections. Each of these patterns of change has considerable significance in terms of estimating the size of the eligible electorate and in interpreting election returns.

In general, and as is well known, the United States has been marked by gradual extension of suffrage rights throughout its history, although reversals have also occurred in particular time periods and areas. This process has been accomplished both by extension of the franchise to formerly excluded population groups and by governmental actions intended to remove extralegal obstacles to participation by particular groups. Since the rules governing voting rights have been largely a matter of state and local jurisdiction, modification of suffrage rights occurred at widely varying times from one state to the next and, for that matter, within states. Apart from formal legal and administrative rules, it is highly likely that enforcement of such rules also varied widely from one area to another. As a consequence, it is difficult to estimate the size of the eligible electorate and, hence, to calculate levels of voter participation, particularly for the nineteenth and early twentieth century. It is also fair to say that currently available estimates of voter participation should be viewed with considerable caution. These factors similarly complicate interpretation of the results of data analyses. For example, to the degree that particular population groups were discriminated against and excluded from voting, their influence upon the distribution of the vote could not have been direct.

Much the same comments apply to residence and registration requirements. Here again, during most of American history these matters were left to state and local jurisdiction and, in the nineteenth and early twentieth century in particular, there was considerable variation in legal and informal practices. Residence requirements obviously work to reduce the size of the electorate, while registration requirements increase the "opportunity costs" of voting and effectively also work to reduce the size of the electorate. In general, the years following the turn of the twentieth century were marked by stiffening of registration and residency requirements, with substantial variation from state to state and from one area to another within states, with some relaxation on a national basis of these requirements in recent years. It may be that the stiffening of these requirements contributed to the general decline in voter participation rates across the twentieth century. On the other hand, relaxation of registration and residence requirements in recent years has seemingly not resulted in an increase in voter participation. The central point is, however, that registration and residence requirements affected historical voting behavior in ways that are not fully known.

Change in ballot form from *viva voce* practices in the late eighteenth and early nineteenth century to the "party strip" system and then to the "Australian ballot" beginning in the latter nineteenth century obviously changed the meaning of the voting act and also introduced variation in opportunities for voter coercion. Both the viva voce and the party strip systems provided greater opportunities for coercing and influencing voters and both probably worked to increase "party line" voting while decreasing ticket-splitting. Where these practices were employed and when changes in them took place is not fully known, but they clearly constitute factors that complicate interpretation and analysis of voting returns.[1]

A final complication of this same sort is introduced by change in the timing of elections. In the earlier nineteenth century in particular, as is noted in Chapter 1, there was wide variation in the dates on which elections, even to the same offices, were held. Elections to Congress were not held on the same days in the various states, and in many states these elections were not held on the same days as presidential elections or elections to other offices. Beginning in the latter nineteenth century, there was a trend toward holding elections on the same day, although complete uniformity has never been achieved. To the degree that elections were held at different times, voters may have been influenced by different issues in different elections and opportunities for the individual to vote for the candidates of different parties were increased, even under the conditions of viva voce or party strip voting. But if that is the case, what do we make of the evidence of high consistency in the partisan distribution of the vote in, for example, gubernatorial, presidential, and congressional elections, even though these elections sometimes occurred on widely separated dates?

These issues clearly complicate interpretation of voting returns, and also have important substantive implications. These implications are illustrated by an extended scholarly exchange which debated, among other issues, the degree to which change in voter participation rates could be explained by change in such "institutional" factors as residency and registration requirements.[2] But these are also to be seen as research questions. Much more can be learned about institutional arrangements governing voting in the past and of their impact upon voting behavior. Research in these areas would be repaid in terms of improved understanding of factors that shape voting behavior and improved capacity to interpret the data provided by voting returns.

The essays included in this section discuss additional characteristics of historical source materials that complicate their interpretation and use in the study of electoral processes. The initial essay in the section is concerned with the political and geographical subunits of the nation for which voting records and social and economic data are most commonly and comprehensively available. One of the most frequently discussed issues in research into historical voting behavior is the necessity of relying upon data aggregated to the level of one or the other of these subunits. The risks involved in employing aggregated data to infer individual level relations are well known and methods that are sometimes employed to reduce these risks are discussed in Chapter 9. Whether these or other methods are employed, the nature and comparability of the various subunits must be taken into account.

It is not the case, of course, that all research into voting behavior is focused upon individuals. As is noted in the Introduction to this volume, many of the conceptualizations employed in research in this area, such as electoral competition, are aggregate in nature. For these issues, data at the level of aggregated units are fully appropriate. Research in electoral behavior also often focuses upon particular population groups, and for these purposes, aggregated data for geographical and political subunits are often appropriate. In research of this sort, however, questions arise as to the ways in which the populations of these various subunits can be seen legitimately as groups. A state, for example, is a polity with governing authority, and for many purposes of research, the population of a state can be seen as a group. Where other subunits are concerned, the issue is often less clear.

The discussion in Chapter 3 raises a number of issues concerning the comparability of the various subunits both from one area of the nation to another and from one time period to the next. Related issues of comparability are addressed in Chapter 4. These concern the rapid population change in the United States throughout its history, and the rapid social and economic change that has been a usual concomitant of population change. One consequence of the continuing and rapid reconstitution of the population that has occurred in most periods and many areas of the nation is that particular geographical units are not fully comparable from one temporal point to the next. This pattern of change and development calls attention to the need to incorporate measures of change into the analytic models employed to examine many historical processes.

In Chapter 5, Shortridge is concerned with a form of distortion characteristic of data provided by the censuses of the United States. While he is concerned only with the national censuses, it is likely that other enumerations, such as the nineteenth-century state censuses, were marked by similar patterns of error. The Shortridge essay illustrates the use of controlled assumptions to correct for error in data and to reach substantive conclusions. Since we know that even contemporary censuses have underenumerated different population groups in systematically varying degree, we can assume that earlier censuses, which were conducted much less scientifically, were also characterized by "biased underenumeration." By making certain plausible assumptions about the age structure of the national population, Shortridge is able to estimate the magnitude of underenumeration of various population groups and arrive at approximations of the actual size. The accuracy of these estimates, of course, depends upon the validity of the assumptions employed.

The pattern of error considered by Shortridge has important substantive consequences. The latter decades of the nineteenth century have been seen as characterized by very high rates of voter participation, substantially higher than those of the middle decades of the twentieth century. If, however, the nineteenth century population was systematically undercounted, then the size of the eligible electorate has been underestimated and the voter participation rates artificially inflated. If this is the case, the political life of the period would appear substantially different than it is described in much of the literature. Moreover, some of the dire commentaries on the low state of health of the political system in the middle decades of the twentieth century, based on evidence of apparent decline in voter participation rates since the end of the nineteenth century, might require reconsideration.

In Chapter 6 the Allens are concerned with other forms of distortion, political corruption, and vote fraud, which may be, in some unknown degree, characteristic of historical voting records. Since corrupt and fraudulent practices are almost always secret and are certainly not publicized by their perpetrators, hard evidence of their nature, extent, and frequency is difficult to come by. In considering these issues, as they make clear, it is centrally important to arrive at a sensible definition of what constitutes fraud and corruption. As they also make clear, some allegations of corruption can be challenged on the simple grounds that the activities in question were not corrupt in terms of the standards of the time or, for that matter, in terms of the standards of later times. Of greater importance, they suggest that many of the allegations of corruption made by contemporary observers and more recent commentators are based upon normative views of how politics *ought* to be conducted rather than upon solid evidence of fraudulent practices that either frustrated the intent of voters or inflated the votes counted. Here again, the importance of the manner in which underlying historical processes are conceptualized is illustrated.

The Allen essay returns us to the scholarly exchange alluded to earlier. One of the issues debated in that exchange concerned the degree to which the very high levels of voter participation during the nineteenth century could be seen as the spurious artifacts of inflation of the recorded vote through corrupt and fraudulent practices. [3] The Allens tend to discount this possibility. While they conclude that there was some inflation of the vote through fraudulent practices, such practices were probably relatively rare and it is unlikely that they can account in total for the observed high rates of voter participation. But if we add even this small inflationary factor to the possible underestimation of the size of the national popula-

tion—and, hence, underestimation of the size of the eligible electorate—
suggested by Shortridge in his essay, it becomes clear that the high voter
turnout rates of the latter nineteenth century remain open to question.

These several essays, then, call attention to problems that work to
complicate and confound investigation of historical voting behavior as well
as various other areas of historical inquiry. They also suggest routes to
partial solution for these problems. Of greater importance, in some
respects, the essays also point to areas of needed methodological and
substantive research. Much more can be learned, for example, about the
nature and extent of error and distortion in major categories of historical
source materials and methodological approaches to circumvent them can
be developed. That in turn would allow these sources to be used in more
meaningful ways.

NOTES

1. Jerrold G. Rusk, "The Effect of the Australian Ballot Reform on Split Ticket
Voting, 1876-1908," *American Political Science Review,* 64 (December 1970),
1220-1238.

2. Walter Dean Burnham, "The Changing Shape of the American Political Universe," *American Political Science Review* 59 (March 1965), 7-28; Rusk, "Effect of
Australian Ballot Reform"; Philip E. Converse, "Change in the American Electorate,"
in Angus Campbell and Philip E. Converse (eds.) *The Human Meaning of Social
Change* (New York: Russell Sage, 1972), 263-337; and the exchange between
Burnham, Converse, and Rusk in *American Political Science Review* 68 (September
1974), 1002-1057.

3. See the references in footnote 2 above.

3

AGGREGATE UNITS OF ANALYSIS

Erik W. Austin
Jerome M. Clubb
Michael W. Traugott

During most of American history, preservation of the secrecy of the individual vote has been a basic value. Reflecting this value, and aside from *viva voce* practices during the early period of the nation, voting returns have been recorded and preserved only in aggregate form at the level of various political and geographical subdivisions. A similar value has also applied where information on the social, economic, and other characteristics of individuals obtained through censuses and other systematic enumerations is concerned. Such data have usually been published or otherwise made publicly available only in aggregated form for various subdivisions in a fashion that does not allow identification of particular individuals. In the case of the censuses of the United States, data for specific identifiable individuals become available only long after the censuses have been conducted. Data at the individual level collected through the census of 1900, for example, have only recently become available for public use. As a consequence, systematic investigations of the behavior of the electorate in relation to social and economic factors in historical depth must rely on data aggregated to the level of various geographical and other subdivisions, even though the conceptual focus of research may be individuals or completely different social groupings.

The inferential difficulties confronted in employing such subdivisions as "units of analysis" have been widely discussed, particularly since the appearance in 1950 of W. S. Robinson's well-known article, "Ecological Correlations and the Behavior of Individuals."[1] For reasons that are not entirely clear, data in this form are frequently referred to as "ecological" data. Their use to infer patterns of individual behavior or relationships at the individual level is often termed "ecological inference," and the potential for erroneous and misleading inferences which this process involves is referred to as the "ecological fallacy."[2] But whatever the terminology employed, stress upon the disadvantages of aggregate data reflects in part excessive preoccupation with the individual voting act. As is noted in the general Introduction and elsewhere in this volume, for many of the research questions of concern to students of electoral behavior, data at an aggregated level are more appropriate than individual level data. Indeed, it is possible to speak of an "individualistic fallacy" that results from inappropriate use of data at the individual level to infer group properties and relationships.[3]

Problems of inference and analysis employing aggregate data are discussed in Chapters 7, 8, and 9 of this volume and are beyond the purposes of the present chapter, which is primarily descriptive. Limited data at the individual level pertinent to mass political behavior are available for particular time periods and areas, and we touch upon these materials briefly. With rare exceptions, however, investigations of historical voting behavior and its correlates must employ data aggregated to the level of one or the other of the geographical and political subunits into which the nation has been divided. These subunits vary widely in functions, size, areal stability, and in terms of availability of data. Our task is to describe some of the characteristics of these subunits and to suggest their implications for research applications.

AGGREGATE UNITS OF ANALYSIS

During the course of American history, voting returns have been recorded and preserved for literally thousands of geographic and political units. Similarly, descriptive data bearing upon the social, economic, and demographic characteristics of the populations of many of these same units have been recorded in considerable abundance. While extensive and diverse data of this sort are available (sources are described in Chapters 1 and 2), these materials were not originally collected and preserved to serve the needs and interests of researchers. Rather, they were originally collected by various levels and branches of government as part of the pervasive and expanding social and political "bookkeeping" systems which have characterized American public affairs. As a consequence, these data often do not fully meet the needs of researchers, nor are the units for which they are recorded consistently optimum for many research purposes.

AVAILABILITY OF DATA

The geographical and political subunits into which the United States has been divided include the larger and more obvious units—states, congressional districts, and counties—as well as such smaller and often regionally idiosyncratic "minor civil divisions" such as towns, townships, wards, precincts, beats, gores, and school and ditch districts. Each of these subdivisions, and others, has served as a recording unit for at least some types of information, and each has served as an electoral unit for particular offices. In relatively recent years, several new units have come into existance as a result of the enumeration and aggregation functions of the Bureau of the Census, including census tracts, enumeration districts, and Standard Metropolitan Statistical Areas (SMSAs). Voting returns for elections to national, state, and the more important local offices have usually been recorded and preserved for only five of these subunits: states, congressional districts, counties, towns or townships, and the wards and precincts of cities and municipalities. As a consequence, we will be concerned here with only these subunits.

Voting returns recorded at the level of the larger geographical and political subunits are readily available. Returns for numerous national and statewide offices have been collected and recorded in published form for all states for the years from the founding of the nation to the present. In addition, returns for elections to the House of Representatives are readily available for congressional districts, and in some states, returns for other national and state offices have been aggregated and published at the congressional district level as well.

Election returns for the other subdivisions are less readily and consistently available. As described in Chapter 1, data for four major offices (President, Governor, United States Senator and Representative) have been collected for nearly all counties in the nation from 1788 to the present by the Inter-university Consortium for Political and Social Research (ICPSR) and are available in computer-readable form. County-level election returns for other (usually statewide) offices, such as attorney general, secretary of state, and state judicial posts, are often also available; these can be located in the sources indicated in Chapter 2. These sources usually also provide returns for elections to state legislatures. In general, returns at the county level for elections to these latter offices are most readily to be found for the late nineteenth and twentieth century. Extensive returns for these offices for earlier years can also be found, although in many cases unpublished manuscript sources must be relied upon.

The county is the smallest subunit for which a wide range of election returns is most consistently available for all time periods and areas of the nation. Electoral data for townships, wards, and precincts are differentially available for particular areas in some but not all time periods, and no centralized source of such data exists. Here again, the sources indicated in Chapter 2—state manuals and reports of secretaries of state in particular—frequently provide data at this level for these units. Unfortunately, not all states have published series of this sort, and of the series that do exist, many began publication only in the latter part of the nineteenth century. Extensive data for these smaller subdivisions are also to be found in locally published sources (such as township and city clerk election reports and local newspapers), as well as in manuscript form. These sources also record the results of local as well as national and statewide elections.

Data on electoral outcomes are, in principle, available for even the smallest subdivisions considered here. Many of the sources of data for subcounty units, however, are little known outside their local areas and major research effort is often required to recover useful information. The costs of collecting data, as a consequence, rise dramatically when research is focused upon such subcounty units and when reliance must be placed upon scattered and idiosyncratic data sources. Even at best, it is rarely possible to collect comprehensive data for wards, townships, and precincts for extensive areas over even modesty extended time periods. Thus, the problems of completeness of coverage are more severe when dealing with these units than in the case of states, counties, or congressional districts.

For many of the purposes of electoral research, however, availability of election returns is only part of the story. Equally important for many purposes are data on the characteristics of the populations of the subunits for which electoral data are recorded. The most readily available and systematic source of data on the characteristics of the national populations are the reports of the periodic censuses of the United States. In the main, the published census reports provide social, economic, and demographic data at the level of states and counties. For most censuses, the only data provided by the published reports for smaller units are total population figures, supplemented in some cases by data on age and sex. The published volumes of the 1910 census, for example, report over twenty general categories of information for states and counties and only one (total population) for smaller geographic and political units. Data for congressional districts are also lacking in the published reports. Such data have been published by the Bureau of the Census only since 1960, although county-level data can be summed to the district level in the case of districts composed of whole counties or which are congruent with county boundaries. We know of no source of systematic data for state legislative districts except insofar as those districts coincided with counties.

As is noted in Chapter 2, state censuses conducted in the latter nineteenth and early twentieth century constitute a further and invaluable source of social and economic data. These sources have the advantage of providing a wider range of data for subcounty units than do the federal census reports. On the other hand, only some states conducted censuses and only during particular periods. Thus, the state censuses do not constitute a temporally, nationally, or regionally comprehensive data source. There are also a variety of other sources of data for subcounty units including the reports of various agencies of the national government, such as the Bureau of Labor Statistics, as well as such state and local sources as the reports of boards of assessors, city directories, and local business surveys.

Beginning with the 1960 census, availability of readily usable data for minor civil divisions changes radically. Beginning in that year and continuing with subsequent censuses, the Bureau of the Census has made available extensive data in computer-readable form for a variety of minor civil divisions, including census enumeration districts and census tracts. (The bulk of these data are not included in the published census reports.) The latter data can sometimes be aggregated to the level of larger units such as state legislative districts. Many of these data are also available from the ICPSR.

It remains the case, however, that data relevant to investigation of electoral behavior in historical contexts are most consistently available at the county and state levels. Extensive data can be found for the smaller minor civil divisions, but the costs and difficulties of collecting such data can be substantial. If the scope of research involves a reasonably extended time period or geographical area, difficulties will also frequently be encountered in assembling complete data when the smaller minor civil divisions are employed as units of analysis.

FUNCTIONS OF SUBDIVISIONS

In selecting geographical or political subdivisions as research units of analysis, it is sometimes tempting to employ availability and size as the primary selection criteria. Given these criteria, the smallest geographical or political subdivisions for which adequate data are available with reasonable consistency appear as the optimum unit of analysis. In fact, the functions of the various subdivisions should also enter into the selection process. For research into the linkages between electoral and legislative behavior, for example, the congressional districts are frequently the appropriate units of analysis since districts are the constituencies and bases of support for members of Congress. If the United States Senate is the focus of research, states are frequently the appropriate units for the same reasons. A further criterion for selection may be temporal and areal comparability of functions. For a number of research purposes, variations in functions within categories of subdivisions can cloud conceptual goals.

The several geographic and political subunits considered in the preceding section vary significantly in functions both from one to the other and, in some instances, from one time period and area of the country to the next. Precincts have usually served as little more than recording units and, in some cases, as representational units in city and local government; wards generally serve as both recording and representational units for city government; and congressional districts serve an exclusively representational function. In contrast, towns and townships, counties, and states serve recording and representational functions, but also have governmental functions including raising and spending revenues, law-making and regulation, electing and employing people, and adjudication, among other functions.

The governmental and political functions of towns and townships, counties, and states also vary from one area of the nation and time period to the other. Many of the governmental functions which townships exercised in the nineteenth and early twentieth century (in the relatively few states which established townships) have been assumed by counties or municipalities over the years. In New England, though, counties have always performed few, if any, governmental functions; these functions were assumed long ago by towns (townships and municipalities). The atrophy of county governments in such metropolitan areas as New York, Philadelphia, St. Louis, and Denver has meant that in these areas, counties have become almost artificial subdivisions with few of the governing functions performed by counties in other areas. Thus, analyses that employ counties or townships often involve implicit comparison of areas that vary considerably in function.

States, of course, are substantially more consistent in functional terms than the smaller governmental units. But even here there has been variation and change. In general, states have been considered of greater governmental and political importance and as more important foci of popular loyalties in some areas of the nation than in others. States have also changed in governmental functions, which have grown at the expense of the lower governmental units. They have probably become more prominent as centers of popular attention as the lower units have declined in importance. At the same time, however, the states have also lost governmental prominence in relation to the national government.

The preceding comments suggest further differences. The several sub-units considered here differ, both from one time period and area to another, in the degree and manner in which their populations can be seen as constituting "true groups." That is, they differ in the degree to which they are seen by their inhabitants as sources of benefits and burdens and as sources of regulation and protection. In this context, it is sometimes tempting to consider the smaller minor civil divisions as constituting neighborhoods or communities composed of similar people conscious of their similarities. Such assumptions should be seen, however, as empirical questions rather than a priori facts. When we consider variations in size, the arbitrary manner in which boundaries were often drawn, and the deliberate gerrymandering that sometimes occurred to increase or reduce the political impact of particular population groups, it becomes obvious that neighborhood and community characteristics cannot be assumed of even the smallest of these subdivisions.

NUMBER, SIZE, AND STABILITY

The subdivisions of the United States are further complicated by regional and temporal variation in the locations of these subdivisions and in their number, population and areal size, and the stability of their boundaries. Limited data bearing upon these variations have been assembled in an appendix to this chapter. Examination of the appendix will suggest the importance of these variations in terms of the comparability of the various subdivisions and in terms of assumptions that often underlie research concerned with electoral behavior in historical contexts.

There are differences in the location and number of the five categories of subdivisions considered here. The three larger subdivisions (states, congressional districts, and counties) are found throughout the country and each (considered separately) comprises all of the territory of the nation.[4] Counties or county equivalents have consistently been the principal geographic subdivisions in all states. Further subdivisions below the county level have existed in some states. Approximately twenty states divided counties into townships (called "towns" in New England and New York); these states are located mainly in the northeast and upper midwest regions of the country. The urban areas of most states are also subdivided below the level of counties; these divisions (municipalities, towns, and cities) are also often further partitioned into wards and, within wards, precincts.

The number of subdivisions in each category has grown historically, as would be expected. Growth in the number of states is well known and requires no comment. The number of congressional districts grew in relation to population from 106 in 1790 to 237 in 1850, and reached the

present 435 in 1910. There has always been wide variation in the number
of districts within states, ranging from the single district in Nevada
throughout its history to the 45 districts into which New York was divided
from 1932 to 1952. Within states, the number of districts has also varied
across time. California districts, for example, progressively increased from
two in 1850 to 43 in 1972, while the number of districts in Kentucky,
thirteen in 1832, gradually reduced to seven in 1962.[5] Similarly, the
number of counties has increased. Table 3.1 in the appendix displays the
number of counties and county equivalents for selected decades from
1790 to 1980. While most of these increases have occurred as new states
entered the Union, some changes in the number of counties have occurred
in established states.

Information on the number of smaller subdivisions (townships, towns,
and municipalities; and wards and precincts of cities) is much less complete due in part to the small size, frequent compositional changes, and
essentially local nature of most of these units. The number of townships
and municipalities is known or can be estimated, however, for various
periods (see Table 3.2 in the appendix). As can be seen, the total has
undergone greater change than in the case of the larger geographic units.
The number of wards and precincts is less well known. Not all cities of
particular sizes established wards, and in those that did, the number has
frequently changed over even relatively short periods of time. (Table 3.3 in
the appendix gives the number of wards and equivalents for selected cities
at various points in time since 1850.) Change in the number of these units
clearly suggests substantial change in their boundaries and incomparability
from one time period to another.

Precincts have traditionally been constituted within wards in cities for
voting purposes; a precinct has usually been defined as the geographical
area served by one polling place. While in principle many cities established
precincts to serve a fixed number of people (often stipulated by the city
charter), in practice the number of precincts varied widely from city to
city as well as between wards in the same city. Information on the number
of precincts in existence at various times is extremely fugitive; in most
cases, local sources for particular areas must be relied upon. Even then, the
frequency with which precinct lines were redrawn (often before each
biennial election) renders assessment of the number of precincts difficult.
Table 3.4 in the appendix indicates the number of precincts in four major
cities at selected times. The range in the number of precincts into which
wards were divided is quite large even within the same city; in Albany in
1950, for example, the number of precincts in each ward varied from 4 to
19, while in Milwaukee the range was 11 to 31, and in Philadelphia the
number varied from 1 to 82.

Geographic and political subdivisions have also varied widely in area and population. States in the continental United States now range in land area from Delaware, with 1,982 square miles, to Texas, with 262,134 square miles, with a mean area of approximately 70,000 square miles. While the land area of the states has not varied greatly over time, the states have varied significantly in population. In 1850 the states varied by 3,009,949 persons: from 87,445 people (Florida) to 3,097,394 (New York); by 1970, the gap had increased to 19,657,333 (Alaska with 300,382 persons and California with 19,957,715). Mean state population increased in the 120-year period from 1850 to 1970 from 748,125 to 4,049,127.

The geographic size of congressional districts has varied with population density. States with few inhabitants (located generally in the West) have constituted single congressional districts, with Nevada (109,889 square miles) being the largest in area. Districts in the heavily populated urban areas have frequently consisted of only a few square miles of territory. While the laws concerning apportionment have been designed to equalize the number of people in congressional districts, in practice the base population figures specified in the acts were used only as very rough guidelines by the states until the 1960s. As a consequence, population size of congressional districts often varied by tens of thousands of people across states and even within certain states. The base population per U.S. Representative (as stated in the statutes) has steadily increased at every decade, growing from 30,000 in 1790 to 93,020 in 1850, and reaching 469,088 in 1970.

Counties have been heterogeneous in population and territorial size. At the present time, the smallest county (New York County, New York) comprises only 23 square miles while San Bernardino County, California, is the largest with 20,119 square miles (larger than eight entire states). In past periods, this discrepancy was even greater, since some large counties in western states have been subdivided to form new counties. In general, counties of the West are larger than their counterparts in the Midwest and East. There has also been little uniformity in the population of counties from one time or county to the other. Not only have counties fluctuated in population from one decade to the next (increases of several hundred percent in a single decade in the nineteenth century were not uncommon), but there has also been great variation within states at any single point in time. California, for example, contains the smallest county in the nation (Alpine County: 1970 population of 484) and the largest (Los Angeles, with 7,032,075 persons in 1970). While such extremes are rather uncommon, the disparities in population size are apparent for most states and between states during all decades in the past. (See Table 3.5 in the appendix for the distribution of counties by population size.)

Townships in those states which have subdivided their counties in this manner also vary widely in areal and population size. In the Midwest, townships were originally laid out as six-mile squares of territory and remain generally similar in size in that region. "Towns" in New England and New York are the equivalent of townships and are more varied in size, averaging twenty square miles in some states and fifty or more in New York. In the western and southern states divided into townships, these subdivisions are usually much larger, approaching seventy or eighty square miles in some states. Population of townships is as disparate as that of counties, ranging from a few hundred people to thousands in townships bordering cities or other urban areas.

The population and area of wards and precincts are much more difficult to determine than in the case of the larger subdivisions. Reference to local statutes (and in some cases, maps) is necessary to determine geographic areas. Although the frequency of boundary changes in these subdivisions makes generalizations about areas very tenuous, wards usually comprised several square miles of territory, while precincts ranged in size from a few city blocks to a very few square miles. Wards and precincts were seldom of equal geographic sizes, even within the same city, and the same can be said of population. Wards have ranged upward from several thousand inhabitants, and precincts have ranged from twenty or thirty people to a few thousand. As mentioned earlier, comparisons of the number and size of wards and precincts are made difficult by wide regional variations, frequency of boundary changes, and the local nature of the documentation describing these subdivisions.

Boundary change has also been characteristic of most of these geographic subdivisions across time. In a relative sense, states have remained the most stable. In only one instance (the creation of West Virginia) has a state boundary been altered in a major way. Congressional districts have generally retained stable boundaries for a decade following reapportionment of U.S. Representatives at the time of decennial censuses, although in the nineteenth century boundary changes between apportionments were common. Often, however, congressional district boundaries were changed every decade, especially in areas and periods of rapid population growth. Congressional districts in predominantly rural areas have, of course, changed less frequently than those in urban locales, for the above-mentioned reason of population growth.

The number of county boundary changes is quite large, although the frequency of changes has varied both spatially and temporally. With the exception of Delaware (which has only three counties), the boundaries of counties in every state have changed at some time since entry into the Union. Most of the boundary changes occurred in the early years after statehood, although some county boundary changes have also occurred even in the 1960s and 1970s. The Midwest, South and West, with more counties of generally larger size than in the Atlantic seaboard states, have experienced the majority of county boundary changes in the nation, with most of these coming in the nineteenth century. While there were a great number of changes in the boundaries of the counties considered as a group, a majority of counties have retained boundaries nearly identical to those which were originally constituted. Thus, counties are, in the main, generally constant in areal composition over most periods of time.[6]

Townships have also been largely geographically constant over time. In many of the states the "survey" or "congressional" township of six-mile-sided squares of territory have predominated and these boundaries, once established by survey, have usually remained constant over time. An exception to the "stable township" pattern can be noted. States that did not follow the "congressional township" approach (the New England states, New York, New Jersey, Pennsylvania, and eastern Ohio), and also townships containing municipalities, have changed boundaries more frequently, largely as a result of the expansion of towns and municipalities.

Wards and precincts have been marked by more numerous boundary changes than the larger subdivisions, particularly in times of rapid growth of the cities in which they are located. Like counties and townships, the boundaries of these subdivisions can be altered at any time and changes in boundaries have been frequent. Many cities have retained the same number of wards, especially in recent years, but have altered ward and precinct boundaries and added precincts to encompass new areas of the cities.

Boundary changes have taken several forms. The most common has been organization of new units from territory formerly included in other, neighboring areas; this has generally occurred as territory has become more settled or developed. Many county boundary changes occurred through the subdivision of existing counties to form new counties during early years of statehood and development. To achieve areal comparability from one time to another, boundary changes of this sort can be compensated for by aggregation of the new counties to the original county from which they were formed. Ward and urban precinct changes frequently have also been of this type as the result of population increase.

More developed units frequently change their boundaries relative to neighboring units by a process of annexation of territory. These annexations may be the result of topographical changes (shifting course of rivers and streams, or resurvey of existing boundary lines) or may be due to the spreading population or influence of one area into the territory of a neighboring subdivision. The most common occurrence of the latter type has been the expansion of municipalities into the areas surrounding them. A third type of boundary change has resulted from incorporation or establishment of municipalities or towns in areas that were not formerly so subdivided. Cases in point include many smaller towns and cities and the various "independent" cities which have been created across time (notably in Virginia, but in other states as well). It is, of course, more difficult to compensate for boundary changes of this form in order to retain comparability than in the case of changes that involve subdivision of original units.

Changes in the boundaries of the various geographic and political units pose major problems of temporal comparability. In general, these problems are most severe in the case of wards and precincts. Where boundary changes do not follow the subdivision pattern referred to above, adjustment to preserve comparability over time is usually difficult. It is rare that reliable data bearing upon the population affected by boundary changes are available.

DATA FOR INDIVIDUALS

As we have noted above, systematic investigations of the behavior of the historical electorate in relation to social and economic factors must rely primarily upon data aggregated to the level of various geographic and other subdivisions, even though the conceptual focus of research is upon individuals. There are, however, significant exceptions to this generalization. Several bodies of data bearing directly upon the behavior and characteristics of individual members of the electorate are available and constitute research resources of major importance. Probably the best known of these are the data collected through sample surveys of the electorate conducted during the middle decades of the twentieth century (see Chapter 1). Detailed discussion of sample surveys as a source of data for electoral inquiry is beyond the purpose of the present volume. Extensive collections of these data are available in more or less readily usable computer-readable form. Thus, it is necessary to discuss briefly some of the characteristics of this data source both to call attention to its value as a research resource and to better elucidate the characteristics of the data resources that are more typically available for historical research.

The advantages of sample survey data are obvious. These data bear more directly upon individual attitudes, behavior, and reactions. Thus, many of the inferential problems confronted in the use of other forms of data are avoided. Of even greater importance, perhaps, sample surveys are designed to provide information that is specifically relevant to research problems and to conceptualizations and theories of mass political phenomena. Where most historical research is concerned, the researcher relies instead upon information that was originally collected and compiled for purposes other than research.

These advantages, and the impressive findings that have resulted from the use of sample survey data, have led to heavy emphasis on this approach in the study of electoral phenomena and processes. But whatever their advantages, sample survey data do not constitute a perfect form of information for all research purposes, nor do they solve all of the problems confronted in the investigation of electoral behavior. The most obvious limitation of this data source is the relatively brief time span which it encompasses. Systematic sample survey research began only in the 1930s, although the approach was employed occasionally and in more limited and less systematic ways in even earlier years. Thus, systematic survey data are available at best for only the limited period from the 1930s to the present.

Even this statement, however, tends to somewhat exaggerate the historical relevance of this data source. The survey approach to data collection has become progressively more sophisticated, beginning particularly in the early 1950s, as the approach came to be increasingly employed as a tool of academic research. Improvements were particularly noteworthy in terms of sample design and procedures, question wording, and construction and design of interviewing questionnaires. In contrast to more recent surveys, those of the 1930s and earlier 1940s often tended to be deficient in terms of the questions posed to respondents, and samples were often small with the consequence of large sampling error. Many of the surveys of the electorate in these years also employed "quota" samples. Samples were designed to represent the electorate in terms of the propensities to vote of the various social and geographic groupings composing the eligible electorate. Thus, social groups with low propensities to vote, such as blacks, are not adequately represented from the standpoint of many contemporary research interests in the products of these early data collection efforts. In contrast, the more recent surveys often employ larger probability samples and an effort is sometimes made through "oversampling" to represent small groups within the eligible electorate.

This is not to say, of course, that the data collected through the earlier surveys are without value. It is only to emphasize the relatively limited temporal reach of extant collections of sample survey data. Research based upon such data necessarily omits vast expanses of American political development and history. As a consequence of this limited historical reach, there is no reason to believe that findings and generalizations based on survey research have relevance beyond the relatively narrow period for which survey data are available. Similarly, because of the limited span of time to which survey data are relevant, critical political phenomena cannot yet be examined through this approach. Because of their limited temporal scope, moreover, survey data do not provide a basis for fully effective investigation of the effects upon mass political processes and behavior of particular contextual factors—such as high education levels and advanced communications facilities—that have been relatively constant across the period of survey research.

The data of sample survey research also present their own inferential problems. In the main, survey investigations have been cross-sectional in nature and concerned with the distribution of political behavior and attitudes at a single time point. "Panel" studies which interview the same individuals several times across a relatively long time period are rare. As a consequence, use of sample survey data to investigate change and continuity in individual attitudes and behavior runs the risk of fallacious inferences. Surveys usually involve rather small samples of the national population and thus they frequently do not provide a means to assess the effects of particular issues and stimuli upon particular local or otherwise limited groups. The sample survey approach has also been criticized on the grounds that it does not permit local contextual factors that are presumed to affect individual behavior and attitudes—such as, for example, the immediate social or economic environment in which the individual is located—to be taken adequately into account. These latter limitations are practical rather than intrinsic and could be reduced or eliminated through larger, and much more costly, samples. Even so, they do impose real limitations upon the research value of the rich stores of sample survey data that are available. To suggest limitations of sample survey data does not, however, detract from their immense research value. Probably without exception, students of historical politics would devoutly wish that systematic surveys had been conducted during earlier years and their data products preserved.

Historians have also unearthed other sources of individual data relevant to electoral processes during earlier historical periods. Chief among these are poll books (recording individual vote choices) and canvass and registration lists, local histories, and biographical and commercial directories which record partisan preferences and, in some instances, other characteristics of significant numbers of individuals. These sources have sometimes been described as analogous to sample surveys; the analogy, however, is far from perfect. Indeed, the characteristics of these sources illustrate the strength and value of the data of sample surveys.

As in the case of sample survey data, the central value of poll books, canvass lists, and other similar historical sources is that they bear directly upon individuals. Hence, they do not present the inferential problems presented by aggregated data. On the other hand, while these sources provide information for periods as early as the late eighteenth and early nineteenth century, they are marked by limitations that are at least as serious as those characteristic of aggregate data. In the first place, only a small number of examples of such sources have been located and these are relevant to widely scattered and limited communities and localities. As yet, it is difficult to ascertain whether or in what ways the patterns of behavior, the partisan preferences, and other individual characteristics reflected in these sources are representative of any population beyond the limited areas and groups to which they are directly pertinent. It may be that additional examples of these sources will be found, and with improvement of theory, such sources may come to provide critical tests of competing formulations.[7]

A second limitation of these sources lies in the nature of the data which they provide. Poll books, for example, provide data on the political behavior—the vote choices—of individuals, but they do not typically provide data on the partisan attitudes, the policy preferences, or the social and economic characteristics of these individuals. Biographical directories, registration lists, and other similar sources sometimes provide an indication of individual partisan preferences and, in some instances, data bearing upon other political attitudes and individual characteristics. These sources do not, however, provide evidence of actual individual voting behavior, and the data on individual social and economic characteristics which they provide are often severely limited.

Sources of data such as these can be supplemented by another more voluminous and comprehensive source of data bearing upon the social and economic characteristics of individuals. Data for all individuals enumerated through the United States Censuses of 1790 through 1900 are available (the so-called "manuscript censuses"), as are individual-level data collected through some of the state censuses of the nineteenth and early twentieth century.[8] Since this source identifies individuals by name, at least in the case of heads of households, it is possible to match these data with the individual-level data obtained from sources of the sort indicated above, and in this way create a substantially more powerful analytic resource.[9] Whatever the strengths of the manuscript censuses, the utility of this approach is limited by both the high costs confronted in recovering and matching data for any substantial number of individuals and by the scattered and fragmentary nature of historical sources providing data on individual voting behavior and political attitudes.

SUMMARY

Extensive individual-level data are available for investigation of electoral behavior. In the main, however, data in this form are the products of sample surveys conducted in the middle decades of the twentieth century. Occasional collections of individual-level data pertinent to electoral processes have been found for earlier years and it is probable that additional "finds" of such data will be made. For the earlier years, however, data of this sort are rare. The underlying values of American politics have worked to preserve the secrecy of the individual voting act.

Data aggregated to the level of one or the other of the geographic and political subdivisions of the United States are abundant and provide the primary basis for research into electoral behavior in historical contexts. These subdivisions, however, vary widely in terms of availability of data, size, functions, and other characteristics which raise questions of comparability both from one area of the nation and from one time period to another. Frequent changes in the boundaries of many of these subunits further complicate over-time comparisons. There are no simple or mechanical solutions to the complexities presented by the aggregated nature of the basic data resources for the study of American electoral history. To the degree that solutions are available, they lie in the area of more careful conceptualization of research problems.

APPENDIX

TABLE 3.1
Number of Counties and County Equivalents by State, Selected Decades, 1790-1980

	1790	1850	1900e	1950	1980
Alabama	--	52	66	67	67
Alaska	--	--	--	--	29
Arizona	--	--	--	14	14
Arkansas	--	51	75	75	75
California	--	27	58	58	58
Colorado	--	--	57	63	63
Connecticut	8	8	8	8	8
Delaware	3	3	3	3	3
Florida	--	28	45	67	67
Georgia	11	95	137	159	159
Hawaii	--	--	--	--	4
Idaho	--	--	21	44	44
Illinois	--	99	102	102	102
Indiana	--	91	92	92	92
Iowa	--	49	99	99	99
Kansas	--	--	105	105	105
Kentucky	9	100	119	120	120
Louisiana	--	47	59	64	64
Maine	--	13	16	16	16
Maryland--a	20	20	24	24	24
Massachusetts	11	14	14	14	14
Michigan	--	43	83	83	83
Minnesota	--	--	83	87	87
Mississippi	--	59	75	82	82
Missouri--b	--	100	115	115	115
Montana	--	--	25	56	56
Nebraska	--	--	90	93	93
Nevada	--	--	14	17	17

TABLE 3.1 (Continued)

	1790	1850	1900e	1950	1980
New Hampshire	5	10	10	10	10
New Jersey	13	20	21	21	21
New Mexico	--	--	--	32	32
New York	15	59	61	62	62
North Carolina	54	79	97	100	100
North Dakota	--	--	40	53	53
Ohio	--	87	88	88	88
Oklahoma	--	--	--	77	77
Oregon	--	--	33	36	36
Pennsylvania	21	63	67	67	67
Rhode Island	5	5	5	5	5
South Carolina	9	29	40	46	46
South Dakota	--	--	68	68	66
Tennessee	--	79	96	95	95
Texas	--	78	243	254	254
Utah	--	--	27	29	29
Vermont	8	14	14	14	14
Virginia--c	78	137	118	127	136
Washington	--	--	36	39	39
West Virginia	--	--	55	55	55
Wisconsin	--	31	70	71	72
Wyoming--d	--	--	13	23	23
TOTAL	270	1590	2784	3099	3140

a. Number of counties in Maryland from 1880-1980 includes Baltimore City.
b. Number of counties in Missouri from 1880-1980 includes St. Louis City.
c. Number of counties in Virginia from 1790 and 1850 does not include independent cities.
d. Number of counties in Wyoming, Idaho, and Montana do not include the portions of Yellowstone National Park which fall within their respective state boundaries.
e. 1900 totals include Indian reservations for the respective states.

TABLE 3.2
Number of Minor Civil Divisions
(including townships and municipalities)

	1850 a	1900 a	1941	1952	1977
Alabama	19	199	268	302	432
Alaska	--	--	--	--	155
Arizona	--	--	33	48	93
Arkansas	408	1,246	387	360	492
California	72	537	284	306	699
Colorado	--	156	245	241	282
Connecticut	160	210	192	185	74
Delaware	26	33	52	49	63
Florida	11	135	281	294	562
Georgia	20	381	459	475	609
Hawaii	--	--	--	--	--
Idaho	--	29	151	193	203
Illinois	389	1,609	2,574	2,590	1,310
Indiana	860	1,016	1,551	1,549	578
Iowa	210	1,654	2,542	934	968
Kansas	--	1,605	2,138	2,119	634
Kentucky	45	357	281	313	429
Louisiana	20	148	192	215	341
Maine	338	631	528	515	104
Maryland	28	96	140	146	255
Massachusetts	364	353	351	351	171
Michigan	512	1,288	1,742	1,753	591
Minnesota	--	2,205	2,634	2,640	855
Mississippi	18	375	271	263	300
Missouri	259	1,240	1,138	1,110	964
Montana	--	271	115	121	135
Nebraska	--	857	1,007	1,010	537
Nevada	--	3	12	15	31
New Hampshire	220	245	235	234	55
New Jersey	186	424	566	567	382
New Mexico	--	--	63	72	113
New York	1,180	1,440	1,543	1,542	877
North Carolina	26	958	369	401	549
North Dakota	--	1,407	1,737	1,741	361
Ohio	1,566	2,024	2,225	2,242	982
Oklahoma	--	--	518	499	582
Oregon	--	92	195	208	261
Pennsylvania	1,512	2,382	2,584	2,554	1,172
Rhode Island	31	38	39	39	20
South Carolina	17	434	248	239	316
South Dakota	--	1,311	1,426	1,397	316
Tennessee	40	144	204	241	350
Texas	23	194	654	738	1,128
Utah	--	61	199	209	228
Vermont	308	252	313	309	71
Virginia	34	168	208	223	280
Washington	--	72	294	310	302
West Virginia	--	110	204	216	251
Wisconsin	352	1,307	1,802	1,815	600
Wyoming	--	16	84	86	95
Nation	9,254	29,713	35,260	33,980	21,158

a. Estimated.

TABLE 3.3
Number of Wards (or Ward Equivalents), Selected Cities, 1850-1970

	1850	1870	1890	1910	1930	1950	1970
New York	30a	44a	50a	63b	62b	68b	68b
Boston	12	16	25	25	22	22	22
Philadelphia	17	28	34	47	48	52	66
Detroit	NA	10	16	18	22	22	26
Chicago	9	20	34	35	50	50	50
St. Louis	6	12	28	28	28	28	28
Los Angeles	NA	NA	9	8b	16b	31b	31b
Atlanta	NA	5	6	10	13	6	9
Milwaukee	5	12	18	23	25	27	19
Cincinnati	11	24	30	24	26	26	26

a. includes Brooklyn.
b. Assembly Districts.
NA — Not subdivided into wards.

NOTES

1. W. S. Robinson, "Ecological Correlations and the Behavior of Individuals," *American Sociological Review* XV, 5 (June 1950), 351-357.

2. See Mattei Dogan and Stein Rokkan (eds.) *Quantitative Ecological Analysis in the Social Sciences* (Cambridge, MA: MIT Press, 1969).

3. See Hayward R. Alker, "A Typology of Ecological Fallacies" in Dogan and Rokkan, *Quantitative Ecological Analysis,* 69-86.

4. Independent cities in Virginia, Maryland, and Missouri, which are not counties in the strict sense, are not included within the boundaries of counties. Louisiana's subdivisions are called "parishes" rather than counties. Both of these subdivisions are considered as the equivalents of counties.

5. For changes in the number of congressional districts by state across time, see *Historical Statistics of the United States, Colonial Times to 1970* (Washington, DC: U.S. Department of Commerce, 1975), 1085.

6. Information concerning changes of the boundaries of the various units can be obtained from quite disparate sources. For changes in state, county, and sometimes minor civil division boundaries, the U.S. Census reports from 1850 onward provide some information. These data, however, were obtained only every ten years in connection with the decennial censuses, and thus often do not provide exact or complete information on changes which, of course, can occur at any time in the

TABLE 3.4

Number of Wards and Precincts in Selected Cities, 1870, 1900, 1950, and 1980

	1870		1900		1950		1980	
	Number of Wards	Number of Precincts	Number of Wards	Number of Precincts	Number of Wards	Number of Precincts	Number of Wards	Number of Precincts
Albany-a	10	24	19	70	19	132	16	121
Chicago-b	20	82	35	1,256	50	4,297	50	3,083
Milwaukee-c	12	23	23	131	27	437	16	334
Philadelphia	31	657	41	1,012	52	1,392	66	1,792

a. Albany calls its precincts "election districts."

b. The 1870 data from Chicago are for 1869; the 1900 data are for 1904.

c. In 1980 Milwaukee relabeled its political voting divisions: Wards were named "aldermanic districts" and precincts were termed "wards."

TABLE 3.5

Number of Counties by Population Size

Population Size	1850 Number	1850 %	1900 Number	1900 %	1950 Number	1950 %	1977 Number	1977 %
Less than 5,000	436	26.9	375	13.8	261	8.4	291	9.6
5,000–9,999	428	26.4	397	14.6	516	16.6	496	16.3
10,000–24,999	544	33.6	1,180	43.5	1,181	38.1	980	32.2
25,000–49,999	157	9.7	542	20.0	647	20.9	596	19.6
50,000 and over	56	3.5	219	8.1	498	16.1	679	22.3
TOTAL	1,621[a]	100.1%	2,713[a]	100.0%	3,103[a]	100.1%	3,042[a]	100.0%

a. Does not include independent cities or those counties not having organized county governments.

respective decades. State manuals, blue books, and the reports of secretaries of state provide some information as to the boundary changes of counties, minor civil divisions, and occasionally wards and precincts of cities. Documents published or available from the offices of city clerks and boards of election are frequently the only sources for information on the constitution and reconstitution of ward and precinct boundaries. Finally, the boundaries of congressional districts are documented in various congressional and census publications; in addition, maps of the districts as they were constituted for each Congress were produced by the Congressional Vote Analysis project of the Work Project Administration in the 1930s and 1940s, and are available at the National Archives. The ICPSR has also collected and integrated information on the boundary changes affecting counties; these documents record the date and nature of the changes (if known) and can be supplied upon request.

7. A useful summary of the locales for which individual-level voting data have been discovered is presented in Paul F. Bourke and Donald A. DeBats, "Individuals and Aggregates: A Note on Historical Data and Assumptions," *Social Science History* 4, 2 (Spring 1980), 229-250.

8. Data at the individual level from the census of 1890 were accidently burned; only a small proportion of these data survived.

9. See, for example, Melvyn A. Hammarberg, *The Indiana Voter: The Historical Dynamics of Party Allegiance During the 1870s* (Chicago: University of Chicago Press, 1977).

4

DEMOGRAPHIC AND COMPOSITIONAL CHANGE

Jerome M. Clubb
Erik W. Austin
Michael W. Traugott

The preceding chapter examined some of the characteristics of the various categories of geographic units for which election returns and social, economic, and demographic data have usually been recorded. That examination raised a number of issues of comparability. During any particular historical period, each of the several categories of subunits (counties, for example) was marked by wide variation in population and geographic size from one region of the nation to another and even within smaller areas such as states. Boundary changes and population growth and decline further complicate the picture, with the consequence that particular subunits are in some respects not fully comparable, often to an unknown degree, from one time period to the other. Change in the functions of various categories of subunits, such as the gradual erosion of the governmental and administrative role of counties, raises other issues of comparability. This chapter is concerned with related patterns of historical change which raise further substantive and analytical issues.

It is sometimes observed that a high rate of geographic mobility has been a particularly pronounced characteristic of the population of the United States during the middle decades of the twentieth century. In fact, there is considerable evidence that a high rate of geographic mobility has been a virtually constant characteristic of the United States throughout its history. Population movement, combined with birth and death rates, resulted in rapid and uneven change in the size and characteristics of the population of the various areas in the nation even over relatively short periods. These patterns of change have been paralleled by rapid and also uneven social and economic change. The consequence has been that the electorates of particular areas were effectively reconstituted and the "interest base" of constituencies substantially modified, even during the short periods from one decennial census to the next.

Change of this sort raises a number of intriguing and in some ways paradoxical research questions. Change in the partisan distribution of the vote is often taken as an indication of change in the partisan loyalties of the electorate or as a reflection of popular responses to particular candidates and public issues. Similarly, shifts in levels of political participation are often seen as indications of change in the political attitudes of the mass electorate. In fact, such patterns of change can sometimes be accounted for, often with equal plausibility, by population and social and economic change. Nor is electoral change produced by these factors to be taken as merely another element of spurious variation that confounds research and analysis. Population, social, and economic change can also obviously be included among the factors that have worked historically to derange electoral alignments and coalitions and to undermine the constituency bases of political leaders and parties.

An obverse pattern is, if anything, more intriguing. We can observe historically numerous areas of the nation in which the partisan distribution of the vote and voter turnout levels persisted with almost incredible stability despite massive population change. At this point, we can only ponder the processes of political socialization and acculturation, or the processes by which areas tended to attract disproportionately the politically similar, that might account for this pattern.

It is obvious that rapid and uneven population, social, and economic change raises a number of interesting methodological issues. There is, of course, the problem of separating the variations in the recorded vote that result from these patterns of change from those that might be taken as a reflection of attitudinal factors operating in the mass electorate. Rapid and, in some respects, erratic population change may also complicate the linear interpolation procedures that are often employed using decennial census data to provide estimates of population levels and social and economic characteristics to match elections between censuses. It is also possible that these characteristics of historical population change may challenge assumptions that underlie the usual applications of regression techniques to estimate individual-level relations from aggregated data for geographical subunits. These factors undoubtedly raise other methodological issues as well.

Our purpose in this chapter, however, is not to explore research problems, however intriguing, or to ponder methodological issues. Our task is simply to describe selected aspects of population and social and economic change in order to provide an indication of rates and loci of change and to call attention to some of the consequent research and methodological issues.

POPULATION CHANGE

The most obvious indicator of demographic and compositional change is population size at different times. Subunits, whether states, counties, or other areas, that are marked by population increase or decline are obvious examples of units that are in some degree not the same in composition at one time as compared to another, and the greater the degree of increase or decline, the greater the compositional change. *Net population change* is a common measure of change from one time to another and is calculated by dividing the difference in population between one time and a subsequent time by the total population at the first time. Usually expressed as a percentage, net population change can be either positive—reflecting population gain, or negative—reflecting population decline. Positive values can exceed 100 percent, signifying that the population size has more than doubled from the earlier time.[1]

Net population change for each of the states and for the nation as a whole for the period from 1820 through 1970 is presented in Table 4.1. As the table suggests, net population change has tended to be uneven across the various states and from one time period to the next. Although growth has been the rule, states have also experienced population decline in various periods. The period of most rapid growth in the various states was usually immediately following entry into the Union with declining growth, or even population decline, thereafter. There are also exceptions including, for example, the burgeoning of population in such "sun states" as Florida, Arizona, and Nevada from the 1940s onward, and California around the turn of the century. In nearly every decade, some states declined or were marked by very limited growth in population, while other states in even the same regions grew at a relatively rapid rate. The general pattern has been decline in state population growth rates, with various exceptions. The decade of the 1930s, for example, was marked by a rather precipitous drop in the growth rates of most states.

TABLE 4.1

Percentage Net Population Change by Decade, 1820-1970

	1820–1830	1830–1840	1840–1850	1850–1860	1860–1870	1870–1880	1880–1890	1890–1900	1900–1910	1910–1920	1920–1930	1930–1940	1940–1950	1950–1960	1960–1970
NEW ENGLAND															
Conn.	8.1%	4.1%	19.6%	24.1%	16.8%	15.9%	19.8%	21.7%	22.7%	23.8%	16.4%	6.4%	17.4%	26.3%	19.6%
Me.	33.9	25.6	16.2	7.7	-0.2	3.5	11.9	5.0	6.9	3.5	3.8	6.2	7.9	6.1	2.3
Mass.	16.6	20.9	34.8	23.8	18.4	22.4	25.6	25.3	20.0	14.4	10.3	1.6	8.7	9.8	10.5
N.H.	10.3	5.7	11.7	2.5	-2.4	9.0	8.5	9.3	4.6	2.9	5.0	5.6	8.5	13.8	21.6
R.I.	17.0	12.0	35.6	18.4	24.5	27.2	24.9	24.0	26.6	11.4	13.7	3.8	11.0	8.5	10.1
Vt.	18.9	4.0	7.7	0.3	4.9	0.5	0.0	3.4	3.6	-1.0	2.0	-0.1	5.2	3.2	14.0
MIDDLE ATLANTIC															
Del.	5.5	1.7	17.2	22.6	11.4	17.3	14.9	9.6	9.5	10.2	6.9	11.8	19.4	40.3	22.8
N.J.	15.6	16.4	31.1	37.3	34.8	24.9	27.7	30.4	34.7	24.4	29.1	2.9	16.2	25.5	18.2
N.Y.	39.8	26.6	27.5	25.3	12.9	16.0	18.0	21.2	25.4	14.0	21.2	7.1	10.0	13.2	8.4
Pa.	28.5	27.9	34.1	25.7	21.2	21.6	22.8	19.9	21.6	13.8	10.5	2.8	6.0	7.8	4.2
EAST NORTH CENTRAL															
Ill.	185.2	202.4	78.8	101.1	48.4	21.2	24.3	26.0	16.9	15.0	17.7	3.5	10.3	15.7	10.2
Ind.	133.1	99.9	44.4	36.6	24.5	17.7	10.8	14.8	7.3	8.5	10.5	5.8	14.8	18.5	11.4
Mich.	255.7	570.9	87.3	88.4	58.1	38.2	27.9	15.6	16.1	30.5	32.0	8.5	21.2	22.8	13.4
Ohio	61.3	62.0	30.3	18.1	13.9	20.0	14.8	13.2	14.7	20.8	15.4	3.9	15.0	22.1	9.7
Wis.	--	--	--	154.1	35.9	24.7	28.2	22.7	12.8	12.8	11.7	6.8	9.5	15.1	11.8
WEST NORTH CENTRAL															
Iowa	--	--	345.8	251.1	76.9	36.1	17.7	16.7	-0.3	8.1	2.8	2.7	3.3	5.2	2.4
Kan.	--	--	--	--	239.9	173.4	43.3	3.0	15.0	4.6	6.3	-4.2	5.8	14.3	3.1
Minn.	--	--	--	2730.7	155.6	77.6	66.7	34.5	18.5	15.0	7.4	8.9	6.8	14.5	11.5
Mo.	110.9	173.2	77.8	73.3	45.6	26.0	23.6	16.0	6.0	3.4	6.6	4.3	4.5	9.2	8.3
Neb.	--	--	--	--	326.7	267.8	134.1	0.7	11.8	8.7	6.3	-4.5	0.7	6.5	5.1
N.D.	--	--	--	--	--	--	--	74.7	80.8	12.1	5.2	-5.7	-3.5	2.1	-2.3
S.D.	--	--	--	--	--	--	--	22.1	45.4	9.0	8.8	-7.2	1.5	4.3	-2.2
SOUTH															
Va.	13.7	2.3	14.7	12.3	0.5	23.5	9.5	12.0	11.2	12.0	4.9	10.6	23.9	19.5	17.2
Ala.	142.0	90.9	30.6	25.0	3.4	26.6	19.8	20.9	16.9	9.8	12.7	7.1	8.1	6.7	5.4
Ark.	112.9	221.1	115.1	107.5	11.3	65.6	40.6	16.3	20.0	11.3	5.8	5.1	-2.0	-6.5	7.7
Fla.	--	56.9	60.5	60.6	33.7	43.5	45.2	35.0	43.4	38.7	51.6	29.2	46.1	78.7	37.1
Ga.	51.6	33.8	31.1	16.7	12.0	30.2	19.1	20.6	17.7	11.0	0.4	7.4	10.3	14.5	16.4
La.	40.6	63.4	46.9	36.7	2.7	29.3	19.0	23.5	19.9	8.6	16.9	12.5	13.5	21.4	11.8
Miss.	81.1	175.0	61.5	30.5	4.6	36.7	14.0	20.3	15.8	-0.4	12.2	8.7	-0.2	0.0	1.8

TABLE 4.1 (Continued)

	1820–1830	1830–1840	1840–1850	1850–1860	1860–1870	1870–1880	1880–1890	1890–1900	1900–1910	1910–1920	1920–1930	1930–1940	1940–1950	1950–1960	1960–1970
N.C.	15.5	2.1	15.3	14.2	7.9	30.7	15.6	17.1	16.5	16.0	23.9	12.7	13.7	12.2	11.5
S.C.	15.6	2.3	12.5	5.3	0.2	41.1	15.6	16.4	13.1	11.1	3.3	9.3	11.4	12.5	8.7
Tex.	--	--	--	184.2	35.5	94.5	40.4	36.4	27.8	19.7	24.0	10.1	20.2	24.2	16.9
Ky.	21.9	13.4	26.0	17.6	14.3	24.8	12.7	15.5	6.6	5.5	8.2	8.8	3.5	3.2	5.9
BORDER															
Md.	9.7	5.1	24.0	17.8	13.7	19.7	11.5	14.0	9.0	11.9	12.5	11.6	28.7	32.3	26.5
Okla.	--	--	--	--	--	--	--	--	--	22.4	18.1	-2.5	-4.4	4.2	9.9
Tenn.	61.2	21.6	20.9	10.7	13.4	22.6	14.6	14.3	8.1	7.0	11.9	11.4	12.9	8.4	10.0
W. Va.	--	--	--	--	--	39.9	23.3	25.7	27.4	19.9	18.1	10.0	5.4	-7.2	-6.2
MOUNTAIN															
Ariz.	--	--	--	--	--	387.5	112.1	30.9	--	63.5	30.3	14.6	50.1	73.7	36.0
Colo.	--	--	--	--	--	--	--	91.7	48.0	17.6	10.2	8.4	18.0	32.4	25.9
Ida.	--	--	--	--	--	--	--	84.1	101.3	32.6	3.0	18.0	12.1	13.4	6.8
Mont.	--	--	--	--	--	--	--	-7.5	54.5	46.0	-2.1	4.1	5.6	14.2	2.9
Nev.	--	--	--	--	519.7	46.5	-26.5	--	93.4	-5.5	17.7	21.0	45.3	78.2	71.3
N.M.	--	--	--	--	--	--	--	33.1	--	10.1	17.5	25.6	28.1	39.6	6.8
Utah	--	--	--	--	--	--	--	52.4	34.9	20.4	13.0	8.4	25.2	29.3	18.9
Wyo.	--	--	--	--	--	--	--	--	57.7	33.2	16.0	11.1	15.9	13.6	0.7
PACIFIC															
Cal.	--	--	--	310.4	47.4	54.3	39.7	22.9	60.1	44.1	65.7	21.7	53.3	48.5	27.0
Ore.	--	--	--	--	73.3	92.2	79.5	31.8	62.7	16.4	21.8	14.3	39.6	16.3	18.2
Wash.	--	--	--	--	--	--	--	48.3	120.4	18.8	15.2	11.1	37.0	19.9	19.5
Alas.	--	--	--	--	--	--	--	--	--	--	--	--	--	--	32.8
Hawaii	--	--	--	--	--	--	--	--	--	--	--	--	--	--	21.5
NATION	34.1	32.7	35.9	35.6	26.6	26.0	25.5	20.7	21.0	14.0	16.1	7.2	14.5	18.5	13.3

-- Not applicable.

Despite variations in net population change from one area and time period to another, it is clear that the population of the states underwent significant augmentation or diminution during most decades. Put differently, the population of the states was in varying degrees reconstituted during each decade.

Net population change as displayed in Table 4.1 reflects the aggregate change characteristic of each state. Just as state population change is rarely the same as change at the national level, there is no reason to assume that rates of change for counties and other units within states paralleled the aggregate state pattern. It is generally assumed that moves of the "short hop" variety, from one neighborhood to the other, for example, are more common than are longer range moves such as those across state boundaries. For over a century, moreover, rural areas have lost population to the cities and other urban concentrations. For these and other reasons we can expect patterns of population change within states to differ from aggregate state patterns.

For purposes of comparison, Table 4.2 presents net population change for selected cities during the period from the 1850s through 1970. As can be seen, change in the population of these cities did not consistently parallel change at the state level. During much of the nineteenth century and well into the twentiety century, the population of most of these cities tended to change at a more rapid rate than did the population of the states in which they are located. In contrast to a general pattern of growth during earlier years, the population of these cities during the last thirty or forty years has tended to decline or has increased at a rate substantially below that of the state as a whole. The latter pattern indicates, of course, that other areas in the state increased in population at a faster rate than did these cities. Rates of city population change also varied within states. Los Angeles, for example, grew at a much faster rate than did San Francisco; Boston and Northhampton grew at similar rates in the nineteenth century but diverged markedly throughout the twentieth century. Examination of other smaller units within states would undoubtedly reveal even more varied rates of change, much of which is concealed by aggregation to the state level.

The data on net population change presented in Table 4.1 clearly, then, underestimate the amount of population change and, hence, the continual reconstitution of the electorate. The data also, however, understate population change and electoral reconstitution for still other reasons. Probably the most serious of these, and certainly the most obvious, is implicit in the word "net." In calculating net population change, the several components of population change (births, deaths, and in- and outmigration) are not treated separately but are lumped together as the product of change in all

TABLE 4.2

Percentage Net Population Change by Decade, 1850-1970 (Selected cities and states)

	1850–1860	1860–1870	1870–1880	1880–1890	1890–1900	1900–1910	1910–1920	1920–1930	1930–1940	1940–1950	1950–1960	1960–1970
MASSACHUSETTS:	23.8	18.4	22.4	25.6	25.3	20.0	14.4	10.3	1.6	8.7	9.8	10.5
Boston	29.9	40.9	44.8	23.6	25.1	19.6	11.7	4.4	-1.3	4.0	-13.0	-8.1
Northampton	28.6	49.7	19.8	23.2	24.4	4.2	13.0	11.1	1.7	17.2	3.4	-1.3
Waltham	43.3	41.7	29.2	59.7	25.5	18.5	11.1	27.0	2.0	17.9	17.4	11.1
NEW YORK:	25.3	12.9	16.0	18.0	21.2	25.4	14.0	21.2	7.1	10.0	13.2	8.4
Poughkeepsie	27.9a	36.4	0.6	9.9	8.2	16.3	25.3	15.1	0.5	1.3	-6.6	-16.4
PENNSYLVANIA:	25.7	21.2	21.6	22.8	19.9	21.6	13.8	10.5	2.8	6.0	7.8	4.2
Norristown	46.9	21.5	21.5	51.5	12.5	25.2	15.9	10.9	6.5	-0.1	2.1	-1.9
Philadelphia	365.9	19.2	25.7	23.6	23.6	19.7	17.7	7.0	-1.0	7.3	-3.3	-2.7
NEBRASKA:	--	326.7	267.8	134.1	0.7	11.8	8.7	6.3	-4.5	0.7	6.5	5.1
Omaha	--	754.1	89.9	360.2	-27.0	21.0	54.4	11.7	4.6	12.2	20.1	15.2
GEORGIA:	16.7	12.0	30.2	19.1	20.6	17.7	11.0	0.4	7.4	10.3	14.5	16.4
Atlanta	271.5	128.1	71.7	75.2	37.1	72.3	29.6	34.8	11.8	9.6	47.1	2.0
TEXAS:	184.2	35.5	94.5	40.4	36.4	27.8	19.7	24.9	10.1	20.2	24.2	16.9
San Antonio	136.1	48.8	67.7	83.3	41.5	81.2	67.0	43.5	9.6	60.9	43.9	11.3
CALIFORNIA:	310.4	47.4	54.3	39.7	22.9	60.1	44.1	65.7	21.7	53.1	48.5	27.0
Los Angeles	172.4a	30.6	95.2	350.6	103.4	211.5	80.7	114.7	21.5	31.0	25.8	13.6
San Francisco	62.3b	163.1	56.5	27.8	14.6	21.6	21.5	25.2	0.0	22.2	-4.5	-3.3

a. Based on Census Bureau estimate for 1850 population.

b. 1850 population counts lost due to fire; hence, net change 1850-1860 based on 1852 population.

-- Not applicable.

components, growth or decline in the total number of people. Thus, equal numbers of births and deaths cancel each other out leaving a net change of zero; outmigration that is nearly as large as migration into the area is partially cancelling with the result of low population change.

Data provided by the censuses of 1850 through 1970 allow calculation for each state of a measure that more nearly approximates *"gross" population change* and which better reflects the reconstitution of the electorates of the various states from one census to the next. Estimates of the deaths of in- and outmigrants and for the static population of each state during each intercensus period, can be calculated, along with births for the nonmigrating population. These totals are then added to the total number of in- and outmigrants, including migrants from both other states and other nations, and divided by the total population of each state at the first of each pair of adjacent censuses. This procedure avoids the cancelling effects involved in the calculation of net population change and sums total births, deaths and in- and outmigration as an approximation of gross or aggregate population change for each state.[2]

This measure, however, also underestimates total population change between censuses. There are no records of the number of individuals who were born in other states or countries but who were residents of a given state at one census and left the state prior to the next census. Similarly, there are no records of individuals who were residents of a state at one census and who left the state for a more or less prolonged period but returned prior to the next census. Despite such limitations, this measure provides a better indication of the degree to which the populations of the states differed, due to loss of inhabitants through outmigration and deaths and to replacements through inmigration and births, at one census from the populations at the preceding census than does net population change.

In many respects gross population change (Table 4.3) is marked by properties similar to net population change. States recently admitted to the Union have the highest gross rates of change with declining rates thereafter. Florida, Arizona, and Nevada again are notable exceptions to this generalization. There are also noteworthy differences. For one thing, the gross population change values tend to be more stable than those for net population change both from state to state and from one period to the next. This is a reflection of the influence of birth and death rates that were relatively similar across the nation and even from one time period to the next, and of the substantial but constant levels of interstate migration.

Of greater importance, and as expected, the gross change rates are substantially higher than the net change rates, reflecting much more in the way of population "turnover" than the latter measure. The net population change in Illinois in the decade from 1850 to 1860, for example, was 101

TABLE 4.3

Percentage Gross Population Change Rates, by Decade, 1850-1970

	1850–1860[a]	1860–1870[b]	1870–1880	1880–1890	1890–1900	1900–1910	1910–1920	1920–1930	1930–1940	1940–1950	1950–1960	1960–1970
NEW ENGLAND												
Conn.	58.0%	47.4%	43.8%	52.9%	56.3%	56.0%	53.3%	42.8%	33.0%	44.8%	51.1%	43.6%
Me.	44.1	34.7	37.7	40.7	40.7	44.1	38.3	42.3	37.2	38.5	40.4	35.0
Mass.	64.3	52.4	57.8	60.8	60.4	52.5	43.6	38.6	34.1	41.2	42.3	39.4
N.H.	39.8	36.4	41.7	45.6	44.2	38.1	37.6	39.5	38.9	42.7	45.3	47.8
R.I.	50.0	51.3	57.2	60.6	62.4	62.2	44.2	41.9	35.2	44.3	43.8	39.2
Vt.	38.1	33.8	33.6	37.5	41.1	42.5	35.4	34.4	36.2	36.3	35.8	41.8
MIDDLE ATLANTIC												
Del.	49.6	44.9	52.5	51.0	50.3	45.0	43.8	40.4	41.6	48.8	65.4	46.8
N.J.	67.5	60.3	56.3	63.6	68.6	68.5	53.1	52.0	30.3	43.8	49.6	41.2
N.Y.	64.8	46.9	51.5	55.0	60.3	60.0	43.8	46.7	33.5	39.2	41.2	35.9
Pa.	58.2	51.4	56.3	54.1	50.6	55.7	47.7	44.1	32.3	37.8	39.1	33.3
EAST NORTH CENTRAL												
Ill.	137.9	80.3	60.1	59.6	57.4	48.4	44.1	44.2	31.8	40.7	43.6	34.5
Ind.	73.2	54.0	52.2	48.7	44.8	40.8	40.8	40.8	34.4	41.5	44.4	34.7
Mich.	115.1	80.0	61.8	56.3	43.4	47.3	61.6	59.1	34.7	46.7	47.7	36.7
Ohio	64.5	48.4	52.1	46.8	43.2	44.6	50.0	42.1	30.9	42.0	47.9	34.0
Wis.	184.1	63.3	58.2	58.7	51.1	43.8	45.3	43.6	35.0	38.2	43.1	38.0
WEST NORTH CENTRAL												
Iowa	298.2	102.0	64.8	52.6	45.1	39.1	40.3	41.9	33.9	33.4	34.5	28.0
Kan.	--	280.0	214.7	71.1	43.2	44.2	41.1	43.3	39.8	37.8	44.1	26.9
Minn.	--	177.6	102.6	96.5	59.3	46.5	46.0	42.6	37.4	39.4	44.6	36.7
Mo.	124.9	95.7	64.3	55.7	48.4	41.7	39.3	40.4	32.4	35.8	38.0	32.6
Neb.	--	--	310.3	162.8	48.9	38.0	40.4	45.3	39.3	36.8	40.6	31.5
N.D.	--	--	--	--	97.6	103.4	46.7	47.7	45.1	39.4	45.5	39.6
S.D.	--	--	--	--	49.3	70.6	41.5	45.4	42.1	37.8	44.4	31.1
SOUTH												
Va.	51.5	39.4	85.6	50.1	45.7	45.2	46.3	40.5	38.3	52.9	44.9	38.8
Ala.	49.8	46.0	63.1	51.8	53.3	50.8	41.7	45.0	37.3	40.1	37.6	32.2
Ark.	144.2	50.0	104.6	72.5	55.8	64.7	51.3	50.3	39.3	38.6	41.8	35.6
Fla.	91.1	49.5	71.0	68.8	61.3	71.0	58.4	83.5	52.5	74.5	104.6	59.6
Ga.	63.2	45.7	64.8	48.1	52.1	47.4	38.5	37.5	34.4	41.3	41.5	38.9
La.	80.2	48.8	71.6	53.4	57.5	57.7	42.6	50.8	38.4	44.2	48.1	35.4
Miss.	59.4	49.1	70.2	49.5	53.2	48.2	38.3	46.9	37.4	41.3	40.1	37.1
N.C.	47.8	38.1	63.5	46.0	45.5	46.0	47.1	56.2	37.0	40.8	38.4	33.6
S.C.	42.9	48.7	78.1	51.9	48.8	45.0	44.7	44.0	38.2	43.6	41.1	30.7
Tex.	214.4	62.0	128.7	67.6	64.9	56.6	44.9	50.6	38.1	46.2	47.8	37.9

TABLE 4.3 (Continued)

	1850–1860	1860–1870	1870–1880	1880–1890	1890–1900	1900–1910	1910–1920	1920–1930	1930–1940	1940–1950	1950–1960	1960–1970
BORDER												
Ky.	64.2	47.5	58.7	44.5	48.5	42.6	40.5	43.1	35.5	35.9	35.1	33.1
Md.	54.8	31.5	53.7	48.2	52.5	45.6	47.2	44.8	39.4	55.2	55.7	47.0
Okla.	--	--	--	--	--	--	95.8	60.3	43.7	38.9	37.1	35.8
Tenn.	56.6	42.9	232.2	49.5	50.5	45.4	40.2	45.0	37.4	41.6	36.6	32.4
W.Va.	--	--	--[d]	59.9	54.9	56.9	49.1	51.0	36.2	36.6	44.0	41.6
MOUNTAIN												
Ariz.	--	--	437.7	141.4	57.1	80.6	--	76.7	55.0	84.6	102.1	58.6
Col.	--	--	--	--	116.8	130.9	50.7	46.7	39.2	50.4	60.8	49.4
Ida.	--	--	--	--	108.2	79.2	57.6	43.8	45.9	44.6	44.8	34.8
Mont.	--	--	72.6	49.7	50.1	130.7	73.2	44.8	37.5	40.5	49.0	35.4
Nev.	--	--	--	--	--	--	36.7	47.8	54.3	80.1	108.3	98.6
N.M.	--	--	--	--	--	--	--	63.5	60.6	62.9	70.0	31.5
Utah	--	--	--	--	63.7	67.2	56.4	51.2	40.6	54.3	55.4	40.9
Wyo.	--	--	--	--	77.7	82.8	60.7	45.9	40.2	47.1	46.4	33.6
PACIFIC												
Cal.	342.6	69.7	81.5	64.7	48.8	89.1	69.0	89.7	44.7	76.1	67.8	45.4
Ore.	--	95.3	119.5	105.7	52.0	86.5	39.6	47.1	39.8	65.7	41.8	41.4
Wash.	--	--	--	--	67.7	146.3	38.8	38.1	36.8	65.4	45.2	43.5
Alaska	--	--	--	--	--	--	--	--	--	--	--	52.0
Hawaii	--	--	--	--	--	--	--	--	--	--	--	38.7

a. Computed on basis of free population, 1870 figures for noncolored population only.
b. 1860 figures for free population, 1870 figures for noncolored population.
c. Virginia computed using an estimate for 1860 BILI for those counties which remained in Virginia after West Virginia split off in 1862.
d. Figures for West Virginia, 1870-1880 could not be computed due to lack of 1870 information on number of persons born.
-- Not applicable.

percent; the gross change in contrast was 138 percent reflecting a high rate of migration into the state. During the decade from 1920 to 1930 the net change rate for the state was low (17.7 percent), but the gross rate was substantially higher (44 percent). Clearly the net change calculation under-estimates population change and works to conceal significant reconstitution of the population and the electorate.

In more general terms, gross population change rates across the states rarely fall below 30 percent and usually range between 40 and 60 percent for nearly all states in most time periods. While net population change often approaches zero and seldom exceeds 30 percent in the twentieth century, the gross change rate reflects substantially greater population movement. For the relatively well-established states, the rate of population change was higher in the nineteenth century than in the twentieth century. The east and west north central regions, while slowing markedly in rate of net population change in the twentieth century, continued to be marked by a gross population change rate of around 40 percent. Here again, the appearance of population stability conveyed by the net change rates masks a pattern of continuing and substantial population change and reconstitution. Population change has not, in short, been confined to a few states and time periods but has been a relatively constant factor in American history.

As in the case of net population change, the gross population change rates given in Table 4.3 are aggregate figures for each of the various states and do not reflect population movement within states. It is impossible to provide here a detailed examination of within-state population movement. To do so would require a data collection effort of very considerable magnitude. It is possible, however, to draw for illustrative purposes upon data developed through the work of social and urban historians carried out over the past decade and a half or more.[3] These historians have provided estimates of population "persistence rates" for a number of cities during the late nineteenth and twentieth century. The persistence rates are estimates of the percentage of people who were residents of the given city at one census, but who were not residents at the next. The counterpart of the persistence rate, of course, provides an indication of the rate at which people left the various cities either through migration or death. Table 4.4 provides estimates of population persistence rates for selected cities at various periods and for the states in which these cities were located. Although the estimates are based upon very extensive research and data collection, they are not completely comparable in every case, and some of the assumptions which they involve have been challenged. They do serve, however, to indicate levels of population movement characteristic of the cities in comparison to those of the states.

As Table 4.4 indicates, the persistence rates for the various cities are by no means identical with those of the states. While the persistence rates tend to rise over time, there are significant differences in the rate at which residents remained in (or left) the various cities. The persistence rates for the states are, understandably, higher and more consistent than those of the cities. Many of the people who left a particular city relocated within the same state, and many, particularly in later years, probably moved just outside the boundaries of the city proper. Comparison of the city and state rates serves to underscore an earlier point. Since they capture only state-to-state movement, and that only at decennial points, the state-level measures are consistently below the actual levels of population movement. Data for substate areas would undoubtedly reveal substantially higher population movement at least in particular areas. Thus, large-scale shifting and reconstitution of the electorate appears to have been a constant historical process.

The estimates of population change given above are all undifferentiated by age. As a consequence, they do not provide a direct indication of change and reconstitution of the eligible electorate. At first glance, moreover, it might appear that they consistently overstate change in the electorate. Obviously, births during a particular decade affect the eligible electorate only after a significant time lag. Indeed, all components of both net and gross population change contain persons too young to be in the eligible electorate. This overstatement of change is partially compensated for by the inherent understating of population change of the intrastate and "short-hop" variety discussed above. The measures of population change given previously in the tables, therefore, provide a rather rough estimate of the magnitude of dissimilarity across decades.

CHARACTERISTICS OF THE POPULATION

Population change was often accompanied historically by change in the economic and social characteristics of the population. In particular areas, moreover, even relatively limited changes in population size were accompanied by substantial social and economic change as industries expanded or declined or as new economic pursuits were undertaken and others abandoned. Change of this sort raises, of course, issues of comparability, particularly from one time period to another, similar to those presented by population change, and it also introduces a variable that may in some instances explain shifts in voting patterns.

TABLE 4.4
Persistence Rates of Population in Selected Cities and States, 1850-1960

City or State	1850–1860	1860–1870	1870–1880	1880–1890	1890–1900	1900–1910	1910–1920	1920–1930	1930–1940	1940–1950	1950–1960
MASSACHUSETTS	73.1%	78.1%	76.3%	77.7%	76.4%	76.8%	78.4%	78.3%	84.3%	79.9%	79.0%
Boston	39.0			64.0			41.0		59.0		
Northhampton	53.0										
Waltham	44.0	45.0	50.0	58.0							
NEW YORK	68.6	74.3	67.5	75.4	73.5	78.0	78.6	83.1	86.5	81.3	79.9
Poughkeepsie		49.0	50.0								
PENNSYLVANIA	76.8	80.4	77.8	81.3	81.2	78.6	78.6	79.0	83.5	80.0	79.8
Norristown							59.0		50.0	53.0	
Philadelphia	32.0										
NEBRASKA	----	----	16.7	49.4	60.0	66.6	70.4	68.1	70.7	68.4	70.4
Omaha				44.0		44.0					
GEORGIA	67.9	85.7	79.6	84.1	81.0	82.7	83.2	72.6	83.5	77.6	80.1
Atlanta		44.0									
TEXAS	74.8	77.1	80.4	82.9	78.3	78.9	81.9	81.8	85.2	80.7	82.0
San Antonio			32.0								
CALIFORNIA	33.1	76.3	75.2	79.7	28.4	79.9	80.6	84.3	85.3	77.3	80.9
Los Angeles				54.0			49.0				
San Francisco			84.0	50.0							

SOURCE: State-level figures appearing in this table were calculated by the authors from data obtained from the ICPSR Archive. Figures for cities were obtained from Thernstrom (footnote 3, The Other Bostonians, Cambridge, MA, 1973).
-- Not applicable.

We cannot examine here all of the many aspects of social and economic change that the United States has undergone since its founding. We can only touch upon several relatively limited aspects of change in order to suggest in approximate ways rates and loci of change and to call attention to the research and methodological issues which they raise. In doing so, we will also call attention at several points to characteristics and limitations of the historical data that are most commonly available.

URBANIZATION

One of the more obvious processes of change which the United States has undergone is the shift of population from villages and rural areas to urban settings. Although a continuing phenomenon in American history, the process has involved widely differing patterns both from one area of the nation to another and from one time period to the next. In some areas and time periods the process occurred with considerable rapidity, and towns and cities of substantial size appeared virtually overnight. Thus, a predominantly rural area at one census became by the time of the next an area of significant urban concentration. In other areas the process occurred much more slowly, and still other areas have remained essentially rural throughout their history. The continuing growth of major cities in the northeastern quadrant of the country was a dominant fact, and often a source of concern, during much of the history of the nation. More recently, this process has slowed or been reversed, and city growth has shifted from the Northeast to the South and Southwest.

There are various ways of measuring urban population and, as will be suggested, some of the approaches that have been employed historically pose significant research difficulties. One measure is simply the proportion of the population of a given area that resides in places of varying population size. This information is given in Table 4.5 for selected time points from 1790 to 1970 and depicts the general pattern of urbanization from a national perspective. The table suggests the shift of the national population away from rural areas and small towns and the corresponding growth of major urban concentrations. As will also be noted, however, the proportion of the population residing in smaller towns (under 25,000) increased more rapidly than did the proportion residing in larger areas, particularly since 1930. The pattern is, of course, in some respects a definitional artifact as the proportion of the population residing in Standard Metropolitan Statistical Areas (also given in Table 4.5) suggests. Many of these smaller towns were suburbs of larger urban areas and in many ways indistinguishable from the larger urban areas, aside from arbitrary city boundaries.

TABLE 4.5

Percentage of U.S. Population in Places, by Size of Place, in Selected Decades, 1790-1970

Size of Place	1790	1810	1830	1850	1870	1890	1910	1930	1950	1970
Under 2,500	94.9%	92.7%	91.2%	84.7%	74.4%	64.9%	54.3%	43.9%	41.2%	34.3%
2,500-4,999	1.1	1.0	1.0	1.4	2.8	3.6	4.1	3.8	4.3	4.0
5,000-9,999	1.2	1.6	1.8	2.6	3.3	3.8	4.6	4.8	5.4	6.4
10,000-24,999	1.2	1.5	1.9	2.4	4.4	5.5	6.0	7.4	7.9	10.5
25,000-99,999	1.6	3.2	2.5	3.9	4.4	6.8	8.9	10.5	11.8	17.0
100,000-249,999	0	0	1.6	2.8	2.6	4.4	5.3	6.1	6.3	7.0
250,000+	0	0	0	2.2	8.1	11.0	16.8	23.5	23.1	20.8
	100.0%	100.0%	100.0%	100.0%	100.0%	100.0%	100.0%	100.0%	100.0%	100.0%
Population in Standard Metropolitan Statistical Areas (SMSAs)	--	--	--	--	--	--	--	--	56.1%	68.6%

-- Not applicable.

119

Urbanization did not occur at the same rate in all areas and time periods. Some of these variations are reflected by another definition of urban, in this case the proportion of the population residing in places of 2,500 or more persons. This information is given in Table 4.6 for each of the states from 1790 to 1970. As can be seen, several of the eastern seaboard states experienced their greatest increase in urban residence, in terms of this definition, during the first half of the nineteenth century; in a number of midwestern states, increase in urban residence was most marked in the latter half of the nineteenth century; while in the South and West the most dramatic increases came in the years since 1940. It can also be noted from the table that the states varied considerably in urban population during the same time periods. In 1860, the urban population varied from zero in Nebraska to over 63 percent in Rhode Island. In 1920, when 51.1 percent of the national population resided in places of 2,500 or more persons, there were only sixteen states that were more than 50 percent urban in terms of this definition, and the states ranged from 13.6 percent urban (North Dakota) to 91.8 percent (New Jersey). By 1970, the states had become more homogeneous in terms of urban population.

In tabulating the various censuses, residence in places of 2,500 persons or more has been used as a definition of "urban" consistently since 1906. For some of the earlier censuses, a higher defining figure was originally employed, but the data for the various states was subsequently retabulated using the 2,500 figure. For more recent censuses, other definitions of urban have been employed while also retaining the 2,500 definition. Thus, data tabulated in terms of the latter definition are most consistently available across the sweep of American history. As will be recognized, of course, this definition is inadequate for a number of purposes and sometimes leads to anomalies. Residence in a town of three or four thousand population is obviously not the same as residence in a major city such as New York or Chicago, but this difference is masked in the 2,500 definition. It is also the case that sparsely populated areas in various time periods appear in terms of this definition to be highly urban. Mining and lumbering areas, for example, sometimes appear in the data as nearly 100 percent urban, signifying only that the small population of these areas was almost entirely clustered in a few small towns.

The information presented in Table 4.6 does, however, demonstrate the differing patterns of urbanization that have characterized the United States. This information also suggests problems of comparability over time. During most periods of forty or fifty years, the urban populations of various states doubled or tripled, and it is obvious that rates of urbanization for particular areas varied widely from the state pattern. Thus, in

TABLE 4.6

Percentage of Population Residing in Places of 2,500 or More Inhabitants, 1790-1970

	1790	1800	1810	1820	1830	1840	1850	1860	1870	1880	1890	1900	1910	1920	1930	1940	1950	1960	1970
NEW ENGLAND																			
Conn.	3.0%	5.1%	6.1%	7.6%	9.4%	12.6%	16.0%	26.5%	33.0%	41.9%	50.9%	59.9%	65.6%	67.8%	70.4%	67.8%	64.1%	78.3%	77.4%
Me.	0.0	2.4	3.1	2.0	3.2	7.8	13.5	16.6	21.0	22.6	28.1	33.5	35.3	39.0	40.3	40.5	41.0	51.3	50.8
Mass.	13.5	15.4	21.3	22.8	31.1	37.9	50.7	59.6	66.7	74.7	82.0	86.0	89.0	90.0	90.2	89.3	87.9	83.6	84.6
N.H.	3.3	2.9	3.2	3.0	5.0	10.0	17.1	22.1	26.2	30.3	39.3	46.7	51.8	56.5	58.7	57.6	56.5	58.3	56.4
R.I.	10.0	20.8	23.4	23.0	31.2	43.8	55.6	63.3	74.6	81.9	85.3	88.3	91.0	91.8	92.4	91.6	88.4	86.4	87.1
Vt.	0.0	0.0	0.0	0.0	0.0	0.0	1.9	2.0	7.0	10.1	15.2	22.1	27.8	31.2	33.0	34.3	36.4	38.5	32.2
MIDDLE ATLANTIC																			
Del.	0.0	0.0	0.0	0.0	0.0	10.7	15.3	18.9	24.6	33.4	42.2	46.4	48.0	54.2	51.6	52.3	46.5	65.5	72.2
N.J.	0.0	0.0	2.4	2.7	5.7	10.6	17.6	32.7	43.7	54.4	62.6	70.6	76.4	79.9	82.6	81.6	79.6	88.6	88.9
N.Y.	11.5	12.7	12.7	11.7	14.9	19.4	28.2	39.3	50.0	56.4	65.2	72.9	78.9	82.7	83.6	82.8	80.2	85.4	85.6
Penn.	10.2	11.3	12.8	13.0	15.3	17.9	23.6	30.8	37.3	41.6	48.6	54.7	60.4	65.1	67.8	66.5	65.8	71.6	71.5
EAST NORTH CENTRAL																			
Ill.	--	--	0.0	0.0	0.0	2.0	7.6	14.3	23.5	30.6	44.9	54.3	61.7	67.9	73.9	73.6	74.5	80.7	83.0
Ind.	--	0.0	0.0	0.0	0.0	1.6	4.5	8.6	14.7	19.5	26.9	34.3	42.3	50.6	55.5	55.1	56.4	62.4	64.9
Mich.	--	--	0.0	0.0	0.0	4.3	7.3	13.3	20.1	24.8	34.0	30.3	47.2	61.1	68.2	66.8	64.3	73.4	73.8
Ohio	--	0.0	1.1	1.7	3.9	5.5	12.2	17.1	25.6	32.2	41.1	48.1	55.0	63.8	67.8	66.8	66.4	73.4	75.3
Wis.	--	--	--	--	--	0.0	9.4	14.4	19.6	24.1	33.3	38.2	43.0	47.3	52.9	53.5	55.5	63.8	65.9
WEST NORTH CENTRAL																			
Iowa	--	--	--	--	--	0.0	5.1	8.9	13.1	15.2	21.2	25.6	30.6	36.4	39.6	42.7	46.9	53.0	57.2
Kan.	--	--	--	--	--	--	--	9.4	14.2	10.5	18.9	22.4	29.1	34.8	38.8	41.9	47.4	61.0	66.1
Minn.	--	--	--	--	--	--	0.0	9.4	16.1	19.1	34.0	34.1	41.0	44.1	49.0	49.8	53.9	62.2	66.4
Mo.	--	--	0.0	0.0	3.5	4.3	11.8	17.2	25.0	25.2	32.0	26.2	42.3	46.6	51.2	51.8	57.9	66.6	70.1
Neb.	--	--	--	--	--	--	--	0.0	18.0	13.5	27.5	23.7	26.1	42.3	35.3	39.1	45.8	54.3	61.5
N.D.	--	--	--	--	--	--	--	--	--	--	5.8	7.3	11.0	13.6	16.6	20.5	26.6	35.2	44.3
S.D.	--	--	--	--	--	--	--	--	--	--	8.7	10.2	13.1	16.0	18.9	24.6	33.1	39.3	44.6
SOUTH																			
Ala.	--	--	--	0.0	1.0	2.1	4.6	5.1	6.3	5.4	10.1	11.8	16.3	21.7	28.1	30.2	40.1	54.8	58.4
Ark.	--	--	0.0	0.0	0.0	0.0	0.0	0.9	2.6	4.0	6.5	8.5	12.9	16.6	20.6	22.2	32.3	42.8	50.0
Fla.	--	--	--	0.0	0.0	0.0	0.0	4.1	8.1	10.0	19.8	20.2	29.1	36.5	51.8	55.1	56.5	73.9	80.5
Ga.	0.0	3.2	2.1	2.2	2.7	3.6	4.3	7.1	8.5	9.4	14.0	15.6	29.1	25.1	30.8	34.4	40.1	53.3	60.3
La.	--	--	22.5	17.7	21.4	29.9	26.0	26.1	27.9	25.5	25.4	26.5	30.0	34.9	39.7	41.5	50.8	63.3	66.1
Miss.	--	0.0	0.0	0.0	2.0	1.0	1.8	2.6	4.0	3.1	5.4	7.7	11.5	13.4	16.9	19.8	27.6	37.7	44.5
N.C.	0.0	0.0	0.0	2.0	1.4	1.8	2.4	2.5	3.4	3.9	7.2	9.9	14.4	19.2	25.5	27.3	30.5	39.5	45.0

TABLE 4.6 (Continued)

	1790	1800	1810	1820	1830	1840	1850	1860	1870	1880	1890	1900	1910	1920	1930	1940	1950	1960	1970
S.C.	6.6	5.4	6.0	4.9	5.8	5.7	7.3	5.9	8.6	7.5	10.1	12.8	14.8	16.5	21.3	24.5	28.8	41.2	47.6
Texas	--	--	--	--	--	--	3.6	4.4	6.7	9.2	15.6	17.1	24.1	32.4	41.0	45.4	59.8	75.0	79.7
Va.	1.6	1.8	2.5	2.6	3.5	5.7	7.1	8.5	11.9	12.5	17.1	18.3	23.1	29.2	32.4	35.3	40.3	55.6	63.1
BORDER																			
Ky.	0.0	0.0	1.1	1.6	2.4	4.0	7.5	10.4	14.8	15.2	19.2	21.8	24.3	26.2	30.6	29.8	33.5	44.5	52.3
Md.	4.2	7.8	12.2	16.3	20.4	24.2	32.3	34.0	37.8	40.2	47.6	49.8	50.8	60.0	59.8	59.3	54.4	72.7	76.6
Okla.	--	--	--	--	--	--	--	--	--	--	--	--	19.2	18.5	34.3	37.7	49.6	62.9	68.0
Tenn.	0.0	0.0	0.0	0.0	0.8	0.8	2.2	4.2	7.5	7.5	13.5	16.2	20.2	26.1	34.3	35.2	38.4	52.3	58.7
W.Va.	--	--	--	--	--	--	--	--	8.1	8.7	10.7	13.1	18.7	25.2	28.4	28.1	31.9	38.2	39.0
MOUNTAIN																			
Ariz.	--	--	--	--	--	--	--	--	--	31.4	45.1	48.3	31.0	36.1	34.4	34.8	36.5	74.5	79.6
Colo.	--	--	--	--	--	--	--	--	12.0	--	--	--	50.3	48.2	50.2	52.6	57.3	73.7	78.5
Ida.	--	--	--	--	--	--	--	--	--	--	0.0	6.2	21.5	27.6	29.1	33.7	39.8	47.5	54.1
Mont.	--	--	--	--	--	--	--	--	--	--	29.4	34.8	35.5	31.3	33.7	37.8	42.8	50.2	53.4
Nev.	--	--	--	--	--	--	--	--	16.5	31.2	35.0	17.0	16.4	19.8	37.9	39.3	52.5	70.4	80.9
N.M.	--	--	--	--	--	--	--	--	--	--	--	--	14.2	18.0	25.2	33.2	46.2	65.9	69.8
Utah	--	--	--	--	--	--	--	--	--	--	36.2	38.1	46.3	48.0	52.4	55.5	59.9	74.9	80.4
Wyo.	--	--	--	--	--	--	--	--	--	--	35.4	28.9	29.6	29.4	31.1	37.3	39.8	56.8	60.5
PACIFIC																			
Cal.	--	--	--	--	--	--	7.4	20.7	37.2	42.9	48.8	52.3	61.8	67.9	73.3	71.0	67.1	86.4	90.9
Ore.	--	--	--	--	--	--	--	5.5	9.1	14.8	28.2	32.2	45.6	49.8	51.3	48.8	48.1	62.2	67.1
Wash.	--	--	--	--	--	--	--	--	--	--	36.4	40.8	53.0	54.8	56.6	53.1	53.6	68.1	72.6
Alaska	--	--	--	--	--	--	--	--	--	--	--	--	--	--	--	--	--	38.1	48.7
Hawaii	--	--	--	--	--	--	--	--	--	--	--	--	--	--	--	--	--	76.5	83.1

-- Not applicable.

terms of their urban character, many areas were not the same at one time as they had been at another.

POPULATION OF FOREIGN ORIGIN

As is well known, the population of the United States was augmented over the years by large numbers of immigrants, some 44,789,000 from 1820 through 1969. The peak period of immigration extended from the mid-nineteenth century through the 1920s, when legislative restrictions drastically slowed the flow of new arrivals. One of the consequences of this influx of immigrants was to significantly change the composition of the nation and to radically and rapidly change the composition of particular areas.

The percentage of the population of each state which was of foreign birth is given in Table 4.7 for each census from 1850 through 1970. As can be seen, the foreign-born distributed themselves quite unevenly across the nation. The northeastern seaboard and upper midwestern states have throughout the years included in their populations substantial numbers of foreign-born (generally, 10 to 30 percent of the total populations). In contrast, foreign-born population rarely accounted for more than 5 percent of the residents of the southern and border states. Three patterns of change in the foreign-born component of the population of the various states can be noted. In the northeastern and middle Atlantic states and in several states of the upper Midwest, particularly Illinois and Michigan, the proportion of foreign-born increased rather steadily from the mid-nineteenth century, peaked around 1910, and declined thereafter. A second large group of states, including less populous eastern states such as Vermont and Delaware, the southern states, and Indiana, Ohio, Iowa, and Kansas in the Midwest, changed only slightly in terms of foreign-born population between 1850 and 1920. A number of western and midwestern states, including Wisconsin, Minnesota, North Dakota, Nevada, California, and Washington, appear to have included substantial numbers of foreign-born among their early settlers. During the first two decades of statehood, individuals of foreign birth accounted for between 30 and 45 percent of the population of these states. These proportions gradually declined until about 1910 when in these states, as in other states, decline became more precipitous.

Thus the potential electoral impact of foreign-born voters varied considerably across the states and from one time period to the next. The potential impact was clearly negligible in the South and in most of the border states. In a large number of states in the Northeast, the Midwest and the West, the foreign-born population tended to be relatively large and to increase throughout the latter nineteenth century and, in some cases,

TABLE 4.7
Percentage of Population Foreign Born, 1850-1970

	1850	1860	1870	1880	1890	1900	1910	1920	1930	1940	1950	1960	1970
NEW ENGLAND													
Conn.	10.1	17.6	21.1	20.9	24.6	26.2	29.5	27.3	23.8	19.2	14.8	10.9	8.6
Me.	5.4	6.0	7.8	9.1	11.9	13.4	14.8	14.0	10.5	9.9	8.1	6.2	4.3
Mass.	16.2	21.2	24.2	24.9	29.4	30.2	31.2	28.0	24.8	19.7	15.2	11.2	8.7
N.H.	4.3	6.4	9.3	13.3	19.2	21.4	22.4	20.6	17.8	13.9	10.9	7.4	5.0
R.I.	15.7	21.5	25.5	26.8	30.8	31.4	32.8	28.7	24.8	19.3	14.3	10.0	7.8
Vt.	10.4	10.4	14.3	12.3	13.3	13.0	14.0	12.6	12.0	8.8	7.6	6.0	4.2
MIDDLE ATLANTIC													
Del.	5.7	8.5	7.3	6.5	7.8	7.5	8.6	8.9	7.1	5.6	4.3	3.3	2.9
N.J.	11.9	18.4	20.9	19.6	22.8	22.9	25.9	23.4	20.9	16.7	13.0	10.1	8.9
N.Y.	21.0	25.8	26.0	23.8	26.2	26.1	29.8	26.9	25.4	21.2	16.9	13.6	11.6
Penn.	12.8	14.9	15.5	13.7	16.1	15.6	18.8	15.9	12.8	9.8	7.4	5.3	3.8
EAST NORTH CENTRAL													
Ill.	13.0	19.0	20.3	19.0	22.0	20.1	21.3	18.6	16.2	12.3	9.0	6.8	5.7
Ind.	5.5	8.8	8.4	7.3	6.7	5.6	5.9	5.1	4.4	3.2	2.6	2.0	1.6
Mich.	13.8	20.0	22.6	23.7	26.0	22.4	21.2	19.8	17.5	13.0	9.5	6.8	4.8
Ohio	11.0	14.1	14.0	12.3	12.5	11.0	12.5	11.8	9.7	7.5	5.6	4.1	3.0
Wisc.	34.9	35.7	34.6	30.8	30.8	24.9	22.0	17.5	13.1	9.2	6.4	4.3	3.0
WEST NORTH CENTRAL													
Iowa	11.0	15.7	17.1	16.1	17.0	13.7	12.3	9.4	6.8	4.6	3.2	2.0	1.4
Kans.	--	11.9	13.3	11.1	10.4	8.6	8.0	6.2	4.3	2.9	2.0	1.5	1.2
Minn.	33.7	34.2	36.5	34.3	35.9	28.9	26.2	20.4	15.2	10.6	7.0	4.2	2.6
Mo.	10.6	15.1	12.9	9.8	8.8	7.0	7.0	5.5	4.5	3.0	2.3	1.8	1.4
Neb.	--	22.1	25.0	21.5	19.1	16.6	14.8	11.5	8.6	6.2	4.3	2.9	1.9
N.D.	--	--	--	--	44.6	35.4	27.1	20.3	15.5	11.6	7.9	4.7	3.0
S.D.	--	--	--	--	27.7	22.0	17.2	12.9	9.5	6.9	4.7	2.7	1.6
SOUTH													
Ala.	1.0	2.3	1.0	0.8	1.0	0.8	0.9	0.8	0.6	0.4	0.5	0.5	0.5
Ark.	0.8	1.1	1.0	1.3	1.3	1.1	1.1	0.8	0.6	0.4	0.5	0.4	0.4

TABLE 4.7 (Continued)

	1850	1860	1870	1880	1890	1900	1910	1920	1930	1940	1950	1960	1970
Fla.	3.2	4.2	2.6	3.7	5.9	4.5	4.5	4.4	4.0	3.7	4.4	5.5	8.0
Ga.	0.7	2.0	0.9	0.7	0.7	0.6	0.6	0.6	0.5	0.4	0.5	0.6	0.7
La.	12.8	22.3	8.5	5.8	4.4	3.8	3.1	2.5	1.7	1.2	1.1	0.9	1.1
Miss.	0.8	2.4	1.4	0.8	0.6	0.5	0.5	0.4	0.4	0.3	0.4	0.4	0.4
N.C.	0.3	0.5	0.3	0.3	0.2	0.2	0.3	0.3	0.3	0.3	0.4	0.5	0.6
S.C.	1.3	3.4	1.1	0.8	0.5	0.4	0.4	0.4	0.3	0.3	0.4	0.5	0.6
Tex.	7.9	10.3	7.6	7.2	6.8	5.9	6.2	7.7	6.6	3.7	3.6	3.1	2.8
Va.	1.6	3.2	1.1	1.0	1.1	1.0	1.3	1.3	1.0	0.9	1.1	1.2	1.6
BORDER													
Ky.	3.0	6.5	4.8	3.6	3.2	2.3	1.7	1.3	0.8	0.5	0.5	0.6	0.5
Md.	9.1	13.3	10.7	8.9	9.0	7.9	8.0	7.0	5.8	4.5	3.6	3.0	3.2
Okla.	--	--	--	--	--	--	2.4	1.4	1.3	0.9	0.8	0.9	0.8
Tenn.	0.6	2.6	1.5	1.1	1.1	0.9	0.8	0.7	0.5	0.4	0.5	0.4	0.5
W. Va.	--	--	3.9	3.0	2.5	2.3	4.7	4.2	3.0	2.2	1.7	1.3	1.0
MOUNTAIN													
Ariz.	--	--	--	--	--	--	22.9	23.4	14.6	7.4	6.1	5.4	4.3
Col.	--	--	16.6	20.5	20.4	16.9	15.9	12.4	9.5	6.3	4.5	3.4	2.7
Ida.	--	--	--	--	20.7	15.2	12.4	9.0	7.0	4.6	3.3	2.3	1.8
Mont.	--	--	--	--	32.6	27.6	24.4	17.1	13.9	9.9	7.3	4.5	2.8
Nev.	--	30.1	44.2	41.2	32.1	23.8	22.0	19.1	15.8	9.6	6.6	4.6	3.7
N.M.	--	--	--	--	--	--	6.9	8.1	5.6	2.9	2.5	2.3	2.2
Utah	--	--	--	--	25.5	19.4	17.0	12.6	9.1	5.9	4.3	3.6	2.8
Wyo.	--	--	--	--	24.6	18.8	18.6	13.0	10.5	6.7	4.6	2.9	2.1
PACIFIC													
Calif.	24.1	38.7	37.5	33.9	30.3	24.7	21.8	19.9	17.6	12.6	9.3	8.5	8.8
Ore.	--	9.8	12.8	17.5	18.3	15.9	15.3	13.0	11.2	8.0	5.5	4.0	3.2
Wash.	--	--	--	--	25.8	21.5	21.1	18.4	15.6	11.7	8.0	6.3	4.6
Alaska	--	--	--	--	--	--	--	--	--	--	--	3.6	3.0
Hawaii	--	--	--	--	--	--	--	--	--	--	--	10.9	9.6

-- Not applicable.

into the twentieth century. Since 1920, the incidence of foreign-born population has tended to decrease; by 1960 only five states, all in the Northeast, included as many as 10 percent foreign-born residents.

Both the diversity of the foreign-stock population and the potential impact of immigration upon electoral patterns are, of course, understated in Table 4.7. The "immigrant" component of the population contained widely varied national groups with highly diverse cultural and economic characteristics. These groups differed significantly in terms of their time of arrival and settlement patterns. Some groups tended, particularly initially, to concentrate themselves in certain and often relatively limited areas of the nation, while others distributed themselves much more broadly. Thus, the potential impact of these various national groups upon electoral processes and the likelihood of retention of cultural attributes and identifications derived from their native countries were significantly more diverse than the table suggests.

Table 4.7 also understates the potential impact of immigration upon electoral processes in even more serious ways. That impact is clearly not adequately reflected by the proportion of the population that was foreign-born. Second- and, for that matter, subsequent-generation members of ethnic groups are obviously also relevant. Information on the numbers of individuals who were native-born but of foreign or mixed parentage was not collected through national censuses until 1870, and information pertinent to third-generation population was never collected.

Considerations of space preclude presentation of any of the available data, but several illustrative observations are in order. The proportion of "foreign-stock" population (native-born of foreign or "mixed" parentage as well as foreign-born) was, of course, consistently much larger than the proportion foreign-born. These proportions increased rapidly, particularly in the late nineteenth and early twentiety century and declined after 1920. In the early years of the twentieth century, these individuals constituted a very substantial segment of the population in a number of areas. In 1910, for example, "foreign stock" population accounted for over half of the total population of thirteen states. As late as 1950, individuals of "foreign stock" in terms of the Census Bureau's definition accounted for over one-third of the population of one-sixth of the states. Clearly, then, immigration had the effect of transforming the population of major areas of the nation.

Here again, the statewide figures given in Table 4.7 obviously understate the impact of immigration upon smaller areas of the nation. In some respects, the transformation of the urban population through immigration was particularly noteworthy, and, indeed, the growth of major cities in the late nineteenth and early twentieth century was closely related to the flow

TABLE 4.8
Percentage Foreign-Born Residents in Selected Cities, 1860-1970

	1860	1870	1880	1890	1900	1910	1920	1930	1940*	1950*	1960	1970
Chicago	50.0	48.4	40.7	41.0	34.6	35.8	29.9	25.5	19.8	14.5	12.3	11.1
Detroit	46.8	44.5	39.2	39.8	33.8	33.8	29.3	25.9	19.8	14.9	12.1	7.9
Philadelphia	30.0	27.2	24.1	25.7	22.8	24.8	22.0	19.1	15.0	11.2	8.9	6.5
Boston	35.9	35.1	31.6	35.3	35.1	36.3	32.4	29.9	23.5	18.0	15.8	13.1
Atlanta	NA	NA	NA	2.9	2.8	2.9	2.4	1.8	1.4	1.3	0.9	1.2
Los Angeles	NA	35.0	28.7	25.3	19.5	20.7	21.2	20.0	14.3	12.5	12.6	14.6
Dallas	NA	NA	NA	10.5	7.9	5.7	5.5	3.6	2.5	1.9	1.9	2.1
Kansas City	NA	23.8	16.7	15.7	11.2	10.3	8.5	6.6	4.8	3.5	2.8	2.0
Cleveland	44.8	41.8	37.1	37.2	32.6	35.0	30.1	25.6	20.4	14.5	11.0	7.5
Pittsburgh	34.7	31.0	27.2	28.9	26.4	26.4	20.5	16.4	12.6	9.6	7.5	6.0
New York	45.5	42.1	37.0	38.9	37.0	40.8	36.1	34.0	27.9	22.6	20.0	18.2

*Foreign-born white.
NA — Not available.

of newcomers from other nations. For illustrative purposes, Table 4.8 presents the proportion foreign-born for selected major cities. The regional distribution of the foreign-born population is again apparent. The largest concentrations were in the cities of the Northeast and upper Midwest, while the numbers in such cities as Kansas City, Dallas, and Atlanta were very significantly smaller. As in the case of the statewide proportions, the influence of immigration is understated in Table 4.8 since these figures include only the foreign-born and omit individuals of second- and third-generation immigrant stock.

POPULATION EMPLOYED IN AGRICULTURE

The transformation of the national economy is one of the obvious facets of American history, bringing with it substantial and, in many areas, rapid change in the context of electoral politics. Stated in the most general terms, that transformation involved decline in the relative importance in the national economy of agriculture and the extractive industries, and growth in the importance of the industrial and tertiary sectors. Numerous indicators of historical economic change are available, none of which, either individually or taken in combination, is entirely satisfactory. One such indicator, the percentage of the labor force employed in agriculture for selected decades from 1850 through 1970, is presented in Table 4.9 to provide a crude summary of the general contour of economic change.

The information presented in Table 4.9 is also a useful illustration of some of the difficulties presented by historical source materials. As noted at several points in this volume, the censuses of the United States are the most comprehensive and consistent sources of systematic, quantitative data bearing upon the national past. Even at best, however, data from this source suffer from numerous inconsistencies. Changes in definitions from one census to the next, particularly during the earlier years, introduce troublesome questions of comparability. Change in the age definition of the labor force, as reflected in Table 4.9, is a case in point, as is the inclusion of forestry and fisheries with agriculture in 1950. Fortunately, efforts have been made to improve the consistency of these data. An example is the work of Simon Kuznets and his colleagues, which provides the data employed in the table for the decennial points from 1870 through 1950. However, such efforts are also limited by the characteristics of the available original data, and fully adequate measures cannot always be developed.

In a still more general sense, of course, the proportions employed in agriculture are a highly imperfect indicator. For the purposes of electoral analysis, for example, this indicator probably tends to understate the importance of agriculture. The tabulations purport to show, with noted

TABLE 4.9
Percentage of Population Employed in Agriculture, 1850-1970
(Selected decades)

STATE	1850[a]	1870[b]	1890	1910	1930	1950	1970[c]
NEW ENGLAND							
Conn.	32.0	24.6	15.7	9.4	5.4	2.5	1.1
Me.	47.4	42.7	33.8	24.0	16.7	8.5	4.1
Mass.	18.9	14.1	7.7	4.4	3.1	1.5	0.9
N.H.	50.2	40.8	27.3	18.0	11.5	5.9	1.9
R.I.	19.5	15.1	8.2	4.5	3.0	1.1	0.9
Vt.	52.4	57.2	45.2	33.8	27.0	17.2	6.1
MIDDLE ATLANTIC							
Del.	35.7	45.9	33.1	26.4	17.6	8.2	2.6
N.J.	25.5	25.3	13.5	7.1	3.7	2.2	0.9
N.Y.	35.3	38.3	18.0	9.3	4.8	2.6	1.3
Penn.	30.3	30.3	19.1	11.3	6.7	3.8	1.8
EAST NORTH CENTRAL							
Ill.	65.5	55.9	35.4	19.5	11.1	6.6	2.7
Ind.	65.6	63.2	49.3	33.1	20.0	11.1	3.4
Mich.	60.4	51.7	41.0	28.9	12.9	6.2	1.8
Ohio	50.9	51.9	35.4	21.8	11.9	6.5	2.1
Wis.	52.4	60.0	44.7	33.2	25.7	18.0	6.5
WEST NORTH CENTRAL							
Iowa	66.5	66.2	54.7	42.8	36.3	27.6	13.1
Kan.	--	63.4	58.8	44.1	33.0	21.9	8.8
Minn.	24.1	63.4	44.5	33.4	30.6	21.9	7.6
Mo.	51.1	58.0	47.4	35.2	25.4	16.9	5.1
Neb.	--	59.8	50.0	45.9	38.9	28.5	13.7
N.D.	--	--	66.8	60.2	55.9	43.2	21.3
S.D.	--	--	62.8	56.9	52.8	39.0	22.2
SOUTH							
Ala.	68.3	82.0	72.3	66.4	48.0	24.0	3.9
Ark.	71.0	82.3	76.7	69.3	57.6	34.0	8.4
Fla.	45.5	75.1	52.4	36.6	22.3	11.0	4.6
Ga.	67.6	78.3	64.8	62.1	42.8	20.4	4.3
La.	24.2	61.5	63.0	49.4	36.4	16.5	4.1
Miss.	67.0	85.6	80.7	76.4	65.9	40.9	7.5
N.C.	58.3	80.1	71.7	63.5	43.8	23.7	5.2
S.C.	60.3	81.8	77.0	70.1	50.1	25.6	4.2
Tex.	59.0	74.9	65.8	59.6	38.1	15.1	4.7
Va.	47.8	64.0	51.3	43.9	30.8	12.9	3.3
BORDER							
Ky.	60.2	67.5	58.1	52.2	39.5	24.7	6.8
Md.	22.9	35.8	26.1	20.1	12.5	5.5	1.9
Okla.	--	--	68.4	58.2	37.0	19.6	5.3
Tenn.	70.7	76.2	63.2	54.3	39.3	21.0	4.3
W.Va.	--	67.9	57.1	35.7	20.7	9.3	2.1
MOUNTAIN							
Ariz.	--	30.0	29.2	24.7	23.2	14.2	4.0
Colo.	--	41.5	21.7	25.0	26.3	14.3	4.6
Ida.	--	13.8	42.3	42.3	40.4	25.6	13.0
Mont.	--	15.7	22.2	29.9	36.7	23.7	13.4
Nev.	--	8.9	24.4	19.2	20.7	9.0	2.4
N.M.	--	72.4	55.2	54.4	41.3	17.0	4.8
Utah	--	58.1	34.7	28.3	24.2	11.8	3.8
Wyo.	--	3 .0	31.0	33.6	33.3	18.6	10.0

(continued)

TABLE 4.9 (Continued)

	1850[a]	1870[b]	1890	1910	1930	1950	1970[c]
PACIFIC							
Cal.	2.7	24.1	27.0	19.1	13.3	6.7	3.1
Ore.	--	47.9	40.1	26.0	20.0	11.3	5.5
Wash.	--	42.9	27.0	18.8	25.7	8.3	4.4
Alas.	--	--	--	--	--	--	2.6
Hawaii	--	--	--	--	--	--	4.6

a. Based on free males over 15 years of age.
b. 1870 through 1950 are based on Kuznets data on percent of gainfully employed.
c. Agriculture, forestry, and fisheries.
--Not applicable.

exceptions, only individuals directly employed in agricultural pursuits. It can readily and plausibly be assumed that in many areas, individuals who were not classified as employed in agriculture were in fact employed in commercial and industrial pursuits which were closely related to and dependent upon agriculture. Hence, their interests and goals may well have been closely allied with the agricultural sector. In these terms, the table underestimates to an unknown degree the likely influence of agricultural interests in many areas.

Despite these and related limitations, the data do provide an illustrative indication of patterns of economic change and, more specifically, of the changing significance of agriculture in the economies of the various states. With the exception of a brief period in the late nineteenth century, the trend in agricultural employment in all states is one of rather consistent and steady decline. The states vary considerably, however, in both the importance of agriculture and in the rate of decline. In 1870, with the exception of the northeastern seaboard states and California, a majority of the employed persons in each of the states was still engaged in agricultural pursuits. In the upper Midwest, the years from 1870 to 1900 witnessed relatively rapid decline in the proportion of agricultural workers, and by 1900, employment in these states was predominantly in nonagricultural pursuits.

A number of states in the far Midwest, along with most of the southern states, remained largely agricultural well past the turn of the century. It was not until the 1930s that agricultural employment in such states as the Dakotas, Arkansas, Georgia, South Carolina, and Mississippi dropped below 50 percent of the labor force. In the western states, probably due to the importance of extractive industries, agricultural employment was never the occupation of a majority of the population, except in New Mexico. In these states, decline in the proportion of the population employed in the agricultural sector was also not as rapid as in other states.

It is probably unnecessary to observe once again that the pattern of economic change imperfectly reflected by the indicator employed in this section was not evenly distributed within the various states. Large areas of many states underwent little in the way of change in this respect and remained predominantly agricultural well into the twentieth century and, indeed, remain so today. The implication is, of course, that other areas within such states underwent more rapid transformation than that suggested by Table 4.9, and in this way the constituencies and voting complexions of numerous areas were probably often sharply deranged.

CONCLUDING COMMENTS

The processes of population, social, and economic change illustrated in this chapter raise obvious methodological and substantive research issues. Continuing processes of change operated at varying rates across the nation. In highly differential degrees, the various subunits of the nation changed in social and economic character, and their populations were effectively reconstituted even during relatively brief periods. Hence, comparisons of voting patterns from one time period to the next contend with populations that were in varying degrees not the same in composition and interest base. Examination of the voting patterns of a few states provides a cursory illustration of the kinds of research issues raised by these processes of change.

The pattern of the presidential vote in Massachusetts and Rhode Island across the latter decades of the nineteenth century strongly suggests V. O. Key's process of "secular realignment," the process by which particular population groups gradually shifted in their loyalties from one party to the other.[4] In Massachusetts, the Democratic vote tended to gradually increase while the Republican vote declined from the 1860s through the 1880s. The same pattern was characteristic of Rhode Island beginning in this case in the early 1870s. Examination of gross population change in the two states during the same period (Table 4.3) suggests a different explanation from that of attitudinal change, which is often involved in the concept of secular realignment. Both states were characterized by very high rates of gross population change during these years, and their populations were effectively reconstituted between the 1860s and 1890s. Thus, we can imagine virtual absence of attitudinal change in partisan loyalties accompanied by the introduction of new population groups with loyalties different from those of longer-term residents.

A contrasting pattern is suggested, however, by the pattern of the presidential vote in Indiana and Wisconsin during the same period. Both of these states were also characterized by rapid population change, although at a somewhat lower rate than either Massachusetts or Rhode Island. But despite a relatively high rate of population change, the partisan distribution of the presidential vote in Wisconsin was essentially stable across the elections of the period, with consistent Republican victories. In Indiana these same elections were highly competitive, and the Republican and Democratic share of the vote consistently hovered close to 50 percent, with at most a very modest decline in Republican strength. In two states, then, rapid population change was seemingly accompanied by partisan change; in two others, in contrast, nearly equal rates of population change were not paralleled by partisan change.

Some apparent clarification of these contrasting patterns is provided by other indicators of change. Both Massachusetts and Rhode Island became highly urban across these years (Table 4.6); in neither state was agriculture a dominant pursuit at the beginning of the period, but in both agricultural employment steadily declined (Table 4.9); and the foreign-born component of the population of both was large and increased steadily across the period (Table 4.7). In Indiana and Wisconsin, urban population (as defined by the census) increased, but both states remained predominantly rural at the end of the period, and neither developed major urban centers on the order of Boston or Providence. The proportion of the population employed in agriculture declined in these states but remained above 50 percent in both until 1890, when it fell to approximately 49 percent in Indiana and 44 percent in Wisconsin. The foreign-born population of Wisconsin was large at the beginning of the period and declined modestly across the period, suggesting a different pattern of immigration from that of Massachusetts and Rhode Island. The foreign-born proportion of the Indiana population also declined across these years but never exceeded 9 percent. Massachusetts and Rhode Island, in short, underwent significantly different processes of population, social, and economic change than did Wisconsin and Indiana, which may help account for differences in partisan change.

These four states illustrate, then, the complex and diverse patterns of population, social, and economic change characteristic of the various areas of the nation and the complex potential interrelations between these patterns of change and voting behavior. In varying degrees and at differing rates, the eligible electorate of the nation underwent a continuing process of reconstitution along numerous dimensions. In a very real sense, the composition of the electorate of the subunits of the nation was in differential degree not the same from one period to the next. Obviously these patterns of complex population, social, and economic change have potential relevance to observed patterns of voting behavior. While change of this sort introduces methodological complexities of considerable magnitude, they also raise substantive research issues of major importance.

NOTES

1. Figures in this and all subsequent tables, unless otherwise noted, were calculated by the authors from data obtained from the Inter-university Consortium for Political and Social Research (ICPSR). The ICPSR is not responsible, of course, for any errors of calculation or for any of the interpretations made herein.

2. In computing gross population change, census data recorded decennially were used in all instances. The elements taken into the calculation of these rates of change were:

NBOLI   number of native-born persons born out of a state but living in that state (the native-born inmigrants)

BILI   number of persons born in a state and living in that state

BILO   number of persons born in a state and living outside that state (the outmigrants)

FBLI   number of foreign-born persons living in the state

D   Number of deaths in any of the above groups

Changes in the first four components above can be calculated between times 1 and 2, becoming:

ΔNBOLI $_{time\ 1 \ldots 2}$

ΔBILI $_{time\ 1 \ldots 2}$

ΔBILO $_{time\ 1 \ldots 2}$

ΔFBLI $_{time\ 1 \ldots 2}$

Death rates in each group were also calculated from average annual death rates in the decade, based on either national-level rates (for outmigrants) or state-specific rates (for those living in the state). For the group born in and living in the state, twice the number of deaths is needed in the final calculation of population change to account for births among that group according to the formula for computing natural change in population:

Population$_{time\ 2}$ - Population$_{time\ 1}$ = births (B) - Deaths (D)

Solving for births we find

$B = Pt_2 - Pt_1 + D$.

Since ($Pt_2 - Pt_1$) is already accounted for in the ΔBILI, accounting of births can be made by incorporating (2xDeaths) in the final formula for computing gross population change.

Thus the symbolic formula for calculating the aggregated components of population change is:

$$\Delta BILI + \Delta NBOLI + \Delta FBLI + \Delta BILO + 2(D_{BILIt_{1 \ldots 2}}) +$$

$$D_{NBOLIt_{1 \ldots 2}} + D_{FBLIt_{1 \ldots 2}} + D_{BILOt_{1 \ldots 2}}$$

The result of this summation, when normalized by dividing by the total population at time 1, is an estimate of the "gross" population change in an area between two points in time (here, decennial census days). It is undoubtedly an underestimation of the persons who were in the state at one point in time but not the other, since outmigration of foreign-born persons and those originally born in another state cannot be accounted for. Two examples should illustrate the computation of this measure. The total population of Kansas in 1930 was 1,880,999; by 1940 this had declined to 1,801,028, or a *net* population change rate of -4.2 percent. When the components of population change are examined, however, the population of Kansas can be seen to change at a considerably higher rate than revealed by the *net* change rate. The difference between native Kansans born and living in the state in 1930 and 1940 is 70,967 people; this represents the net natural change in this population group during the decade. However, deaths, births, and outmigration are not being taken into consideration in this difference: births (augmentations of the population group) are being somewhat cancelled out by deaths and outmigration of this "native" group. Using census information on the death rate for Kansas in this decade, we can obtain estimates of the number of deaths (120,608) and births (191,575) of this native group. Outmigration during the decade of the native Kansans can also be estimated (128,725) by using the difference in Kansas-born persons living outside of Kansas between the two censuses. It is necessary to account for deaths in this outmigrant group also, and use of a national death rate provides an estimate of this component as well (87,771).

The population of any state also contains two groups of persons not born in the state of their residence. They are persons born in a foreign country; and individuals born in the United States but living in a state other than their state of birth. In- and outmigration of these population subgroups can also be estimated using census data on birthplace of each state's inhabitants; for the decade 1930-1940 in Kansas, the net difference in the foreign-born population in Kansas was -28,648, while the net difference in the numbers of native persons born outside of Kansas was -122,119. Since deaths in each of these groups must also be taken into consideration (to avoid the "cancelling effect" of migrants replacing, in the computations, those who died), national and state-specific death rates were used, respectively to estimate the number of deaths in the resident foreign-born group (6,892) and in the group born out of Kansas but living in that state (63,137). It is not necessary, of course, to account for the births in these two population groups; they are included in the estimates of persons born and living in Kansas.

The elements described above may be seen as the components of population change. They include not only persistence of the population resident in the state at time 1 but also the augmentation (or diminution) of the population between two points in time. All of the elements can then be aggregated without regard to sign, producing for Kansas in the 1930-1940 period a sum of 749,475 people. Normalizing this aggregated component figure by dividing the sum by the total population in the state at the earlier time point produces a measure of population turnover for Kansas of 39.8 percent. This figure is considerably higher than the net population change rate for the same period (–4.2 percent) and presumably captures more accurately the magnitude of population movement than does the "net change" figure.

In a similar manner, the gross population change rate can be computed for Washington from 1900 to 1910, in this case producing a rate of 146.3 percent. Here the largest component is inmigration of native-born persons (364,295), although this is augmented by births, deaths and outmigration of native Washingtonians, and by an influx of foreign-born residents. The figures given below are the components of Washington's population change in this decade:

364,295	inmigration (U.S. natives born outside Washington)
28,203	outmigration of Washington-born persons
148,976	births in Washington
19,217	deaths of Washington natives who died in Washington
5,914	deaths of Washington natives who died outside Washington
44,294	deaths of U.S. natives born elsewhere but residing in Washington
129,833	inmigration of foreign-born persons
17,125	deaths of foreign-born persons residing in Washington
757,857	aggregated components of population change in Washington 1900-1910

The gross population change rate for Washington in this period, 146.3 percent, is again somewhat higher than the net population change rate (120.4 percent) and serves to illustrate the "cancellation effect" inherent in the net change rate.

3. Stephen Thernstrom, *The Other Bostonians: Poverty and Progress in the American Metropolis, 1880-1970* (Cambridge, MA: Harvard University Press, 1973), 22.

4. V. O. Key, Jr., "Secular Realignment and the Party System," *Journal of Politics* 21 (May 1959), 198-210.

5

ESTIMATING VOTER PARTICIPATION

Ray M. Shortridge

With the compilation of extensive machine readable census and election data archives, systematic analysis of American electoral behavior over the past century and a half has become an important line of scholarly inquiry. One dimension of electoral behavior frequently analyzed is voter turnout— the proportion of the electorate which casts a ballot in an election. Equation 1 presents the formula which defines turnout.

$$\% \text{ Turnout} = (\# \text{ Votes Cast} / \# \text{ Eligible to Vote}) \times 100 \qquad [1]$$

As an illustration, if sixty ballots were cast in a district with one hundred eligible voters, then the turnout for the election was 60 percent. Although the concept of turnout is clearly defined, one confronts a serious measurement problem when trying to operationalize the concept for research purposes.[1] The difficulty lies in obtaining from the historical records accurate measures for the two terms in the definition.[2] This chapter discusses deficiencies in the data used to operationalize turnout and explores the implications they pose for research.

THE NUMERATOR

The numerator is measured by researchers as the number of votes cast as recorded in official election returns. The problem lies in the accuracy of

137

the official vote tally. Since the early days of the Republic, political observers have decried the presence of fraud in American elections. In the popular press and scholarly pieces, contemporary commentators contended that the number of votes recorded by the election officials often had been inflated by scurrilous means. Methods such as ballot box stuffing, whereby an individual insidiously inserted more than one ballot in the box; repeat voting, in which an individual voted more than once; surrogate voting for nonexistent or dead voters; and padding the count by election officials have often been employed by political machines in rural and urban areas to control the outcome of an election. These techniques were designed to result in recording more votes than were truly or rightfully cast. A review of this literary evidence led some scholars to conclude that the numerator was indeed significantly inflated by these fraudulent means.[3]

The magnitude of the turnout inflation attributable to fraud has yet to be determined with precision. Not all kinds of fraud inflated the vote count. The Allens have usefully categorized vote fraud into a type which violated the voter's intent and a type which did not violate the voter's intent.[4] Practices such as violence, ballot box stuffing, repeating, and miscounting clearly seriously distorted the intentions of the voter. On the other hand, acts such as purchase of the vote, favors, patronage, or a shot of whiskey did not necessarily lead to a distortion of the voter's intent. The Allens conclude that much of the hue and cry in the literary evidence dealt with the type of acts which served largely to mobilize the electorate and not the type which thwarted the voter's intent. Moreover, with the advent of the secret ballot, party managers could no longer observe whether their paid voter voted correctly. The best strategy for investing funds in the electorate lay in paying a partisan for the other party to abstain. Consequently, in this context, fraud would lead to a decline in the number of votes cast.[5]

THE DENOMINATOR

THE UNDERENUMERATION PROBLEM

A neglected line of inquiry lies in examining the denominator of the turnout equation—the number of eligible voters. Here the historical record manifests grave deficiencies. Voter registration came to most American jurisdictions late in the nineteenth century, and even then the differences in eligibility criteria, enforcement practices, registration procedures, and extant records make it impossible to specify the size of the electorate. As a consequence, one cannot with certitude provide a figure for the denominator in the turnout equation for any nineteenth-century election. The margin for error in this term is potentially quite large.

As an operational matter, the typical recourse of the scholar is to derive some approximation from a population list, usually the United States Census. The standard approach is to use the decennial census enumeration of eligible people for the census years, with the intercensus years estimated by linear interpolation. Although admittedly an approximation, this source provides a standard and replicable base for computing the size of the electorate.

Reliance on the census, or any population list from the nineteenth century, poses a difficult problem for scholars because of the serious underenumeration problem. Errors in the nineteenth-century census were discussed by contemporary observers; General Francis Walker, chief administrator of the ninth census testified before a congressional committee in 1878:

> The censuses of 1850, 1860, and 1870 are loaded with bad statistics. There are statistics in the census of 1870, I am sorry to say, where some of the results are false to the extent of one-half. They had to be published then, because the law called for it; but I took the liberty of branding them as untrustworthy and in some cases giving the reasons therefore at some length.[6]

Noncensus enumeration also suffered from serious sources of error. In reviewing a city's register for death certificates, Walker reported:

> [Walker's chief clerk] found that the certificates of death upon which burial permits were issued were, so far as he could find out, in charge of a woman who appeared to perform menial service; the certificates were often made in pencil, not upon regular printed forms, but on scraps of paper of various shapes and sizes. My clerk reported that he did not believe that one-half of these certificates for the preceding year could be found: they had not been copied into any register, they had not been filed in order or even numbered, but were thrown into a drawer where it was presumed they would remain, but where the manner in which they were kept gave no security that they were not raided upon for the purposes of lighting fires or wiping pens.[7]

A persuasive case cannot be made for a full enumeration of the population by officials a century ago.

Students of the census ascribe two general reasons for underenumeration. First, the technical aspects of census-taking involving the training of personnel and the procedures of enumeration usually result in a uniformly distributed level of underenumeration. In the nineteenth century, census takers were untrained. The qualifications for the job in the field varied from census to census and from district to district. In many localities, positions would be low-level patronage plums, so that the quality of the enumeration would vary dramatically from individual to individual. The census takers were paid under a piece-work program and were rarely adequately supervised. According to Knights, the protracted period of time over which the census was taken also led to underenumeration, particularly in the ante bellum period when often more than three months was required to conclude the count.[8] These inefficiencies doubtlessly introduced a significant amount of underenumeration in the nineteenth-century censuses.

The second general source for underenumeration results from characteristics of the population or conditions of their environment. Irregularity in the respondent's work and leisure patterns inversely affects the likelihood of their being found at home by the census taker. Poor and uneducated people are disinclined to understand or trust the intentions of the census taker who, as an agent of the government, is associated with the government's proclivity to tax, draft, or arrest the poor. The social environment, particularly anomalous and congested housing, contribute to under-counting, as General Walker recognized a century ago:

> When it is considered how many thousands of persons in every large city, how many tens of thousands in a city like New York, not only live in boarding houses, but change their boarding houses at every freak of fancy or disgust, not to speak of those who leave under the stress of impecuniosity and therefore are not likely to leave their future address or advertise their residence, it will be seen how utterly unfitted is such a system of enumeration to the social conditions of the country at the present time.[9]

Crowded tenements, alleys, back-country shanties and sheds clearly are not conducive for a comprehensive population count.

Underenumeration means that the denominator of the turnout equation contains fewer eligible voters than were actually present. This fact has serious implications for turnout estimates. If one hypothetically assumes that eighty people voted in a district and that the census counted one hundred people meeting the qualifications to vote, then the estimated turnout rate is 80 percent (80/100 x 100). However, if the census takers overlooked twenty people and hence the number of eligible voters was in fact one hundred twenty, then the turnout rate should have been 67 percent (80/120 x 100). Underenumeration inversely affects the level of estimated turnout. If underenumeration assumed substantial proportions, then the true turnout rate for the nineteenth century could be markedly lower than the levels commonly estimated in the scholarly literature.

AN ESTIMATE FOR UNDERENUMERATION

The true population of eligible voters actually present, P, is equal to the number of eligible voters enumerated in the census, E, plus the number of eligible voters not enumerated, $\overline{E}$:

$$P = E + \overline{E} \qquad\qquad [2]$$

Since P, the true eligible population, is unknown, one must solve for it by using information which is available. The proportion of a population not enumerated is the underenumeration rate, U. The number of eligible people not enumerated, $\overline{E}$, is the product of U and P:

$$\overline{E} = U \times P \qquad\qquad [3]$$

Substituting for $\overline{E}$ in equation 2:

$$P = E + (U \times P) \qquad\qquad [4]$$

Simplifying and solving for the unknown P:

$$P = E / (1 - U) \qquad\qquad [5]$$

Therefore, to estimate the true eligible voting population, P, one needs the census figures for the eligible population, E, and an estimate for the underenumeration rate, U.

The level of underenumeration present in the modern census is difficult to ascertain. A direct approach to this problem has been devised by census experts and consists of sending the census takers back into the field to enumerate with extraordinary care a sample population and then comparing these results with those obtained by the initial canvass. Obviously, this approach is not feasible for scholars working with the nineteenth-century census. Using city directories or other lists as an approximation for a recount poses serious problems. The scholar cannot be assured of the completeness of the collateral list, which complicates the problem of obtaining a count of the true population.[10] Moreover, locating, compiling, and correlating these collateral lists for the American people throughout the nineteenth century comprises an impossible task in data recovery and analysis. Consequently, scholars are without a direct means for measuring the magnitude of underenumeration in the nineteenth-century census.

The indirect approach for measuring underenumeration draws upon certain types of analysis of the aggregate census statistics.[11] The strategy consists of examining the census for internal error, both within a given census and between consecutive censuses. A comparison can then be made to the amount found in the nineteenth-century census. The results of this comparison along with the underenumeration levels directly estimated for modern censuses permit an informed judgment about the relative under-enumeration level to be expected in the earlier census. Resting as they do upon a precarious set of logical and empirical assumptions, the indirect approach results in only tentative estimates for the underenumeration rate in the nineteenth-century census. However, this appears to be a fruitful strategy for obtaining these underenumeration estimates because the assumptions are explicit and can be refined in light of the subsequent research.

This inquiry approaches an estimate for the underenumeration rate by examining the amount of variation in the age ratios computed for the nineteenth- and twentiety-century censuses. This approach draws upon my collaborative study with John Sharpless of the effect of underenumeration on population mobility studies.[12] The age ratio statistic does not measure underenumeration; however, the technical aspects of census-taking and the characteristics of the social environment discussed above which give rise to underenumeration are also related to age ratio error. A reasonable assumption, then, is that a measure of the extent of age ratio error also measures, albeit imperfectly, the extent of underenumeration. Although a direct measure of underenumeration is not possible, this approach does permit a probable conclusion predicated upon an empirical study of the census.

The age ratio is calculated by dividing the number of people in an age bracket by the mean of the number of people in that and the two adjacent age brackets. In a closed population, the age ratio should equal one, but enumeration error tends to overstate the proportion found in some brackets and understate the proportion found in others. The greater the error, the greater is the deviation from one. Because of the enormous immigration flow into America in the nineteenth century, the assumption of a closed population is of course violated. Using five-year age cohorts reduces the impact of the nonrandom distribution in the age of immigrants. Moreover, statistical techniques advanced by Coale enable the age ratio to be adjusted to control for this immigration effect.[13] The adjusted age ratio produces a measure for the relative under- or overenumeration of one age bracket compared to the adjacent ones within a census. Computing a coefficient of variation for the adjusted age ratios for a census provides a useful summary statistic for the amount of internal consistency of that census's age enumeration. The coefficient of variation from one census can be compared to that from another in an analysis aimed toward assessing the relative accuracy of the tally.

In modern census studies, more direct methods for measuring under-enumeration are possible. Perhaps the most reliable approach consists of counting a sample of the population again with a more rigorous canvass and comparing that result with that obtained from the use of standard census-taking procedures. The amount of underenumeration observed for modern United States censuses can be used with the age ratio error statistics for both the modern census and the older census. The critical assumption in the estimating procedure for underenumeration presented in equation 6 is that the relationship between age ratio error and under-enumeration in a given census is proportional.[14]

$$\frac{U_{t1}}{CV_{t1}} = \frac{U_{t2}}{CV_{t2}} \qquad [6]$$

The coefficient of variation for the adjusted age ratios (CV) can be computed directly from both the modern census (t2) and the earlier census (t1). The underenumeration rate for the modern census (U_{t2}) is available from systematic critiques of modern censuses. Solving for the remaining unknown term, the underenumeration rate in the earlier census (U_{t1}), results in equation 7.

$$U_{t1} = CV_{t1} \left(U_{t2}/CV_{t2} \right) \qquad [7]$$

The underenumeration estimate for the earlier period will be made for the adult male population. Prior to the Nineteenth Amendment, only men were enfranchised in most jurisdictions. Although foreign-born males were commonly subject to requirements such as filing for citizenship, they were on the whole eligible to vote. The multiplicity of state regulations pertaining to immigrant franchise must be considered carefully in any state level analysis. However, nineteenth-century census error for adult males is biased along a nativity dimension—native-born whites were more accurately recorded than foreign-born males.[15] Table 5.1 presents the coefficients of variation computed for the adjusted age ratios for native-born whites, native-born blacks, and foreign-born adult males for the 1880, 1890, and 1900 censuses. The 1950 coefficients of variation for white and black adult males were estimated from Coale's graphs; data for foreign-born whites were unavailable so the coefficient for white males is presented for both foreign born and native born.[16] From these coefficients of variation and from the 2.7 percent underenumeration for white males and the 15.0 percent underenumeration for nonwhite males in the 1950 census, the estimated underenumeration for the nineteenth century can be

TABLE 5.1   Coefficients of Variation for Adjusted Age Ratios for Male
            Adults

NATIVITY GROUP	CENSUS YEAR			
	1880	1890	1900	1950
Native-Born White	5.4%	3.6%	2.9%	2.0%
Foreign-Born White	17.0%	16.1%	26.3%	2.0%
Nonwhite	12.4%	10.4%	5.1%	8.0%

TABLE 5.2   Estimated Underenumeration of Male Adults

NATIVITY GROUP	CENSUS YEAR			
	1880	1890	1900	Mean
Native-Born White	7.3%	4.9%	3.9%	5.4%
Foreign-Born White	23.0%	21.7%	35.5%	26.7%
Nonwhite	23.3%	19.5%	9.6%	17.5%

calculated according to equation 7. Table 5.2 presents these estimates for
the three groups of males.

In the latter part of the nineteenth century, about two-thirds of the
adult male population was native-born white, about one-fourth was foreign-
born white, and about one-tenth was nonwhite.[17] The top of Table
5.3 presents the number enumerated in the 1880, 1890, and 1900 censuses
which were native-born white, foreign-born white, and nonwhite adult
males. These numbers derived from the census must be adjusted to
compensate for the extent to which they underenumerate the true population for each group. For example, in 1880, the census reported 8,669,094
native-born adult males. The estimated underenumeration rate for that
group found in Table 5.2 is 7.3 percent—that is, an estimated 7.3 percent
of the group were not counted by the census-takers. Adjusting for the
estimated underenumeration rate produces an estimated population of
native-born white males of 9,351,774. Table 5.3 also presents the
number of adult males in each group adjusted for underenumeration.
When adjusted for underenumeration, the estimate for the total eligible
voting population increases substantially in each census. A fully refined
figure for the denominator would further adjust the foreign-born increment by estimates for the proportion of that group which is eligible to

TABLE 5.3   Number of Adult Males Reported by the Census and
             Adjusted for Underenumeration

	Census Year		
Census Count	1880	1890	1900
Native-Born White	8,669,094	10,957,496	14,482,870
Foreign-Born White	3,123,516	4,242,360	4,969,842
Nonwhite	1,559,801	1,740,455	2,134,101
Total	13,352,411	16,940,311	21,586,813
Adjusted Estimate			
Native-Born White	9,351,774	11,522,078	15,070,624
Foreign-Born White	4,056,514	5,418,084	6,780,139
Nonwhite	2,033,639	2,162,056	2,586,789
Total	15,441,927	19,102,218	24,707,552

vote in each state. The numbers presented here presume that all adult foreign-born males were eligible, which simplifies the actual situation and leads to a marginally larger denominator and therefore to a slightly lower turnout estimate. Nevertheless, according to these estimates, in order to compute turnout levels for this period, the denominator in the formula must be increased by more than two million in 1880 and 1890 and by more than three million in 1900.

This adjustment to increase the estimated voting age population by the number presumed to have been overlooked by the census-takers markedly affects the turnout levels computed for the period. Row 1 in Table 5.4 presents the estimated turnout for presidential elections conducted between 1880 and 1900 using the number of adult males enumerated by the census. (Intercensus year figures are obtained by linear interpolation.) Row 2 in Table 5.4 presents the estimated turnout for those elections using the adult male population adjusted for underenumeration. During this period, turnout using the unadjusted denominator averaged 68.9 percent; while using the adjusted denominator produced an average turnout estimate of 60.4 percent. Clearly, using an unrefined estimate for the denominator in the turnout formula leads to a substantially higher turnout computation than is derived from using the denominator adjusted for underenumeration error in the census.

TABLE 5.4   Voter Turnout Levels Estimated with Denominator
             Unadjusted and Adjusted for Underenumeration

| | | | Election Year | | | | |
Denominator	1880	1884	1888	1892	1896	1900	Mean
Unadjusted	69.0%	68.0%	70.2%	67.6%	70.7%	67.9%	68.9%
Adjusted	59.7%	59.5%	62.0%	59.7%	62.1%	59.5%	60.4%

RESEARCH DESIGN IMPLICATIONS

LONGITUDINAL ANALYSIS

The denominator problem poses considerable difficulty for longitudinal analysis. Since the advent of survey research methods, enormous depth to the theoretical understanding of voter behavior has been developed as a consequence of the systematic study of voter attitudes and behavior.[18] The results of over three decades of inquiry suggest that the voter's orientation towards politics seems somewhat mutable—that the electorate manifests some variation over time along various dimensions of political awareness and cognition.[19] Yet the limits of these variations in political involvement cannot be set with certitude due to the relatively brief period for which the vast array of individual-level attitude data are available. Utilizing indices of political involvement in a longitudinal analysis covering both the nineteenth and twentieth centuries has been an approach adopted to shed light on the magnitude and causes of variation in political involvement.

The computations for voter turnout in the nineteenth century have not as yet employed a denominator adjusted for underenumeration. As a consequence, the unadjusted levels, such as the unadjusted estimates presented in Table 5.4, suggest a highly active electorate. Moreover, these estimates for the earlier period markedly exceed those for the twentieth century. The seminal work by Burnham contended that these data strongly suggest that the earlier electorate was on the whole more involved in politics than is the modern one.[20] Burnham stressed the theoretical importance of this apparent phenomenon—that the social and political environment shapes the citizen's response to political stimuli and affects the electorate's overall level of involvement and competence. The large turnout estimated for the nineteenth century suggested to Burnham and others that when presented with real alternatives and meaningful choices, the electorate could manifest higher levels of political consciousness and activity. As a consequence, the nineteenth-century political universe might be qualitatively different from the current one and, hence, the theory derived from studying the contemporary electorate might be intellectually parochial.

However, an adjustment for underenumeration in the denominator substantially reduces the turnout estimates for the nineteenth-century elections. As Table 5.4 shows, the unadjusted estimate for presidential elections from 1880 to 1900 averages 68.9 percent, while the mean for the adjusted estimates drops to 60.4 percent. As the above discussion of the numerator concluded, a modest further reduction in the turnout level should be made to compensate for the likely inflation of the number of votes counted for the election. Consequently, the general turnout level in the nineteenth century attained a level possibly 10 percent lower than the estimates derived from using unadjusted numerators and denominators.

As time wore on, census techniques improved so that the census takers managed to record a higher proportion of the people who were actually present. A crucial area for research lies in a systematic study of census-taking practices and an assessment of the effect which changes in these procedures had on underenumeration. To remove the likely trend in underenumeration from the turnout time series, it is necessary to have reliable estimates for the magnitude of this artifact through time. The existing histories of the census do not permit one to say when and to what degree the census was improved by the advent of new techniques. However, it is reasonable to presume that the underenumeration rate declined over the last century or so, although probably not linearly. Consequently, less of an adjustment in the turnout estimates would be required for the twentieth-century turnout estimates than for the earlier period. With these adjustments, the sharp differences in turnout between the nineteenth century and the twentieth century tend to diminish.

The methodological problem in longitudinal analysis of turnout is that of trend. A general trend of turnout declining with time emerges from an examination of the unadjusted estimates. Scholars readily constructed intriguing theories to explain that trend. However, many things correlate with time, including improvement in census-taking practices. This factor plausibly influences the turnout estimates. When this factor is controlled by adjusting the denominator for underenumeration, the negative trend in turnout is not so pronounced. The correlation of turnout with time appears to be somewhat spurious. The theory positing a profoundly different political universe for the earlier period is thereby left without a strong empirical foundation. Changes in the data collection process which are a function of time must be explicitly controlled by the research design employing a longitudinal analysis.

TABLE 5.5   Hypothetical Ecological Regression Statistics:
            Underenumeration (10%) Randomly Distributed

Coefficients	Raw Data	Adjusted Data
Intercept	0.3	0.2
Regression Coefficient	0.5	0.5
Estimated Turnout Levels:		
Group X	80%	70%
Group not X	30%	20%

CROSS-SECTIONAL ANALYSIS

The denominator problem also introduces bias into the results obtained from a cross-sectional analysis, which compares the turnout rates for different groups. A large corpus of work inquires into the effect of individual-level characteristics on turnout through ecological regression or other techniques. For example, an important dimension of post-bellum southern history has been to contrast the turnout levels attained by blacks with those attained by whites.[21] The voting history of the North in the mid-nineteenth century has been informed by the differences in turnout observed for the native born and the foreign born.[22] Similarly, electoral-flow analysis compares the turnout levels in an election estimated for those who voted and those who abstained in a preceding contest.[23] Other cross-sectional studies assess the impact of aggregate level factors on turnout.[24]

The effect of underenumeration varies with the general pattern with which it is distributed across the units in the analysis. The basic consideration lies in the relationship between underenumeration and the independent variable—either underenumeration varies with the independent variable or it does not. Turning to the latter possibility, if there is no correlation between underenumeration and the independent variable, then the underenumeration is randomly distributed relative to that variable. The effect of underenumeration would be to lower the value of the intercept, while the regression coefficient would remain the same, relative to the value for these coefficients obtained from the analysis of unadjusted data. Table 5.5 presents the regression coefficients and derived estimates for the turnout levels of group X and not X under the assumption that a hypothetical 10 percent overall underenumeration rate does not covary with X. The overall turnout level declines by 10 percent, the underenumer-

TABLE 5.6   Hypothetical Ecological Regression Statistics:
Underenumeration (10%) Nonrandomly Distributed

| | (a) Positive Correlation with Independent Variable | |
Coefficients	Raw Data	Adjusted Data
Intercept	0.3	0.25
Regression Coefficient	0.5	0.4
Estimated Turnout Levels:		
Group X	80%	65%
Group not X	30%	25%

| | (b) Negative Correlation with Independent Variable | |
Coefficients	Raw Data	Adjusted Data
Intercept	0.3	0.1
Regression Coefficient	0.5	0.7
Estimated Turnout Levels:		
Group X	80%	80%
Group not X	30%	10%

ation rate; the decline is present for both the X and not X people. The difference between X and not X remains 50 percent when the data are adjusted for underenumeration. When underenumeration is random relative to the independent variable, the general turnout level shifts downward uniformly across the groups in the analysis, while the between group difference remains constant.

The impact is different when underenumeration covaries with the independent variable. In this situation, underenumeration could correlate either positively or negatively with the independent variable, with different effects for each case. Table 5.6 presents the hypothetical regression coefficients and derived group turnout levels for the case with a positive correlation and the one with a negative correlation. In the situation in which underenumeration is positively correlated with X, adjusting the denominator serves to moderate the decline of the intercept and markedly shifts the regression coefficient downward. As a consequence, turnout differences between the two groups observed in the raw data tend to narrow when the independent variable is positively correlated with under-enumeration. On the other hand, when the independent variable inversely correlates with underenumeration, the intercept value declines considerably while the regression coefficient increases substantially. Consequently, an inverse correlation leads to an exacerbation of the observed differences in group turnout.

Clearly, the scholar must be conscious of the risk of spurious correlation affecting the conclusions drawn from the cross-sectional analysis of voter turnout. From a research design perspective, it is necessary to identify explicitly the likely factors which correlate both with an independent variable in the model and also with the level of underenumeration. In ordering these factors, a components of variance approach usefully partitions the variation in underenumeration.

$$U_{ij} = (f)^I n_{ij} + {}^A k_{ij} + {}^I n {}^A k_{ij} \qquad [8]$$

where the level of underenumeration for the ith person in the jth unit is equal to some function of a set (n) of individual level factors (I), plus a set (k) of aggregate level factors (A), plus a set of interactive factors (I · A). Specifying and measuring these factors pose a serious research agenda for scholarship in the field, but the task should prove invaluable for refining the analysis of past electoral behavior.

In the absence of a pure set of behavioral measures, the scholar is not totally without recourse. A systematic discussion of the possible correlation between the independent variables of interest and underenumeration with an eye toward selecting the most likely relationship should be an essential passage in the research design section of a scholarly work. This sort of commentary could also elaborate the effect which the "worst case" would have on the conclusions drawn from the research. Such tactics would not serve as a proof, but would provide the reader with a rational basis for assessing the amount of credence to invest in the conclusion. This approach may appear to be a modest step, but it does permit cumulative scholarship, which is the purpose of scientific inquiry.

CONCLUSIONS

The object of this study does not lie in advancing a specific constant for adjusting turnout levels. The assumptions underlying the argument which led to the values in Table 5.3 are too tenuous for such confidence. Toilers in the voting behavior vineyard should not rush off to the terminal to correct the data file. The effort has been to show first that the denominator derived directly from the census most probably understates the true value for the denominator. Second, the underenumeration is rather substantial in size and varies across groups of analytic interest. Finally, adjusting for underenumeration markedly reduces the turnout level estimated for the nineteenth century.

The significance of these points lies not in the technical side of specifying underenumeration, but in the substantive conclusion that such an adjustment must be made. The denominator in the equation typically used now to compute nineteenth-century turnout understates the number of eligible voters present at the time of the election. As a consequence, the turnout levels commonly attributed to the nineteenth century probably overstate the actual turnout attained. The exigency of adjusting the denominator for underenumeration is great for both cross-sectional and longitudinal analyses. Cross-sectional studies must exercise care to control for differential underenumeration rates for the groups being compared. Longitudinal studies must ensure that an artifact of the data collection process has not introduced trend into their data. Manifestly, a research design for a study of nineteenth-century turnout must explicitly control for the effect of factors relating to the collection of the data as well as to factors pertaining to the theory being tested.

NOTES

1. Hubert M. Blalock, Jr., "The Measurement Problem: A Gap Between the Languages of Theory and Research," in H. M. Blalock, Jr. (ed.) *Methodology in Social Research* (New York: McGraw-Hill, 1968), 5-27.

2. Eugene J. Webb and others, *Unobtrusive Measures: Nonreactive Research in Social Sciences* (Chicago: Rand McNally, 1966).

3. Philip E. Converse, "Change in the American Electorate," in A. Campbell and P. E. Converse (eds.) *The Human Meaning of Social Change* (New York: Russell Sage Foundation, 1972), 263-337; Jerrold G. Rusk, "Comment: The American Electoral Universe: Speculation and Evidence," *American Political Science Review* 68 (September 1974), 1028-1049.

4. Howard W. Allen and Kay Warren Allen, "Vote Fraud and Data Validity," Chapter 6 of this volume.

5. Gary W. Cox and J. Morgan Kousser, *Turnout and Rural Corruption: New York as a Test Case,* Social Science Working Paper 292, Division of the Humanities and Social Sciences, California Institute of Technology, October 1979.

6. "Interview of the Select Committee of the Senate . . . and of the House of Representatives to make Provision for the Taking of the Tenth Census with Professor Francis A. Walker, Superintendent of the Census," *Senate Miscellaneous Documents,* Doc. No. 26, Vol. I, 45th Congress, 3rd Session (December 17, 1878), 15.

7. *Ibid.,* 13.

8. Peter R. Knights, "A Method for Estimating Census Under-Enumeration," *Historical Methods Newsletter,* 3 (December, 1969), 5-8.

9. *Ninth Census,* 1870, Vol. I, xxii.

10. Melvin A. Hammarberg, "Designing a Sample from Incomplete Historical Lists," *American Quarterly* 23 (1971), 542-561.

11. Jacob S. Siegel and Melvin Zelnik, "An Evaluation of Coverage in the Census Population by Techniques of Demographic Analysis and by Composite Methods," *Proceedings* of the Social Statistics Section, American Statistical Association (1966), 71-85.

12. John B. Sharpless and Ray M. Shortridge, "Biased Underenumeration in Census Manuscripts: Methodological Implications," *Journal of Urban History* 1 (August 1975), 409-439.

13. Ansley J. Coale, "The Population of the United States in 1950 Classified by Age, Sex and Color—A Revision of Census Figures," *Journal of the American Statistical Association* 50 (1955), 16-54.

14. Although an arbitrary assumption, positing proportionality is not a capricious act but follows from an understanding that both types of enumeration stem from common deficiencies in census-taking. One would expect, then, that the relationship between the external error (underenumeration) and the internal error (adjusted age ratios) would tend to remain constant. Efficiently conducted censuses would produce reduced error, both internal and external. Consequently, the precise statistical relationship between the underenumeration and age ratio coefficients of variance—whether one is weighted relative to the other—is not germane to this discussion. The crucial point is that the statistical relationship is roughly the same regardless of the accuracy between internal and external error of the census.

15. Sharpless and Shortridge, "Biased Underenumeration."

16. Coale, "Population of the United States."

17. The census age groups included in the "adults" described in this analysis are aged twenty and above.

18. Angus Campbell, Philip E. Converse, Warren E. Miller, and Donald E. Stokes, *The American Voter* (New York: John Wiley, 1960); Philip E. Converse, "The Nature of Belief Systems in Mass Publics," in D. Apter (ed.) *Ideology and Discontent* (London: Macmillan, 1964).

19. Gerald M. Pomper, "From Confusion to Clarity: Issues and American Voters, 1956-1968," *American Political Science Review* 66 (March 1972), 415-428; Norman H. Nie, Sidney Verba, and John R. Petrocik, *The Changing American Voter* (Cambridge, MA: Harvard University Press, 1976).

20. Walter Dean Burnham, "The Changing Shape of the American Political Universe," *American Political Science Review* 59 (March 1965), 7-28.

21. J. Morgan Kousser, *The Shaping of Southern Politics: Suffrage Restriction and the Establishment of the One-Party South, 1880-1910* (New Haven: Yale University Press, 1974).

22. Ray Myles Shortridge, "Voting Patterns in the American Midwest, 1840-1872" (Ph.D. dissertation, The University of Michigan, 1974).

23. Ray M. Shortridge, "The Voter Realignment in the Midwest During the 1850s" *American Politics Quarterly* 4 (April 1976), 193-222; "Voting for Minor Parties in the Antebellum Midwest," *Indiana Magazine of History* LXXIV (June 1978), 117-134; "Democracy's Golden Age?—Voter Turnout in the Midwest, 1840-1872," *Social Science Quarterly* 60 (March 1980), 617-629.

24. Ray M. Shortridge, "An Assessment of the Frontier's Influence on Voter Turnout," *Agricultural History* 50 (July 1976), 445-459.

6

VOTE FRAUD AND DATA VALIDITY

Howard W. Allen
and
Kay Warren Allen

Stories of fraudulent election practices color the political history of the United States, and anecdotes about vote buying, the dishonesty of election officials, and the like suggesting the widespread prevalence of election fraud in the American past are an integral part of the lore of American politics. Many scholars, moreover, have accepted this depiction. In the 1880s, Henry George found that elections in all parts of the nation were corrupted with vote buying and excessive campaign expenditures. He cited the "large cities" and several western states as examples and added that "the most flagrant election corruption" actually was not to be found in the major urban centers but in "the older agricultural communities." Joseph P. Harris, in a book published in 1929 by the prestigious Brookings Institution, declared that "indifference, fraud, corruption and violence have marked the operation of our electoral system. Nor has this condition existed sporadically or in a few particular localities. It has been a more or

AUTHORS' NOTE: The authors wish to express special thanks to Michael C. Batinski, Robert E. Burke, W. Dean Burnham, Ronald P. Formisano, Richard L. McCormick, Samuel T. McSeveney, Gail O'Brian, John L. Stucker, and the editors of

less permanent condition in all parts of the country." L. E. Fredman in 1968 in *The Australian Ballot* agreed. "By the middle decades of the nineteenth century," Fredman claimed, "it was obvious to many Americans that the manipulation of the ballot had made voting a meaningless procedure."[1]

The contention that elections in the United States at most times and in most localities were "meaningless" poses a serious issue to all Americans. To students of American politics, however, this view of election practices is a matter of even graver concern. Election data have long been an important source of evidence for the study of American political history and behavior, and they are one of the very few sources which permit measurement of mass responses to political candidates, parties, and issues for the years before the development of public opinion sampling. If elections were universally fraudulent, then the results of those elections are distortions of popular attitudes and of dubious validity. If election data are invalid, then the study of mass voting behavior is an exercise in futility, and our capacity to understand mass behavior in previous historical eras is significantly diminished. Doubts concerning the validity of election data seem even more serious in view of the vast increase in interest and use of election data in recent years. Since election data are now available in machine-readable form from the Inter-university Consortium for Political and Social Research (ICPSR), in fact, a rather impressive array of political studies based heavily upon analysis of election statistics has appeared, and the validity of this work is brought into question by the possibility that election returns were fraudulent.[2]

THE SIGNIFICANCE OF FRAUD

The significance of the role of fraud in American elections has been raised only recently by Philip E. Converse. Citing the work of W. Dean Burnham, Converse pointed to important configurations of county election data of the late nineteenth century and early twentieth century. These configurations included, compared to more recent standards, a high rate of voter turnout in both presidential and midterm elections, a high frequency of straight ticket voting, and a tendency for all voters to vote

this volume for their helpful comments and criticism of this chapter. Very special thanks also to Charles Holliday who provided invaluable aid in collecting the research materials cited here. A grant from the National Science Foundation (GS-28910) and financial assistance from the Office of Research Development and Administration, Southern Illinois University at Carbondale helped bring this research project to completion.

for all contests in an election. These characteristics began to change in unison early in the twentieth century, and by the 1920s, voter turnout and straight ticket voting had declined sharply, turnout rates in midterm elections had declined even more drastically than in presidential elections, and many voters no longer cast votes for all contests in an election. Part of this change, particularly that which occurred after World War I, Converse suggested, most likely reflected the impact of a number of progressive political reforms enacted by 1920 which eliminated a significant portion of election fraud that had falsely increased vote totals, created an illusion of straight ticket voting, and so on. "By midcentury," said Converse, "there was widespread recognition of the prevalence of voting fraud. The literature on the subject, while everywhere anecdotal, is large and colorful over the whole latter portion of the nineteenth century." Thus it is quite possible, he concluded, that changes which Burnham discovered in election data to a considerable extent merely reflected the decline of fraud brought about by reforms in election procedures.[3]

Samuel P. Huntington's observations on the function of political corruption in modernizing societies, furthermore, gives the role of election and other kinds of fraud in American politics broad functional significance. "Impressionistic evidence," said Huntington, indicates that political corruption "correlates reasonably well with rapid social and economic modernization." Thus, corruption in British politics seemed most prevalent in the seventeenth century and in the United States during the nineteenth century when each of the two societies underwent extensive social and economic change. Political corruption, therefore, tended to occur at times when "new sources of wealth and power" emerged and also to provide "the means of assimilating new groups into the political system by irregular means because the system has been unable to adapt sufficiently fast to provide legitimate and acceptable means for this purpose."[4]

Fraudulent election practices, it is fair to say, deserve more careful analysis. This chapter will attempt to examine the published literature on election practices as an early step in the examination of the extent and function of vote fraud in American politics. A definitive study of illegal or irregular electoral behavior must rest finally upon an analysis of election data, but it seems necessary to precede the quantitative analysis with a review and evaluation of the documentary evidence. It is important to know what participants, observers, and students of the electoral process have said about vote fraud and to identify where and when these participants, observers, and students thought vote fraud occurred, how they thought it was carried out, and who they thought was most likely to commit such acts. The very nature of the subject matter, of course, like other illegal, immoral, or irregular activities, makes it unlikely that conclusive documentary evidence of fraud will be found. Few individuals were likely to have recorded for posterity their involvement in such acts. The literature on vote fraud is vast and rich, however, and a careful consideration of this valuable body of evidence is a prerequisite to the quantitative analysis of vote fraud.

CLASSIFICATION

A useful classification of types of election fraud was provided by James Bryce in *Modern Democracies* in 1921: "The rational will which the citizens are expected to possess and to express by their votes may be perverted in three ways: by Fear, when the voter is intimidated; by Corrupt inducements, when he is bribed; by Fraud, when the votes are not honestly taken or honestly counted." Bryce's categories effectively describe and differentiate the types of activities described as election fraud in the literature. In the context of this study, however, the relevant consideration is the degree to which vote fraud distorted the voters' "rational will," to use Bryce's words. From this point of view, the most serious violation of a voter's "rational will" would certainly include such activities as the manipulation and falsification of the vote count by election officials or others, and by a practice known as repeating, that is, the casting of two or more votes by the same individuals. Some forms of voter intimidation no doubt would also seriously reduce the capacity of the voter to express his "rational will."[5]

Other kinds of political behavior which commonly were treated as forms of intimidation in the literature, however, would not have brought about a conflict necessarily between the voter's "rational will" and his vote. In the election of 1896, for example, it has been suggested that employers intimidated their workers into voting for William J. McKinley by warning their employees that unemployment would result if William Jennings Bryan were elected. Political activity of this nature could be regarded more accurately as heavy-handed political campaigning, unless of course there was evidence that the employer actually monitored the voting and retaliated against those employees who violated his recommendations or unless the employee thought that this might happen. Evidence of large campaign expenditures, as well, do not prove ipso facto that the voter's "rational will" had been misrepresented. Bribery, Bryce's third type of vote fraud, seemed even less likely to have violated the "rational will" of the voter. In such cases the voter *willingly* accepted a sum of money, a job, or some other favor in exchange for a vote. Certain kinds of bribery such as the distribution of free drinks at the corner saloon—a practice often denounced by reformers in the late nineteenth and early twentieth century—or a free ride the polls seem in retrospect very unlikely to have altered the voter's voting behavior, except probably to encourage him to vote. At any rate, in this circumstance the voter cast his vote of his own free will. Free drinks at the neighborhood saloon, in fact, seemed little different in intent from the suburban coffee-klatsch, a form of campaigning widely used by many political candidates in recent elections. Few today would regard the coffee-klatsch as a form of vote fraud.[6]

GEOGRAPHIC AND CHRONOLOGICAL DISTRIBUTION

While some students of American elections have suggested that dishonesty in elections has been more or less a constant characteristic at most times and places in nineteenth- and twentieth-century voting, most have emphasized a geographic and chronological unevenness in the distribution of election frauds; and most authorities have found urban areas most guilty of fraudulent election practices. Bryce, in *The American Commonwealth*, had the impression that "there is the widest possible difference between different regions of the country," and that "the greater part of the Union is pure"; but the areas where fraud was most prevalent, Bryce believed, were the largest American cities.[7] Earl R. Sikes in 1929 concluded that election corruption was widespread "especially in city elections," and Joseph P. Harris asserted in 1929, "Without question, most voting frauds are now to be found in cities, and especially in the larger cities." Urban centers where election fraud was said to have flourished included virtually every major city in the United States.[8]

NEW YORK CITY

Vote fraud in New York City, particularly in the nineteenth and early twentieth century, however, has attracted a disproportionate share of attention. Recognizing that voting fraud and violent elections were not new to New York even in the earliest years of the nineteenth century, Gustavus Myers, one of the many historians of Tammany Hall, noted that corruption in New York elections increased sharply in the elections of 1827. He cited examples of men who were said to have voted several times, and he specifically mentioned a ward "where the foreign population had full sway" and "the Jackson men" controlled by violence and intimidation. Myers seemed convinced, moreover, that most, if not all, pre-Civil War New York elections were influenced by fraud. In 1828: "That hundreds, if not thousands, of illegal votes were counted was admitted." In 1832: "Both sides were guilty of election frauds." In the primary of

1852: "Fraud and violence occurred at nearly every voting place." In 1860: "The frauds practiced against the Lincoln electors surpassed anything the city had known."[9]

Other students of pre-Civil War New York politics accepted Myers's assessment. Ostrogorski declared that the first and most corrupt political machine in the United States was Tammany Hall, and he laid the greatest responsibility upon the "tide of immigration" that became "the prey of the leaders of Tammany in search of heedless or corrupt votes." Samuel P. Orth's study, *The Boss and The Machine,* reflected more or less the same view: "From its very earliest days, fraud at the polls has been a Tammany practice." But "wholesale frauds," continued Orth, became commonplace after "the adoption of universal suffrage." Orth singled out the election of 1854 when Tammany leader Fernando Wood recruited supporters from "about 40,000" shiftless citizens who engaged in repeating and other dishonest practices. He observed, furthermore, that Wood's organization had utilized a speedy naturalization process in order to swell the number of immigrants eligible to vote.[10]

A more recent study of the early history of Tammany Hall by Jerome Mushkat has not substantially altered the judgment of earlier writers. While discussing the late 1820s, Mushkat observed that domination of the New York police was especially important to Tammany "since election frauds were a fact of political life." According to Mushkat, Tammany even at this early date relied upon fraudulent practices. Later, Fernando Wood's "henchmen instructed some voters, barred others, stole ballot boxes, and used every illegal trick imaginable to win the [1856] contest."[11] While Mushkat's study does not emphasize the significance of the role of the Irish and other immigrants in corruption and violent elections, as did earlier studies, it does find that New York City elections were replete with fraud, violence, and intimidation, and hence differs little in this respect from earlier treatments of pre-Civil War New York politics.

Literature dealing with election corruption in New York City in the years between 1865 and 1930 is considerably more extensive. The post-Civil War decades saw the rapid population growth of New York fed by a mammoth increase in foreign immigration. Most observers were convinced that Tammany's grip on New York City government was based in large part upon wholesale election fraud in the foreign-born, working-class districts. Throughout this period, reformers persistently organized campaigns to eliminate alleged election fraud and to reduce the political power of Tammany Hall. *The Nation,* for example, charged in October 1868 as election time approached that the political leaders of the city were using foreigners to pad the roles of those eligible to vote. The "naturalization mill," as *The Nation* put it, "ground out 35,000 voters in this city alone."

According to this article, 10,000 of these aliens were probably legally qualified to vote, 10,000 had not been in the United States the required number of years, and "the other 15,000 have never ... been near the court room; indeed, from 5,000 to 7,000 of these latter are nonexistent." A similar charge was made somewhat later about the "Tweed Ring" by Frank Goodnow in an essay published in Bryce's *American Commonwealth.* Tweed's candidate for governor of New York in 1868, claimed Goodnow, "was secured by the grossest and most extensive frauds ever perpetrated in the city, e.g., illegal naturalization of foreigners, false registration, repeating of votes, and unfair counting."[12]

Similar charges were made in the 1880s by William M. Ivins, who had served as City Chamberlain, in two articles and a well-publicized speech before the New York Commonwealth Club. Ivins reviewed the history of the role of Tammany Hall since the 1860s, when he believed New York politics had become thoroughly corrupt. This involved, according to Ivins, "the open use of immense sums of money at the polls, and the almost equally open frauds in polling and canvassing the votes." He laid much of the blame upon Assemby District leaders who had "come into possession of the ... vital part of the election machinery. They could meet on the night before election and destroy the tickets, and no election could take place." While Ivins' charges were general and he offered little specific evidence, he was convinced that fraud and bribery had been widely practiced in New York elections at least since the "Tweed Ring" gained control of the city.[13]

The Republican opposition to the Tammany Democrats also made serious charges about the prevalence of election fraud in New York. A committee of the Republican-dominated state legislature chaired by Senator Clarence Lexow investigated the New York City police in 1894 in response to repeated charges by Reverend Charles H. Parkhurst, pastor of the Madison Square Presbyterian Church, that corruption in the city was rampant. The committee report concluded among other things that it has been conclusively shown "that in a very large number of the election districts of New York, almost every conceivable crime against the elective franchise was either permitted or committed by the police, invariably in the interests of the dominant Democratic organization ... Tammany Hall." The Republican leader Thomas C. Platt, or "Boss Platt" as he was known to Democrats and other critics, repeated the charges of the Lexow committee with approval. "Conservative estimates," said Platt, "placed the total fraudulent vote in New York County alone in the campaigns of 1891 and 1892, at from thirty to fifty thousand." Platt was not alone in his belief that New York City voters were corrupt, for in the New York State Constitutional Convention of 1894, the Republicans succeeded in adopting an amendment that required voter registration only in towns and cities of more than 5,000 inhabitants, despite Democratic objections that this amendment implied that rural voters were more honest than urban voters.[14]

Platt's charges and those of the Lexow committee and other critics of the conduct of elections in New York City differed little from the observations of presumably more detached and scholarly commentators. Abram C. Bernheim in the *Political Science Quarterly* in 1889 expressed the view that election bribery and fraud were common in the "foreign population and crowded city wards." Relying upon the findings of the City Reform Club, he charged that election fraud had occurred in the 1887 election in the eighth assembly district. "There were 132 voters registered from one lodging house, most of which are known to have been fraudulent." M. Ostrogorski's *Democracy* also charged that dishonest elections continued to be very common after the Civil War in New York. Tammany Democrats "perpetrated frauds" and bribed foreigners who "blindly adopted the tickets given out at the party conventions and supplied the Organization with what was called 'voting cattle.'" In *How the World Votes,* published in 1918, two historians, Charles Seymour and Donald P. Frary, gave added support to the same view of New York elections. They described several techniques widely used since the Tweed era and observed, "So efficient was the Tweed ring in New York City in 1868-1871, that the votes cast were eight percent in excess of the total voting population." These two scholars were firmly convinced, moreover, that vote fraud was still a major problem in New York as they wrote their book at the end of the Progressive era. Vote repeating was common in New York—"The only fraud which flourishes practically unabated in spite of all efforts to check it.... The same man votes in district after district, sometimes casting ten or twelve votes in a day." They singled out the election of 1910 in New York when, they asserted, "it was conservatively estimated that the number of fraudulent registrations and votes prevented equalled the total number of votes cast." Unfortunately, sources of information or other documentation to support these rather precise allegations were not provided.[15]

Post-World War I scholarly studies of New York politics during the 1865-1929 era changed the general verdict little. Harold F. Gosnell, in *Boss Platt and His New York Machine,* repeated without qualification a Republican charge made in the 1890s that "fraudulent naturalizations [were] common in the great Democratic cities," and Gosnell claimed that in 1905 in New York City "one investigator estimated that there were in excess of 170,000 venal voters." M. R. Werner's *Tammany Hall* provided a variety of examples of corrupt election practices, as did Florence E.

Gibson's 1951 study of New York City's Irish. Even more recently, Fredman's *The Australian Ballot* reiterated earlier charges of New York City election corruption. Writing about the 1880s, Fredman said, "The burgeoning metropolis at the mouth of the Hudson River absorbed the teeming masses from Europe and much of the corporate wealth of the nation. The abuses of elections and the vested interests which profited thereby appeared at their worst, and reformers were compelled to use the utmost vigor and persistence."[16] Studies by presumably more detached observers, in sum, differed little from studies of New York politics written in the late nineteenth and early twentieth century on the issue of election corruption in New York City, but these similarities should not seem surprising, since the more recent studies of political corruption have relied in large part upon the writings of earlier reformers and observers.

OTHER CITIES

Philadelphia's reputation as a center of fraudulent election practices was second only to New York's, and the literature suggests that vote fraud was rampant in Philadelphia after about 1860 and until approximately 1930. Orth in *The Boss and The Machine* was quite explicit in his discussion of organization of the "Gas Ring" in the 1880s: "So began in Philadelphia the practice of fraudulent registering and voting on a scale that has probably never been equalled elsewhere in America." These practices, Orth believed, continued on into the twentieth century, and many other authorities agreed. Lincoln Steffens, for example, declared in *Shame of the Cities* that in Philadelphia "the machine controls the whole process of voting, and practices fraud at every stage." The Republican organization in Philadelphia was dominated by Senator Bois Penrose during the first two decades of the twentieth century and in the 1920s by William S. Vare. Both leaders were frequently accused of manipulating the black voter, and Vare's election to the United States Senate in 1926 touched off a much-publicized Senate investigation of election practices and spending in Philadelphia. Charges of election fraud in Philadelphia appeared less frequently after 1930, but as late as 1944 Charles W. Van Devander asserted that "Pennsylvania and Philadelphia have been hardened to the expenditure of tremendous amounts of money to buy elections. The state is accustomed to vote fraud in Philadelphia on a big scale."[17]

An examination of the literature on Chicago politics shows that allegations that Chicago elections were dishonest were made even before the Civil War, but it was only more recently that civic leaders and reformers became alarmed at the extent of election fraud. Books on Chicago politics have preserved many humorous anecdotes about the fraudulent political antics of Michael "Hinky Dink" Kenna and "Bathhouse" John Coughlin,

First Ward Aldermen at the turn of the century. Charles E. Merriam, a political science professor at the University of Chicago and a Chicago reform leader in the early twentieth century, however, believed that large-scale vote fraud did not exist in Chicago until after 1915 when William H. "Big Bill" Thompson became mayor. Then, said, Merriam, "calamity descended upon the city." The 1920s, in Merriam's view, was a decade when wholesale election fraud occurred in Chicago: "It is estimated in Chicago that election frauds in a poll of 1,000,000 votes may reach as high as 50,000 to 100,000." Other observers agreed that vote fraud was rampant in the 1920s in Chicago, and Harold F. Gosnell, Merriam's colleague at the University of Chicago, concluded that election corruption was still prevalent in that city in the 1930s. Since the 1930s, charges of election fraud in Chicago have focused upon the activities of the dominant Democratic organization, and in the years since World War II, Mayor Richard J. Daley's administration frequently has been accused of committing vote fraud. Daley's critics would have little difficulty accepting Mike Royko's assessment of the Chicago Democratic organization: "It never misses a chance to steal a certain number of votes and trample all over the voting laws."[18]

Charges that election fraud has been practiced by one or both parties at various times have been made about most other American cities as well. In Boston, especially during the administration of James M. Curley, the honesty of elections has been questioned,[19] and many are convinced that elections in Jersey City and other cities in New Jersey were corrupt, especially during the reign of Frank Hague in the 1920s and 1930s.[20] Election corruption was alleged to be rife in Cincinnati during the rule of George B. "Boss" Cox in the Progressive Era,[21] in Kansas City under Tom Pendergast's domination in the 1930s,[22] and in Memphis under Edward H. "Boss" Crump's leadership in the early twentieth century.[23] There were also charges of vote fraud in Denver, Detroit, New Orleans, St. Louis, and San Francisco,[24] and there is little doubt that most political observers were convinced that urban life in the United States, roughly from the Civil War to the 1930s, was fertile ground for election fraud and corruption.

RURAL AREAS

While the preponderance of those who have commented on vote fraud in American politics were convinced that the greater share of corruption in elections was in the great cities, there were still many observers who maintained that vote fraud was also very much a characteristic of the politics of the small city, town, and the farm as well. A recent student of vote fraud in the early twentieth century, in fact, argued that "in most histories of the Progressive era, such rural waywardness at the polls has been obscured by the attention given to municipal voting frauds."[25] Indeed, this survey of the literature on political corruption produced a considerable array of examples of fraudulent election practices in the rural areas and small towns in the United States. As was the case with urban vote fraud, the great bulk of the allegations of rural vote fraud fell into the years roughly between the Civil War and 1930, and politicians in every geographic section of the nation have been accused at one time or another of conducting at least some fraudulent elections.

Vote fraud in the rural Northeast has been the subject of several commentators on American politics. "Even in New England, inhabited by the descendants of the Puritans," exclaimed Ostrogorski, "votes are sold ... openly like an article of commerce; there is a regular market quotation for them!" Ostrogorski's comments on vote fraud in New England were based upon a much publicized study of rural and town voting by J. J. McCook which appeared in *The Forum* in 1892. McCook examined the voting behavior of a selection of twenty-one Connecticut towns and wards and concluded that vote purchasing was ubiquitous in Connecticut—he estimated that precisely 15.9 percent of the voters in these towns in Connecticut were for sale. An article published just a year later made similar accusations about New Hampshire voters. This study estimated the number of "purchasable" voters in New Hampshire at about 10 percent of the total state vote. Somewhat later, Lincoln Steffens insisted that politics in Rhode Island "is grounded on the lowest layer of corruption that I have found thus far—the bribery of voters with cash at the polls."[26] Charges of a similar nature have been made about the purchase of votes and other varieties of election fraud in the late nineteenth and early twentieth century in other northeastern states including upstate New York, rural New Jersey, and Delaware.[27]

The rural Midwest has also been mentioned prominently in the literature on fraudulent political practices. R. C. Buley found evidence as early as 1836 of money used to bribe voters in Ohio, and Matthew Josephson stated categorically that there was extensive fraud committed by Republicans in Ohio and elsewhere in the Midwest in the late nineteenth century. "In Ohio," Josephson wrote about the election of 1896, "there was one vote cast for every four living persons (with women then not voting), surpassing all previous records by 25 percent." The most celebrated example of rural vote fraud in Ohio, however, was in Adams County, where in 1910 and 1911 an enterprising local judge brought to trial and convicted 1,690 voters, 26 percent of the eligible voters in the county, for selling votes.[28]

Indiana's rural and small town voters during the last half of the nineteenth century, judging from the literature, ranked among the most corrupt voters in America. Matthew Josephson repeatedly emphasized the prevalence of vote fraud in Indiana. "The floater vote in Indiana," Josephson maintained, "had been estimated at 10,000 in 1880, 15,000 in 1884, but was now [1888] reckoned at 20,000," and he claimed that in the election of 1896 in Indiana "there were 30,000 floaters reported by watchers as receiving besides sandwiches and liquor only $5 a head in this year of depression."[29] A much publicized letter to county chairmen in Indiana supposedly written by William S. Dudley, treasurer of the National Republican Committee during the campaign of 1888, provided heavy ammunition for the advocates of ballot reform. "Divide the floaters into blocks of five," Dudley was supposed to have instructed his Indiana followers, "and put a trusted man with the necessary funds in charge of those five, and make him responsible that none get away." In that same election, according to Buley's account, the Republicans imported five hundred blacks from Chicago to vote in northern Indiana, and "Cincinnati repeaters" were used in Indianapolis. An account of efforts to reform election procedures in Terre Haute in 1913 also reported that a wide variety of vote fraud was practiced in that Indiana town.[30]

Charges of violence, intimidation, and other forms of election fraud are found in great abundance in most studies of politics in the South between the Civil War and the beginning of the twentieth century. E. Merton Coulter, for example, insisted in *The South During Reconstruction* that vote fraud was widespread among black voters in most southern states during the Reconstruction era. After the passage of the Reconstruction Act of 1867, said Coulter, Union generals were instructed to register all eligible voters. "It was . . . good business to enter onto the record as many names as possible, and so it came about that sometimes Negroes were registered two or three times, under different names." Coulter believed that the newly enfranchised freed men were particularly susceptible to the temptation to commit election fraud. Many black voters, he said, were simply duped or manipulated by Republican leaders, but other blacks sold their votes. "A Negro who was too cunning to be tricked," concluded Coulter, "could generally be bought. . . . Many Negroes were bought with a few drinks of whiskey or a handful of cigars." More frequently, however, commentators on southern politics in the Reconstruction period and the late nineteenth century have placed greater emphasis upon the use of violence, intimidation, and fraud by white southerners, who used extraordinary means in these years to prevent blacks from voting. Williams A. Dunning in his well known study of the Reconstruction era cited numerous examples of the use of violence, intimidation, and other illegal and fraudulent acts to prevent blacks from voting, and he specifically mentioned examples in Georgia, Louisiana, and Mississippi. In 1874, Dunning reported, there "appeared, in many of the regions where the black population was most dense, open and unmistakable injunctions to the negroes that they must vote with the conservatives or not at all." The penalty for a black voter who failed to heed such warnings included "no employment, no credit, no land to cultivate." A study of black voting in the South during the late nineteenth century published in 1932 made essentially the same point: "It is hardly necessary ... to attempt to demonstrate that Southern elections since the beginning of Reconstruction were notably corrupt.... The fact has been quite generally admitted by Southern politicians and publicists." More recently, C. Vann Woodward concluded that elections in the South until after the beginning of the twentieth century were characteristically corrupt. According to Woodward, "Elaborate extralegal devices of fraud and chicanery which had developed during Reconstruction became habits that lingered long after Redemption. The stuffing of ballot boxes, the use of boxes with false bottoms, the casting of tissue ballots, the doctoring of returns, the manipulation of counts, the repeating of votes, and the tampering with registration books were all highly developed acts."[3][1]

The frequency of allegations of vote fraud in the South declined considerably after the beginning of the twentieth century (and after blacks had been driven from politics), although published examples of such accusations can be cited. Perhaps the most well publicized recent charge of vote fraud in the South involved former President Lyndon B. Johnson's first campaign for the Senate in Texas in 1948. In that election, the unofficial results first indicated that Johnson's opponent, Coke Stevenson, who had received the largest plurality in the first primary, had won by a very slim margin. Then a precinct in southern Texas, which already had been carried overwhelmingly by Johnson, "corrected" its vote, thereby giving Johnson the extra votes he needed to win the election. Johnson's opponent charged that he had been "beaten by a stuffed ballot box," but Johnson was declared the victor. In general, however, since early in this century, charges of vote fraud in the South have appeared no more frequently than they have in other nonurban sections of the nation.[3][2]

Published accounts of vote fraud in the rural west were considerably less frequent than accounts of fraud in other geographic sections of the United States. The infrequency of references to voting irregularities in the West may only reflect a lack of interest on the part of easterners in western politics, since most of the commentators on vote fraud lived in the East. In the West, furthermore, the voting population was smaller and there were relatively few large concentrations of foreign-born and black voters; groups which, as shall be seen, many political observers thought were most likely to commit voting irregularities. At any rate, allegations of illegal election procedures in the West were of sufficient number to support the view held by many political observers that election fraud was an endemic national affliction.[33]

RELIABILITY AND ACCURACY OF THE LITERATURE

Despite the mass of literature about political corruption, there are reasons to doubt the reliability and accuracy of many generalizations which have been made about vote fraud in American politics. It is clear, in the first place, that very few of the sources consulted in this survey attempted to define vote fraud carefully or to differentiate between the kinds of political acts alleged to be fraudulent. Acts which caused serious distortions of the voter's "rational will" such as repeating, intimidation, and manipulation of the vote count regularly were grouped indiscriminantly with other activities such as excessive campaign expenditures, vote buying, the purchase of drinks at the corner saloon, political barbecues, and free rides to the polls which, as noted above, are not evidence that the voter's intent had been misrepresented.

Charges of vote buying and other forms of direct or indirect bribery appeared perhaps more consistently in the literature than any other type of election fraud, but vote buying and free drinks at the corner saloon, like the coffee-klatsch, probably can be seen more accurately as a means utilized by the political organizations to mobilize the vote. In a sense, vote buying and other small favors probably were regarded as a form of patronage distributed to loyal party voters at election time. "In most instances," wrote Genevieve Gist about Adams County, Ohio, "it was simply a case of paying the Democratic farmer to come out and vote the Democratic ticket." A critic of voting behavior in 1905 in New York State made the same point: "A large percentage of the venal voters are paid to vote for the party to which they belong and against which they would be very unlikely to vote." George Kennan made a similar point about black voters in Delaware: "The Negroes could hardly be induced, by any temptation, to support a Democrat; but their choice as between one Republican and another might be influenced by money."[34] The generalizations about vote fraud, in brief, actually had reference in large part to political techniques that either were or are now illegal or "undesirable" but which probably did not significantly distort the "rational will" of the voter nor reduce the historical value of election data.

PROBLEMS OF SUBSTANTIATION

The evidence to demonstrate the existence of election fraud in the literature is not only anecdotal, it is unsystematic, impressionistic, and by and large inconclusive. Almost all contemporary allegations of vote fraud were based primarily upon sweeping, generalized, often highly emotional charges substantiated in most cases by only the most fragile evidence, if supported at all. The charges made about New York politics by William M. Ivins in the late 1880s, for instance, were given high credibility by the reform press at the time, apparently because Ivins had been a city official. Certainly it was not because of the evidence produced in his published articles. Likewise, Charles E. Merriam's assertion that there were from 50,000 to 100,000 fraudulent votes in Chicago elections in the 1920s was made without evidence. Most of the studies published since the 1920s, moreover, tended to rely heavily upon the charges and allegations of political fraud made by these contemporary observers.

Attempts to analyze fraudulent voting practices systematically and dispassionately were rare. Most of the studies which concerned themselves with vote fraud were written before 1930 when hostility to "bosses," "machines," immigrants, blacks, and working class, urban politics ran high among middle- and upper-class reformers and political observers. Most commentators simply assumed vote fraud was rampant, and few recognized a need to document these allegations.

One of the few endeavors to try to demonstrate quantitatively the existence of widespread vote buying in Connecticut elections was the widely cited article by J. J. McCook which appeared in *The Forum* in 1892. McCook presented tables of data concerning towns in Connecticut claiming to show precisely the percentage of voters in various categories who sold their votes. In "Rural Town I," he maintained, vote selling was practiced by 9.8 percent of the voters, and in "Rural Town II," 20.9 percent. His tables also showed, to use "Rural Town II" as an example, that while only 21 percent of "American stock" sold votes, much higher percentages of most other ethnic groups were venal, including 100 percent of the "colored" and 100 percent of the first generation French Canadians. The article also attempted to show that there was a very high relationship between the consumption of alcohol and selling votes. Among the "American stock" in "Rural Town I," for example, only 1.69 percent of the "Temperate" were venal, but 70.0 percent of the "Intemperate" and 100 percent of the "Drunkards." The "Shiftless" and those who had been arrested or imprisoned were also stamped 100 percent venal. These data, McCook reported, were derived "from books which have been actually used in campaigns by town committeemen," and from oral testimony given him by other local political leaders; or, in other words, from members of local elites. Aside from the fact that McCook's social and moral values seemed to have influenced his conclusions, the reliability of his sources of information seemed insufficient to justify the supreme confidence he and others displayed in his results.[35]

Other attempts to document fraudulent voting activities included, in New York City for example, the results of accusations of excesses in Tammany Hall under William M. "Boss" Tweed's leadership and the findings of the state senate (Lexow) committee report on New York City police and politics in 1894. Another investigation was conducted in 1894 by a delegation of "gentlemen" representing the Bar Association of the City of New York who volunteered to serve as poll watchers in the election of 1893. Their observations led to grand jury indictments of several election officials and to the conclusion, according to one of the group, "That false registration, false voting, and bribery are as easily and as safely practised as they ever were." Some studies of Philadelphia relied upon evidence such as that produced by the United States Senate investigation of the election of 1926, when the Vare "machine" was charged with padding and manipulating registration lists to the extent that unanimous or nearly unanimous counts for machine candidates were found in the poor, working-class districts. Joseph P. Harris, moreover, cited the earlier impact of the personal registration law of 1906 upon registration lists in Philadelphia as evidence of fraud. Harris reported that in 1904 there were 385,036 names registered in Philadelphia, but after the registration reform law was implemented, only 250,950 legal voters remained. "In the corrupt wards of the city the decrease was very pronounced," Harris concluded, and he apparently believed that the new registration law had stricken over 134,000 illegal voters from the lists. Harris also produced extracts of a postelection study conducted by a Chicago reform group, the Citizens' Association of Chicago, to show that in the 1920s fictitious names, names of the deceased, and names of persons who did not live at the address provided were found in the official registration records in some Chicago wards. He presented tables of data to show that voter turnout in the center city, slum wards of New York, Chicago, and Philadelphia and several smaller cities in the 1920 presidential election was very high—higher even than in some very prosperous wards in both cities. In San Francisco, by contrast, Harris's data showed that wards of similarly low socioeconomic characteristics produced low voter turnout. Harris accepted this as evidence that there was widespread corruption in the poor wards of Chicago, Philadelphia, and other cities, and that elections in San Francisco were comparatively honest.[36]

Evidence such as the inability to find registered voters in postelection surveys, an excessive number of names on registration lists, nearly unanimous counts, and very high voter turnout in "machine" wards is consistent with the view that there was large-scale vote fraud. Such evidence, however, is not conclusive, and there are other equally plausible explanations that should be considered. Center city, tenement house districts where fraudulent activity was allegedly concentrated were by all accounts highly transient, overcrowded areas where it would have been highly likely that many legal voters changed addresses very frequently. A recent examination of Boston in the nineteenth century, for example, concluded that in the 1880s, if a city official returned one year later to the same address, he would have "less than a fifty-fifty chance of finding its former inhabitants living there." Undoubtedly an attempt to locate registered voters would have encountered similar difficulties. If Boston was not typical of large American cities in this period, the authors of this study argued, it probably had a "*less* fluid and volatile population than more rapidly-growing cities like New York or Chicago." It is not surprising, in short, that investigations of registration lists and postelection surveys conducted in urban areas failed to locate large numbers of voters at the legal address given at the time of voter registration. It is also quite conceivable that the more than 134,000 names purged from Philadelphia's registration lists in 1906, which Harris accepted as evidence of fraud, were in large part a manifestation of urban population mobility, not election fraud. This conclusion seems even more tenable in view of the fact that the actual vote cast for President in Philadelphia county in 1904 was only 281,654, well below the 385,036 voters registered before the imposition of the reform law of 1906.[37]

The contention of many observers that incredibly large numbers of voters claimed to live at the same address proved the existence of vote fraud can be discounted, at least to some extent. One of the most persistent characteristics of living conditions in the tenement house neighborhoods in the late nineteenth and early twentieth century was high population density. Jacob Riis's classic study of New York tenement life in the late nineteenth century, for example, emphasized repeatedly the extreme overcrowding in these neighborhoods. He referred to the "East Side" as "still the most densely populated district in all the world, China not excluded"; and he described an Italian settlement where "something like forty families are packed into five old two-story and attic houses . . . and out in the yards additional crowds are, or were until very recently, accommodated in sheds." Blake McKelvey in *The Urbanization of America* agreed with Riis's assessment of overcrowding in the slums of New York

170 ANALYZING ELECTORAL HISTORY

and cited a federal study of 1894 indicating that there was only somewhat less congestion in Chicago, Philadelphia, and Baltimore. Humbart Nelli's study of the Italians in Chicago provided an essentially similar picture of families crowded together, one or two to an apartment, "and frequently lodgers or boarders as well. . . . Inhabitants often ate and slept in shifts." Overcrowding of this magnitude was surely beyond the experience of members of the American middle and upper class who conducted studies of vote fraud; and quite possibly most reformers and investigators, already convinced that fraud prevailed in the slums on a massive scale, simply misinterpreted the facts. Understandably, they probably assumed that it was flatly impossible for such large numbers of voters to reside at a single tenement house address.[38]

The overcrowded and transient nature of many center city wards may also help explain how at times turnout rates in the low-income, working-class wards appeared to be excessively high, as Harris and others have noted. Probably census statistics for these areas tended to undercount the actual population. If so, voter turnout percentages would have been correspondingly exaggerated, since the actual number of eligible voters would have exceeded the official number used to calculate the rate of turnout. Jacob Riis was convinced that the census takers failed to count many slum dwellers. "It is their instinct," Riis said of the New York poor, "to shun the light, and they cannot be corralled in one place long enough to be counted." Peter R. Knights found evidence in pre-Civil War Boston that appeared to corroborate Riis's impression. The Boston city directories "discriminated against the lowest economic orders, who were among the most mobile of the population," according to Knights. The work of other students of population also indicate that Riis's impression was probably valid. "We are," wrote a member of the United States Bureau of the Census in 1973, "still concerned about the possibility that undercoverage is more serious in large cities, although we do not have solid evidence to prove or disprove this hypothesis." High turnout rates in the northern states, furthermore, were normal until the beginning of the present century, as W. Dean Burnham has shown.[39] Most of the authors mentioned in this chapter wrote in the twentieth century, when the turnout rate was much lower. It is not surprising therefore that many attributed evidence of high turnout to vote fraud rather than to long term changes in voter behavior.

The most systematic examination of vote fraud in the literature is Samuel J. Eldersveld's and Albert A. Applegate's analysis of the recounts of the Michigan gubernatorial elections of 1950 and 1952. This study attempted to measure the level of "error" committed by voters and by election officials by comparing the original results in these elections with the recounts. The study calculated that the votes cast or counted in "error" in these two elections was about 2 percent of the total vote cast. The rate of "error" varied somewhat by county, and in the 1950 election two Michigan counties showed levels of "error" slightly above 5 percent. Most of this "error" was committed by election officials, but "error" included factors such as incompetence, carelessness, and other honest mistakes which served to distort the voter's intent but were probably not deliberate attempts to commit fraud. Thus, the amount of fraud was considerably less than the total "error" committed. The study also utilized a measure of "partisan bias" which probably fairly accurately identified counties where there was vote fraud, since it measured the tendency of "errors" to benefit one party over the other. This statistic indicated that the highest rates of "partisan bias" did not appear in the urban, industrial precincts of Detroit, as the literature on vote fraud would suggest, but in the highly partisan, rural, Republican counties of Michigan.[40] For some purposes, an overall 2 percent error level may seem high, but on the other hand, it is not high enough to substantiate the view that this election was "a meaningless procedure." The conclusions of this study of Michigan in the 1950s of course may not be regarded as having broad application to elections at earlier times or in other parts of the United States, but they do suggest the possibility that vote fraud was considerably less prevalent than the literature has indicated.

ATTITUDES OF OBSERVERS

The lack of hard evidence of vote fraud and the scarcity of systematic studies of vote fraud in American politics is not surprising in view of the attitudes and values of those who have shown the greatest interest in political corruption. Most of the literature on election fraud was overtly hostile and unsympathetic to the Irish, more recent immigrants, and blacks, and to the urban political leaders ("bosses") and the political organizations ("machines") which represented virtually the only means of political expression available to these minority groups. To some extent, the charges of vote fraud seemed to reflect an inability of the critics of the "machines" to appreciate the "lifestyle" of the urban poor. To some extent the charges seemed but part of a political campaign of elite groups to regain or retain control of city politics. It seems significant in this context that the charges of election fraud appeared most frequently in the years of heaviest immigration and for about a decade after the flow of foreign born was curtailed—roughly from about the Civil War to 1930. Most writing about the immigrant in politics, especially before 1920, was openly condescending, moralistic, and prejudiced toward the new arrivals, and rarely was there an expression of sympathy or even awareness of the suffering and misery of life in the "machine" wards.[41]

Bryce in *The American Commonwealth* described urban populations as "an ignorant multitude, largely composed of recent immigrants," and Ostrogorski was even less restrained. The "clannish habits" of the Irish, he said, were "peculiar to the Celtic race" and made them especially vulnerable to the machinations of the "party Organization" which "flung at a single stroke into the political balance of the United States all the ignorance and all the corruptibility represented by the Irish."[42] These two highly respected foreign commentators found many Americans who shared their low esteem of the politics of the urban poor and foreign born. The *Nation,* a leading mugwump journal, in 1871 pointed out with emphasis that "most of Tweed's subjects are Irish Catholics" and that the Irish were not ready for self-government:

> Irish Catholics—putting aside for the moment the difficulties in the way of constitutional government which in their case, as well as in that of the French, are created by temperament—are really, as regards political development, still in what we may call the clan stage—that is, they have not passed through the same process of political and social development as the other European races.[43]

Theodore Roosevelt in 1886 insisted that in New York City "a large proportion of the members of every political machine are recruited from the lower grades of the foreign population." He declared, furthermore, that "in the lower wards, where there is a large vicious population, the condition of politics is often fairly appalling, and the boss is generally a man of grossly immoral public and private character." Even one as sympathetic to the new citizens as Jane Addams found fault with the Irish. "Many a politician has come from Ireland," she wrote in 1898, "not only with the desire to feed at the public crib, but with a conviction that it is perfectly legitimate to do so, and it is the Irishmen who largely teach political methods to the others living in their vicinity." E. A. Ross, a prominent sociologist at the University of Wisconsin in 1914, also believed that the Irish were a major source of corruption in urban politics. "These Irish immigrants had neither the temperament nor the training to make a success of popular government." Ross, however, did not limit his explanation of election corruption to the venality of the Irish. The "simpleminded foreigner or negro," he felt, was also guilty. Some foreigners were honest, he recognized; and others did not choose to vote or were not permitted to vote ("No doubt the country is better off for their not voting"). Still, he asserted, "it is in the cities with many naturalized foreigners or enfranchised negroes that the vice interests have had the freest hand in exploiting and degrading the people."[44]

After 1920, some observers and students of American politics continued to view the immigrants and their children in the poor, urban wards with suspicion and lack of sympathy, although open hostility by this time was less frequently expressed. Orth's *The Boss and The Machine* in 1921 stated categorically that "the foreign immigrants who congested our cities were alien to American institutions," and even Harris' work, completed later in the 1920s, reflected vestiges of the mugwump-progressive's patronizing attitude toward the immigrant and the urban poor. Frequently Harris used such value-laden descriptions as "best" wards, "better class Negro wards," and "down-town, lodging house, 'riffraff,' and machine controlled wards." Harris maintained, moreover, that the "establishment of universal manhood suffrage, and the influx of immigrants from foreign countries have given votes to a large number of persons without political experience, education, or ideals." Writing in the 1930s, the historian Matthew Josephson was no less hostile to the new citizens from abroad. New York City immigrants, said Josephson, comprised "one of the most ignorant, violent, *lumpen* proletariats in the modern world. For this rabble, traditionally, the rulers of the city's dominant political organization provided bread and even circuses in the form of annual clambakes and excursions." And even Mike Royko slipped into the same style in locating vote fraud in Chicago: "Most of it goes on in the wards where the voters are lower middle class, black, poor white, or on the bottle."[45]

Many of these observers were particularly offended by the importance of the saloon and the bartender in the political life of the urban poor. "The old custom of personal house-to-house canvass has, in our cities, degenerated into a visiting of liquor saloons and 'corner groceries,' " declared Henry George in 1883. "So large in the aggregate are the amounts of money thus disbursed by candidates, that in many towns it is said that one-half of the saloons could not be kept open but for the elections." Three years later, Theodore Roosevelt likewise emphasized the importance to the New York machine of the saloon. The "liquor-sellers," Roosevelt maintained, have "enormous influence in politics," and, he maintained, "bartenders form perhaps the nearest approach to a leisure class that we have at present on this side of the water." In that same year, William M. Ivins in his celebrated exposé of New York politics declared that money spent in "barrooms" at election time contributed much to the "demoralization of the community. . . . I am credibly informed that on the evening of the last great Democratic parade in the late Presidential campaign they took in $2200 for liquors over the Hoffman House bar." About 20 percent of the immigrants, *The Nation* declared in 1887, were corrupt—"They are the worst element in our population, whose natural meeting-place is the liquor saloon." The crusade to make the consumption of alcohol illegal in these same years, furthermore, was regularly justified as a method of purifying politics by keeping strong drink from the Irish and the immigrants. One leader of the Anti-Saloon League declared in 1914 that some cities in the United States were "well-nigh submerged" by "an element which gathers its ideas of patriotism and citizenship from the low grogshop." This group "is manipulated by the still baser element engaged in the un-American drink traffic and by the kind of politician the saloon creates." The association of vote fraud with demon rum declined in frequency in the literature after the adoption of the Prohibition Amendment in 1919, but as late as 1928, Sikes asserted "that treating voters to drinks, cigars, or giving them presents in some other form is one of the most insidious ways of influencing votes."[4][6]

Black voters were also singled out in the literature as especially prone to commit election fraud. Ostrogorski was convinced that honesty in politics in the South greatly declined after the enfranchisement of blacks, or, as he called them, the "besotted negroes." "After the Civil War," he wrote, "the victors gave the suffrage to the whole ignorant and degraded mass of freed negroes" who "without understanding anything of the issues of politics . . . grasped its externals admirably." Porter's *A History of the Suffrage in the United States* echoed Ostrogorski's observations. The price of black suffrage in the post-Civil War South, said Porter, was "political vice, corruption, villainy, and outrage." Charles Seymour and Donald P. Frary were equally specific. Blacks, they suggested, "had been corrupted en masse." James Bryce endorsed a similar view of black voters in 1921 by writing that "bribery is, or recently was, common" in certain rural areas and "in some cities, where a section of the less intelligent voters, especially the negroes in the Middle States, have been corruptible."[4][7]

The literature on election fraud, in sum, corresponded roughly with the years of the mugwump-progressive reform movements and can be seen as a manifestation of the middle- and upper-class reform of these years. The mugwumps, as *The Nation* sympathetically described them in 1871, were "mostly of New England origin or education, or . . . are peculiarly and strongly American in the best sense of the term," and more recently Gerald W. McFarland has provided very convincing collective biographical data to document *The Nation's* characterization of the mugwumps. This description applied almost as well to many of the progressive reformers. Studies of the backgrounds of these individuals in American society during the Progressive era indicate that most progressive reformers were largely native-born American, white, mostly Protestant members of the middle and upper class. As *The Nation* perceptively noted, to most New York

City reformers, "the region over which Tweed rules is as much a *terra incognita* as Montenegro or Albania." The sources of many of the charges of vote corruption originated from this middle- and upper-class group and from the slick-paged, relatively expensive mugwump and "muckrake" magazines such as *The Nation, Harper's Weekly, Outlook, McClure's,* and *The World's Work,* which obviously catered to an elitist, middle- and upper-class audience.[48] Most of the writing on political corruption since the 1920s, moreover, has tended to accept uncritically the accusations of these reformers who were in fact themselves political partisans, highly unlikely to have had a detached assessment of the immigrant-based "machines." To most of the mugwumps and progressives, the mere existence of a well-organized urban "machine" seemed enough to conclude that vote fraud had been committed; to them isolated instances of vote fraud often were sufficient to believe that urban, immigrant, politics was wholly corrupt. "What they were really asking for," as Richard Hofstadter has noted about the mugwumps, "was leadership by an educated and civic-minded elite."[49]

Evidence exists to show that some of those accused of committing vote fraud categorically denied guilt, insisting instead that the charges were politically motivated. A forceful statement to this effect in defense of Tammany Hall's conduct of elections, for example, was the minority report which appeared in the published proceedings of the 1894 Lexow committee's investigation of the New York City Police Department. The minority report was filed by Jacob A. Cantor, the only member of the Lexow committee from New York City. Cantor branded the findings of the majority as "astonishingly false and absolutely unsustained by the testimony." The committee counsel, Cantor pointed out, was a Republican, not from New York City, and unacquainted with "either the geographical, political or social condition of the metropolis." Cantor accused the Republican majority of making no effort to find evidence of Republican corruption, and he insisted that the witnesses brought before the committee "were those whose testimony had been secured beforehand by the Republican clubs of the city." Cantor admitted that probably "there were certain irregularities at the polls, but not," he maintained, "of a character to warrant the wholesale indictment made against the entire city in the report presented by the majority." The Republican allegations, Cantor went on, had exaggerated a few instances of fraud out of proportion: "The testimony ... simply shows that but in a very few of the election districts, not fifteen in all, out of about 1,100, were there any charges, even of irregularity." There was "not a scintilla of proof," added Cantor, to show that the police had used their position to influence elections in Tammany Hall's favor, as the majority report argued. Finally,

Cantor concluded, in New York City "crimes against the ballot box have been more sternly prosecuted and severely punished than in any other town, city or village in the State, and its elections . . . have been more free from fraud." Cantor's point of view, of course, did not fit the preconceptions of most of Tammany's critics, and his arguments went virtually ignored in the many discussions of the findings of the Lexow investigation of vote fraud and political corruption in New York City.[50]

CONTESTED ELECTIONS

The rarity of legal documentation of election fraud also casts suspicion upon the accuracy of the charges of election fraud. Given the competitive nature of the two-party system and the unrestrained quality of the charges of vote fraud, one ought to find innumerable contested elections and references to court cases in the literature, even though in many areas the courts were controlled by the "machine." Some elections were contested, to be sure, but relative to the total number of elections, the number actually contested apparently was minuscule. In Kansas City in the 1930s the Pendergast "machine" was convicted of vote fraud, and in notorious Adams County, Ohio, many were convicted of accepting vote bribes, but there are relatively few examples of proven instances of vote fraud.

Few political leaders, quite understandably, have admitted to committing vote fraud. A rare exception was Richard "Big Dick" Butler, who told of a rebellion against Tammany Hall in the early twentieth century in which he used repeaters to defeat the Tammany candidate. "Ballots were easy to get," he said, "and we took plenty." He folded marked ballots in sets of ten and had his wife iron them flat. "One of my repeaters went to the polls twenty times and dropped in ten ballots every time." By these means, claimed Butler, the mighty New York Democratic machine was defeated; and, said Butler, "it was wonderful to see how my men slugged the opposition to preserve the sanctity of the ballot and stop the corruption of Tammany Hall."

On the other hand, there were also election recounts brought about by charges of vote fraud which seemed to show that elections were honest. William E. "Boss" Lorimer's enemies in Chicago, for example, were absolutely convinced that Lorimer's control of his wards on the west side was based on fraud, but a recount in 1903 actually awarded Lorimer six additional votes. Conclusive information about recounts and contested elections, unfortunately, is widely scattered and difficult to obtain.[51]

Compilations of contested elections to the House of Representatives however do exist. These have been compiled from the First through the

TABLE 6.1 Contested Elections to the House of Representatives Involving Charges Of Election Fraud[a]

| Congresses | 1-5 | 6-10 | 11-15 | 16-20 | 21-25 | 26-30 | 31-35 | 36-40 | 41-45 | 46-50 | 51-55 | 56-60 | 61-64 | Total |
Dates	1789-1799	1799-1809	1809-1819	1819-1829	1829-1839	1839-1849	1849-1859	1859-1869	1869-1879	1879-1889	1889-1899	1899-1909	1909-1917	
New England	1			1			1		1	2		1		7
Mid-Atlantic	1					3	2	3	5	2	6	1	4	27
East N. Central				1			2	3	4	6	2	3	3	24
West N. Central							3	3	2	3	1			12
South	3	1	4		4	1		1	23	14	32	5	4	92
Border			2	1	1		1	10	5	2	10	3	5	40
Mountain							2	1		2		1		6
Pacific									1	2	2	1		6
Totals	5	1	6	3	5	4	11	21	41	33	53	15	16	214

[a]First through Sixty-Fourth Congresses (1789-1917), arranged by decades and sections.

Sixty-Fourth Congresses (1789-1917), and distribution of these cases by state and decade appears in Table 6.1. Of about 16,000 elections to the House held in these years, only 452 were contested at all, and in only less than half of these, 214 altogether, was election fraud, bribery, or intimidation given as justification for the challenge. In ninety, or about 42 percent, of the latter elections, evidence of fraud sufficient to justify action by the House was determined.[52]

Examination of Table 6.1 shows that elections contested for vote fraud were very heavily concentrated in the South and border states during the decades of the late nineteenth century when southern and border state elections were primarily concerned with the issues of Reconstruction and the participation of blacks in the political process. Well over half of all such elections (132 out of 214) were in the southern and border states, and over 30 percent (86) occurred in this single geographical area between 1869 and 1899. This takes on greater significance in view of the relative small size of the southern and border state delegations in the House. In the decade of the 1890s, for instance, the southern and border states held about 35 percent of the seats in the House (126 out of 357), and, if elections contested for vote fraud had been randomly distributed, about 35 percent of them should have occurred in this section. As Table 6.1 shows, however, almost 80 percent of these elections (42 out of 53) in the 1890s were in the southern or border states. Other sections, such as the mid-Atlantic and east north central, where the literature alleged that there was much vote fraud, by contrast, had relatively few House elections contested for vote fraud. In the 1890s the mid-Atlantic region which included New York, Pennsylvania, New Jersey, and Delaware had almost 21 percent (73 out of 357) of the seats in the House but only about 11 percent (6 out of 53) of the elections contested for fraud.[53]

Information about the nature of the charges in contested House elections for the Congresses which have met since 1917 has not been compiled, but between 1917 and 1961 only 81 elections were contested for all reasons. Undoubtedly, charges of fraud were not involved in every contested election in this period, but at least a rough impression of the level of fraud in House elections in these years is reflected in these figures. Of the more than 9,500 individual elections to the House held between 1917 and 1961, in other words, only slightly less than 1 percent were contested for any reason. If vote fraud was common in elections to the House of Representatives, it was not revealed by an examination of contested elections considered by that institution. The highest frequency of charges of vote fraud occurred, moreover, in the post-Reconstruction South and border states when political conditions were unstable and highly unusual.

CONCLUSION

A small number of political observers, finally, have also expressed doubts that fraud in elections was widespread, although some of these thought vote fraud had been more prevalent at an earlier time. Seymour and Frary concluded as early as 1916 that the adoption of the secret ballot had brought an end to large-scale dishonesty in elections. "Fraud is not common," they asserted, "and where it exists, it is usually confined to single localities." In 1928 Frank Kent expressed a similar view: "Such cheating as there is now is on a scale so small as to be negligible." V. O. Key, Jr. in *Southern Politics,* was quite skeptical of accounts of vote fraud ("legends," he called them) allegedly committed by "Boss" Crump in Memphis. Said Key, "the chances are that arithmetical enthusiasm is of less importance than the herding of the voters to the polls." Richard Jensen in his study of the Midwest in the late nineteenth century concluded that midwestern elections at least were generally free of vote fraud: "By nineteenth-century standards, American or European, the midwestern elections were quiet, decorous affairs—hard fought, but basically honest," and more recently Leo Hershkowitz has argued that the charges of corruption against William M. Tweed in New York were a "myth" created by Tweed's political enemies. [54]

The unsystematic, undocumented, partisan, and emotional nature of most of the literature indicates that the charges of vote fraud were probably gross exaggerations, and it seems unlikely that a significant portion of the sharp decline in voter turnout rates after 1900 can be explained by the elimination of vote fraud. This explanation is open to question, even if one were to accept the most unrestrained charges of corruption, since many observers believed that election fraud continued to be practiced extensively in several major urban centers and in some rural areas long after 1920 when the decline in voter turnout rates began to level out. Charges of fraud in elections in New York City did seem to decline in frequency after about 1900 or 1910, but many clearly thought that vote fraud was as widely practiced as ever or even had increased in the 1920s and later in such cities as Philadelphia, Chicago, and Kansas City. The frequency of charges of vote fraud in the literature, in short, did not appear to be associated with the decline in voter turnout.

But even if the allegations of vote fraud were accepted at face value, the greatest portion of fraudulent election activities probably posed no major threat to the validity of election data. Election irregularities described in the literature tended to fall generally into two categories, those which violated the voter's intentions and those which did not (Table 6.2). Acts of violence and falsification of election results (Type I and II) were the kinds

TABLE 6.2   A Crude Classification of Vote Fraud

VIOLATED THE VOTER'S INTENT

Type		Area		Period
I.	Violence	1)	cities with large immigrant populations; especially:	
			New York	1840-1930
			Philadelphia	1870-1930
			Chicago	1890-1940
			Kansas City	1900-1940
			The South	1866-1900
II.	Ballot box stuffing;	2)	The South	1870-1900
	repeating; miscounting, and the like	3)	Other Rural Areas	general

DID NOT VIOLATE THE VOTER'S INTENT

III.	Purchase of Votes	1)	very widespread in both urban and rural areas, but most common among poor, urban populations.	general
IV.	Patronage; personal favors; treating			general

of fraudulent activity which clearly pose the most serious threat to the student of political history. These types of fraud, however, were infrequently mentioned in the literature and episodic in nature. Hence, these types should be relatively easy to pinpoint from manuscript and printed sources and presumably more prominently manifested by "unexpected" and idiosyncratic fluctuation in the election data. Fraudulent election practices (Types III and IV in Table 6.2) such as vote buying, use of patronage, personal favors, and treating received the greater proportion of attention in the literature and were probably much more widely committed than those included in the first category. The second category of fraud (Types III and IV), to be sure, includes illegal and irregular activities, but these involved voters legally entitled to vote whose *intent* was not misrepresented. These types of election practices, while practiced in most parts of the nation at most time periods, probably were practiced by only a marginal element of the voting population.

Vote fraud, along with certain other forms of political corruption, seems a particularly appropriate illustration of Huntington's view that political corruption performed an essential function in the modernization of American society. Rapid industrialization, Huntington argued, attracted to urban areas a massive, largely unassimilated, foreign population with serious social and economic problems long before the United States provided legitimate means to deal effectively with these problems. The United States, of course, did not enact a national social welfare system until the 1930s, over two decades after the flow of immigration had subsided. By all accounts, before the enactment of the New Deal welfare legislation, public and private social welfare agencies had been wholly inadequate to the task of providing aid and assistance to the unemployed and the poor. Thus, as Huntington suggested, in exchange for political support the urban political machine used irregular and illegal practices to help the poor and the immigrant and to assimilate these new urban groups "into the political system," a system which had "been unable to adapt sufficiently fast to prove legitimate and acceptable means for this purpose." In the absence of a legitimate institutional response, in short, the "boss" and the "machine" illegitimately performed essential social functions. "The machine," according to D. W. Brogan, "was the social service state; the precinct captain and all the other members of the hierarchy were the bureaucracy of that state. They gave away coal and food, got the sick into hospital, the unlucky out of jail." And the machines also provided jobs, even if at times the work was "wasteful" and "unnecessary" from the point of view of the tax-conscious middle- and upper-class reformers. "I can always get a job for a deservin' man," George W. Plunkitt of Tammany Hall boasted. "I make it a point to keep on the track of jobs, and it seldom happens that I don't have a few up my sleeve ready for use."[55]

More importantly, the urban machine treated the immigrants, as well as other urban working class groups, with respect, or at least with more respect than these groups could expect to receive from most mugwump or progressive reformers and, in fact, most other Americans. "Boss" Richard Croker of Tammany Hall made much of this point in a defense of Tammany in 1897. Tammany, he claimed, was the only institution in America which attempted to transform foreigners into citizens—"There is not a mugwump in the city who would shake hands with them." Somewhat later, in 1933, "Boss" Vare expressed a similar attitude in his instructions to the Philadelphia Republican City Committee: "Keep close to the plain people.... The Republican party is the people's party. Its place is to keep close to the working man."[56]

The immigrants and other working class groups in the center city in return supported the "machines" with their votes and their loyalty. It seems reasonable to assume that the kinds of vote fraud which distorted the voters' intentions most of the time were unnecessary, although one can readily think of elections when it would have been advantageous to the urban "machine" to amass huge majorities in the city in order to overcome the opposition's majorities in the rural counties. Usually the "machine" was capable of carrying the center city districts with massive majorities without recourse to large-scale vote fraud. "The poor," as Plunkitt of Tammany Hall observed, "are the most grateful people in the world." Historian Gustavus Myers, as well, remarked upon the "lasting fidelity" to Tammany Hall among the foreign born which endured even "in the days of the most flagrant corruption, and formed a phalanx which could always be relied upon." In Chicago, according to E. A. Ross, a similar condition existed. Ross said he was told that the ward leader " 'will go through hell-fire for his people and they for him!' " Charles E. Merriam described the Chicago voter's view of the typical boss "at worst a sort of Robin Hood whose banditry is for the common benefit," and Jane Addams discovered that despite her best efforts, she could not dislodge Alderman Johnny Powers from his domination of Chicago's nineteenth ward. "I may not be the sort of man the reformers like," Powers declared, "but I am what my people like, and neither Hull House nor all the reformers in town can turn them against me." A public opinion survey in Boston in the 1940s indicated a similar loyalty to "Boss" James M. Curley. Although under federal indictment at the time, Curley was very highly regarded, especially among the "lower-middle and lower class" Irish, Italian, and Jewish voters. It is not surprising, in short, that some center city wards were nearly unanimous in their support of the "machine," and it seems to be the case, as D. W. Brogan has noted, that "the real strength of the machine . . . is in the genuine loyalty of the voter who cannot see why he should not do a good friend a trifling favor."[57]

This survey of literature on vote fraud in the United States during the nineteenth and twentieth centuries, in sum, indicates that most political observers were convinced that vote fraud existed at least to some degree in most elections. Most observers also seemed confident that fraud in elections was most flagrantly practiced in the densely populated sections of the major industrial cities inhabited by immigrants, blacks, and the poor generally. Instances of rural and small town fraud committed by native, "old-stock" Americans also received attention, but frequently examples of vote fraud in rural areas triggered a reaction of shock, dismay, and even disbelief. It seems clear that these middle- and upper-class observers held a somewhat vague, but nonetheless definable normative view of the American voter. In this view, the voter was expected to be a well-educated, informed citizen with no special interest to protect. Immigrants and other voters in the "machine-dominated" wards simply failed to measure up to the mugwump/progressive ideal. As Robert H. Wiebe suggested, "Mugwumpish complaints about the boss and his immigrant clients . . . merely stated a preference for one set of cultural credentials over another." [58]

The great preponderance of the literature on vote fraud, moreover, appeared roughly between the end of the Civil War and the Great Depression, and most of the examples of fraudulent voting practices were said to have occurred in that same historical era. The incidence of charges of vote fraud, as well as charges of many other kinds of political corruption, tended to multiply as the rate of immigration and urbanization increased, and such charges became less frequently expressed in the 1930s as the urban populations and the city "bosses" aligned themselves behind Franklin D. Roosevelt and the New Deal. The political goals of New Deal intellectuals, the "bosses," and the immigrants (and their children) seemed to have converged in the 1930s, and many New Dealers, not all of course, unlike the reformers of earlier decades, found it less fashionable to denounce the political practices of the urban "machines." Thus, the immigrants and their children were assimilated into the Democratic Party and the political system as they became a major component of the "Roosevelt coalition." [59] This reconciliation of the "machine" and the middle- and upper-class reformers was never altogether successful, of course, and the hostility which emerged in the election of 1968 between Mayor Daley's "machine" in Chicago and the intellectuals and students who most ardently supported the candidacies of Eugene McCarthy and George McGovern is strongly reminiscent of pre-Depression conflicts. E. L. Godkin and Charles Merriam would have found much to admire in the attacks of the 1960s and 1970s upon the Chicago Democratic "machine."

NOTES

1. Henry George, "Money In Elections," *North American Review,* CCCXVI (March 1883), 201-202; Joseph P. Harris, *Registration Of Voters In the United States* (Washington, 1929), 2; and L. E. Fredman, *The Australian Ballot: The Story of an American Reform* (Lansing, 1968), ix. See also George C. S. Benson, *Political Corruption in America* (Lexington, MA, 1978), especially 17-72; Robert D. Marcus, *Grand Old Party: Political Structure in the Gilded Age, 1880-1896* (New York, 1971), 13 and 277 n. 71; and Paul T. Ringenbach, *Tramps and Reformers, 1873-1916: The Discovery of Unemployment in New York* (Westport, CT, 1973), 47-48.

2. See for example W. Dean Burnham, *Critical Elections and the Mainsprings of American Politics* (New York, 1970); Jerome M. Clubb, William H. Flanigan, and Nancy H. Zingale, *Partisan Realignment: Voters, Parties, and Government in American History* (Beverly Hills, 1980); Ronald P. Formisano, *The Birth of Mass Political Parties: Michigan, 1827-1861* (Princeton, 1971); Melvyn Hammarberg, *The Indiana Voter: The Historical Dynamics of Party Allegiance During the 1870s* (Chicago, 1977); Paul Kleppner, *The Cross of Culture: A Social Analysis of Midwestern Politics, 1850-1900* (New York, 1970) and *The Third Electoral System, 1853-1892: Parties, Voters, and Political Cultures* (Chapel Hill, 1979); J. Morgan Kousser, *The Shaping of Southern Politics: Suffrage Restriction and the Establishment of the One-Party South, 1880-1910* (New Haven, 1974); Richard Jensen, *The Winning Of The Midwest: Social and Political Conflict, 1888-1896* (Chicago, 1971); Allan J. Lichtman, *Prejudice and the Old Politics: The Presidential Election of 1928* (Chapel Hill, 1979); Samuel T. McSeveney, *The Politics of Depression: Political Behavior in the Northeast, 1893-1896* (New York, 1972); Gerald M. Pomper, *Elections in America: Control and Influence in Democratic Politics* (New York, 1970); and Joel H. Silbey, Allan G. Bogue, and William H. Flanigan (eds.) *The History of American Electoral Behavior* (Princeton, 1978). Some of the most important analyses of voting data have appeared as articles. See those included in Jerome M. Clubb and Howard W. Allen (eds.) *Electoral Change and Stability in American Political History* (New York, 1971); and Joel H. Silbey and Samuel T. McSeveney (eds.) *Voters, Parties and Elections: Quantitative Essays in the History of American Popular Voting Behavior* (Lexington, MA, 1972).

3. Philip E. Converse, "Change In The American Electorate," in Angus Campbell and Philip E. Converse, (eds.) *The Human Meaning of Social Change* (New York, 1972), 268-301; and W. Dean Burnham, "The Changing Shape of the American Political Universe," *The American Political Science Review,* LIX (March 1965), 7-28.

4. Samuel P. Huntington, *Political Order In Changing Societies* (New Haven, 1968), 59-64. Other studies that have examined the social functions of political corruption include Robert K. Merton, *Social Theory and Social Structure: Toward The Codification Of Theory And Research* (Glencoe, IL, 1949), 70-81; Eric L. McKitrick, "The Study Of Corruption," *Political Science Quarterly,* LXXII (December 1957), 502-514; and James C. Scott, "Corruption, Machine Politics, And Political Change," *American Political Science Review,* LXIII (December 1969), 1142-1158.

5. James Bryce, *Modern Democracies* (New York, 1921), 417.

6. James A. Barnes, "Myths Of The Bryan Campaign," *Mississippi Valley Historical Review,* XXXIV (December 1947), 367-404; Harold U. Faulkner, *Politics, Reform And Expansion, 1890-1900* (New York, 1959), 208-209; and William Allen White, *Autobiography* (New York, 1946), 285. For a more recent discussion of coercion in the election of 1896 and in late nineteenth-century elections generally, see R. Jensen, *The Winning Of The Midwest,* 45-57; and S. T. McSeveney, *Politics of Depression,* 183-184.

7. James Bryce, *The American Commonwealth* (2 vols.; London, 1889), II, 129-130 and I, 608-619.

8. Earl R. Sikes, *State And Federal Corrupt-Practices Legislation* (Durham, 1928), 56-57; and J. P. Harris, Registration of Voters, 9. Other observers who have expressed the view that vote fraud was more extensive in urban areas include Purley A. Baker in *The Anti-Saloon League Yearbook, 1914,* as quoted in Andrew Sinclair, *Era Of Excess: A Social History Of The Prohibition Movement* (New York, 1964), 9; Kate H. Claghorn, "Our Immigrants And Ourselves," *The Atlantic Monthly,* LXXXVI

(October 1900), 535-548; John I. Davenport, *The Election And Naturalization Frauds In New York City, 1860-1870* (2nd ed.; New York, 1894), 5; Charles E. Merriam and Louise Overacker, *Primary Elections* (Chicago, 1928), 6-7; "The Scientific Basis of Municipal Politics," *World's Work*, III (November 1901), 1362; M. Ostrogorski, *Democracy And The Organization Of Political Parties* (2 vols.; New York, 1902), II, 344-345, 349; and James A. Woodburn, *Political Parties and Party Problems In The United States* (3rd ed.; New York, 1924), 420.

    9. Gustavus Myers, *The History of Tammany Hall* (New York, 1917), 73-76; 90-91, 158-159, and 195-196.

    10. M. Ostrogorski, *Democracy*, 156-157; and Samuel P. Orth, *The Boss And The Machine: A Chronicle Of The Politicians And Party Organization* (New Haven, 1921), 91-92.

    11. Jerome Mushkat, *Tammany: The Evolution Of A Political Machine, 1789-1865* (Syracuse, 1971), 298 and 368.

    12. *The Nation*, VII (October 29, 1868), 341; and Frank J. Goodnow, "The Tweed Ring In New York City," in J. Bryce, *The American Commonwealth*, II, 341.

    13. William M. Ivins, *Machine Politics And Money In Elections In New York City* (1884; reprint ed., New York, 1970), 65 and 52. See discussions of Ivins's presentations in "The Money Power In Politics Again," *The Nation*, LXIV (March 10, 1887), 204; and "Money And Political Machines," *Ibid.*, (March 17, 1887), 222-223.

    14. New York Legislature, Senate Committee On the Police Department Of The City Of New York, "Report And Proceedings Of The Senate Committee Appointed To Investigate The Police Department Of The City Of New York," (5 vols.; Albany, 1895), 1, 15 and Thomas C. Platt, *The Autobiography Of Thomas C. Platt* (New York, 1910), 234-236, and 265. See also William T. Stead, *Satan's Invisible World Displayed: Or Despairing Democracy* (London, 1897), 52-55 and 151-157; William J. Murphy, "Richard Croker of Tammany Hall," M.A. thesis, Fordham University, 1951, 30-40; S. T. McSeveney, *Politics of Depression*, 102-103 and 111-112; and M. R. Werner, *Tammany Hall* (New York, 1928), 434-440.

    15. Abram C. Bernheim, "The Ballot In New York," *The Political Science Quarterly*, IV (March 1889), 130-152; Ostrogorski, *Democracy*, II, 157 and 96; and Charles Seymour and Donald P. Frary, *How The World Votes: The Story Of Democratic Development In Elections* (2 vols.; Springfield, MA, 1918), I, 259-261.

    16. Harold F. Gosnell, *Boss Platt And His New York Machine: A Study Of The Political Leadership Of Thomas C. Platt, Theodore Roosevelt, And Others* (Chicago, 1924), 50 and 147; M. R. Werner, *Tammany Hall*, 130-149 and 558-559; Florence E. Gibson, *The Attitudes Of The New York Irish Toward State And National Affairs, 1848-1892* (New York, 1951), 256-267; and L. E. Fredman, *The Australian Ballot*, 40-41. For additional discussion of vote fraud in New York City by observers and scholars see: Lewis Abrahams, *It's All Politics* (New York, 1944), 89; Herbert J. Bass, *"I Am A Democrat": The Political Career Of David Bennett Hill* (New York, 1961), 96-98; Matthew P. Breen, *Thirty Years Of New York Politics* (New York, 1899), 25-26 and 42-44; Richard J. Butler and Joseph Driscoll, *Dock Walloper: The Story Of "Big Dick" Butler* (New York, 1933), 65-76; Andrew B. Callow, Jr., *The Tweed Ring* (New York, 1966), especially 204-214; John I. Davenport, *The Election Frauds Of New York And Their Prevention,* (2 vols.; New York, 1881), I, 29, 34-35, 79, 100-101, 107, and 260-261; John I. Davenport, *The Election and Naturalization Frauds in New York City, 1860-1870,* (2nd ed.; New York, 1894), 192; Bruce L. Felknor, *Dirty Politics* (New York, 1966), 160; Edward Ridley Finch, "The Fight For A Clean Ballot," *The Independent*, LXVIII (May 12, 1910), 1020-1026; Allan Franklin, *The Trail Of The Tiger* (New York, 1928), 194-197, and 214-217; R. B.

Fosdick, "The Police And The Good Old Days," *Outlook,* CII (October 19, 1912), 346-349; E. L. Godkin, "Criminal Politics," *North American Review* CL (June 1890), 706-723; John W. Goff, "Juggling With The Ballot," *North American Review,* CLVIII (February 1894), 203-210; Matthew Hale, "How The New York Senate Was Captured," *Forum,* XIII (April 1892), 179-192; Charles Stearns Hartwell, "Fraud By Marked Ballots," *Outlook,* LXXV (November 14, 1903), 656-658; George F. Howe, *Chester A. Arthur: A Quarter Century Of Machine Politics* (New York, 1934), 39-40; "Is Tammany Vindicated?" *Literary Digest,* CXI (November 14, 1931), 10; John A. Lapp, "Elections–Identification of Voters," *American Political Science Review,* III (February 1909), 62-63; Seymour Mandelbaum, *Boss Tweed's New York* (New York, 1965), 85; Amicus Most, "Everybody Votes For Tammany," *Nation,* CXXXIII (November 25, 1931), 566-567; Gustavus Myers, "The Secrets of Tammany's Success," *Forum,* XXXI (June 1901), 488-500; Ernest Poole, " 'Reform' On The Bowery," *World Today,* VIII (January 1905), 57-62; Allen T. Rice, "The Next National Reform," *North American Review,* CXLVIII (January 1889), 82-85; Theodore Roosevelt, "Machine Politics In New York City," *Century,* XXXIII (November 1886), 74-82; Edward M. Sait, *American Parties And Elections* (New York, 1927), 583; Earl R. Sikes, *State And Federal Corrupt-Practices Legislation,* 57-58; John G. Speed, "The Purchase Of Votes. 1) How Votes Are Bought And Sold In New York City," *Harper's Weekly,* XLIX (March 18, 1905), 386-388; "Stealing Votes From The Radicals," *New Republic,* LXXIII (February 1, 1933), 312; Lincoln Steffens, *Shame Of The Cities* (New York, 1904), 270-306; Norman Thomas, "Twisting Tammany's Tail," *Forum,* LXXXV (June 1931), 335-341; and Norman Thomas and Paul Blanshard, *What's The Matter With New York* (New York, 1932), 89-90.

17. Orth, *The Boss And The Machine,* 96-97; and Charles W. VanDevander, *The Big Bosses* (New York, 1944), 135-147 and Steffens, *Shame Of The Cities,* 193-229. On vote fraud in Philadelphia see also: Abrahams, *It's All Politics,* 92; Charles C. Binney, "Merits And Defects Of The Pennsylvania Ballot Law Of 1891," *Annals Of The American Academy Of Political And Social Science,* II (May 1892), 751-771; Robert C. Brooks, *Corruption In American Politics And Life* (New York, 1910), 193; J. Bryce, *American Commonwealth,* II, 358-359 and 364-365; "Digging Into Election Frauds," *Literary Digest,* CXIV (December 3, 1932), 9; David H. Kurtzman, "Methods Of Controlling Votes In Philadelphia," Ph.D. dissertation, University of Pennsylvania, 1935, 122-136; William B. Lex "Election Frauds Go Unchecked," *National Municipal Review,* XXXIII (May 1944), 226-228; "Lost, Strayed Or Stolen: Millions Of Votes," *U.S. News And World Report,* L (March 6, 1961), 76-80; Charles E. Merriam and Harold F. Gosnell, *The American Party System* (rev. ed.; New York, 1929), 342-343; M. Ostrogorski, *Democracy,* II, 169 and 188; Louise Overacker and Victor J. West, *Money In Elections* (New York, 1932), 38-40; John Salter, "Party Organization In Philadelphia: The Ward Committeeman," *American Political Science Review,* XXVII (August 1933), 618-627; Seymour and Frary, *How The World Votes,* I, 260-261; Sam Bass Warner, Jr., *The Private City: Philadelphia In Three Periods Of Its Growth* (Philadelphia, 1968), 214-221; and Herbert Welsh, "The Degradation Of Pennsylvania Politics," *Forum,* XII (November 1891), 330-345.

18. Ray Ginger, *Altgeld's America: The Lincoln Ideal Versus Changing Realities* (New York, 1958), 92-94; Lloyd Wendt and Herman Kogan, *Bosses In Lusty Chicago: The Story of Bathhouse John And Hinky Dink* (Bloomington, 1967), 19, 102-103, 107, 108, 147, 164, and 291; Charles E. Merriam, *Chicago: A More Intimate View Of Urban Politics* (New York, 1929), 17-20, 33; and Mike Royko, *Boss: Richard J. Daley Of Chicago* (New York, 1971), 77. For additional charges of

vote corruption in Chicago see Harold Baron, "Vote Market," *Nation,* CXCI (September 3, 1960), 109-112; Allen F. Davis, *Spearheads For Reform* (New York, 1967), 162; Bruce L. Felknor, *Dirty Politics,* 160-161; L. E. Fredman, *Australian Ballot,* 59-60, 85, and 120; Harold F. Gosnell, *Negro Politicians: The Rise Of Negro Politics In Chicago* (Chicago, 1967), 115 and 145-146; Harold F. Gosnell, *Machine Politics: Chicago Model* (Chicago, 1937), 19, 34, 42-43, 86-88, and 190; Bruce Grant, *Fight For A City: The Story Of The Union League Club Of Chicago And Its Times, 1880-1955* (Chicago, 1955), especially 67-80; Illinois General Assembly, "Grand Jury Report Of November, 1908," Chicago Voting Machine Investigation, Report Of The Legislative Committee, 1915, 160-163; "Illinois Goes To The Polls," *New Republic,* LXXXVI (April 29, 1936), 331; Ted Leitzell, "Chicago, City Of Corruption," *American Mercury,* XLIX (February, 1940), 143-151; Thomas B. Littlewood, *Horner Of Illinois* (Evanston, 1969), 183; "How To Beat A Voting Machine–And A Drive To Make It Honest," *U.S. News And World Report,* LIV (April 8, 1963), 63; Charles E. Merriam and Harold F. Gosnell, *Non-Voting: Causes And Methods Of Control* (Chicago, 1924), 228-230; Seymour and Frary, *How The World Votes, I,* 264; Steffens, *Shame Of The Cities,* 233-276; William H. Stuart, *The Twenty Incredible Years* (Chicago, 1935), Studs Turkel, *Talking To Myself: A Memory of My Times* (New York, 1973), 583; Richard Wilson, "How To Steal An Election," *Look,* XXV 71-92 (February 14, 1961), 51-61; C. VanDevander, *The Big Bosses,* 278; "Vote Frauds. Can They Be Stamped Out This Time?" *U.S. News And World Report,* LXV (November 4, 1968), 8; and Carroll H. Wooddy, *The Chicago Primary Of 1926. A Study In Election Methods* (Chicago, 1926), 144-156.

19. Jerome S. Bruner and Sheldon J. Korchin, "The Boss And The Vote: A Case Study In City Politics," *Public Opinion Quarterly,* X (Spring 1946), 1-23 apparently did not subscribe to the view that "Boss" Curley's administration was corrupt, but they attested that such a view was widely held.

20. Richard P. McCormick, *The History Of Voting In New Jersey: A Study Of The Development Of Election Machinery, 1664-1911* (New Brunswick, NJ, 1953), 159-161 and 185-186; Dayton D. McKean, *The Boss: The Hague Machine In Action* (Boston, 1940), 22-23, 126-127, and 132-33; William E. Sackett, "New Jersey And The Bosses," *Harper's Weekly,* LV (April 8, 1911), 8; and C. VanDevander, *The Big Bosses,* 90-94.

21. Matthew Josephson, *The Politicos, 1865-1896* (New York, 1938), 704-705; Zane L. Miller, *Boss Cox's Cincinnati: Urban Politics In The Progressive Era* (New York, 1968), 71, 90-92, 183-185, 202, and 213; and S. P. Orth, *The Boss And The Machine,* 104-105.

22. Lyle W. Dorsett, *The Pendergast Machine* (New York, 1968), 59, 70, 75, and 122-124; Maurice M. Milligan, *The Inside Story Of The Pendergast Machine By The Man Who Smashed It* (New York, 1948), 52, 140-165; and William M. Reddig, *Tom's Town: Kansas City And The Pendergast Legend* (Philadelphia, 1947), 78, 286-287.

23. Jonathan Daniels, "He Suits Memphis," *Saturday Evening Post,* CCXII (June 10, 1939), 22-34; James Street, "Mista Crump Keeps Rollin' Along," *Colliers,* CI (April 9, 1938), 16, 26, and 28-29; and C. Van Devander, *The Big Bosses,* 167, 170-172, and 180-181.

24. On corrupt voting practices in Denver see Arthur Chapman, "Colorado's Election Frauds," *World Today,* VIII (March 1905), 290-297; Ben B. Lindsey and Harvey J. O'Higgins, *The Beast* (New York, 1910), 158-163; Lawrence Lewis, "How Woman's Suffrage Works In Colorado," *Outlook,* LXXXII (January 27, 1906), 167-178; and E. M. Sait, *American Parties And Elections,* 584. On Detroit see Arthur

C. Millspaugh, *Party Organization And Machinery In Michigan Since 1890* (Baltimore, 1917), 39. On New Orleans see George M. Reynolds, *Machine Politics In New Orleans, 1897-1926* (New York, 1936), 129-131; and V. O. Key, Jr., *Southern Politics In State And Nation* (New York, 1950), 623; on Pittsburgh see Steffens, *The Shame Of The Cities*, 181-182 and Bruce M. Stave, *The New Deal And The Last Hurrah: Pittsburgh Machine Politics* (Pittsburgh, 1970), 30; on St. Louis see Steffens, *The Shame Of The Cities*, 39, 106-107; on San Francisco see Walton Bean, *Boss Ruef's San Francisco* (Berkeley, 1952), 57; L. D. Fredman, *Australian Ballot*, 25-27; and Henry George, "Bribery In Elections," *Overland Monthly*, VII (December, 1871), 497-504. Ostrogorski, in addition, referred generally to Washington, New Orleans, San Francisco, and Cincinnati as having reputations for dishonest elections, but there were many others: "Almost all cities whose population exceeded 100,000, or even a lesser figure, had their Rings." *Democracy*, II, 175.

25. Genevieve B. Gist, "Progressive Reform In A Rural Community: The Adams County Vote-Fraud Case," *Mississippi Valley Historical Review*, XLVIII (June 1961), 60.

26. M. Ostrogorski, *Democracy*, II, 345; J. J. McCook, "The Alarming Proportion Of Venal Voters," *Forum*, XIV (September 1892), 1-13 and "Venal Voting: Methods And Remedies," *Forum*, XIV (October 1892), 159-177; J. B. Harrison, "The Sale Of Votes In New Hampshire," *Century*, XLVII (November, 1893), 149-150; and L. Steffens, "Rhode Island: A State For Sale," *McClure's* XXIV (February 1905), 337-353.

27. "Digging Into Election Frauds," *Literary Digest*, CXIV (December 3, 1932), 9; Henry Christman, *Tin Horns And Calico: A Decisive Episode In The Emergence Of Democracy* (New York, 1945), 29-30; "Corruption In Rhode Island," *Outlook*, LXXIII (March 28, 1903), 698-699; J. B. Harrison, "The Sale Of Votes In New Hampshire," *Century*, 149-150; George Kennan, "Holding Up A State. The True Story Of Addicks And Delaware. I," *Outlook*, LXXIII (February 14, 1903), 386-392; James K. McGuire (ed.) *The Democratic Party Of The State Of New York* (New York, 1905), 489-490; "Money In Elections," *The Nation*, XXXIX (October 9, 1884), 303; "Rural Corrupt Practices," *The Nation*, LXXXII (April 19, 1906), 315-316; Newman Smyth, "Political Corruption In Connecticut," *Outlook*, LXXIX (March 18, 1905), 690-695; and John G. Speed, "Purchase Of Votes. 2) How Votes Are Bought And Sold In New York State," *Harper's Weekly*, XLIX (March 25, 1905), 422-424 and "Purchase Of Votes. 4) The Use Of Money In Doubtful States," *Harper's Weekly*, LXIX (April 8, 1905), 498, 500, and 513.

28. R. Carlyle Buley, *The Old Northwest Pioneer Period, 1815-1840* (2 vols.; Indianapolis, 1950), 219; M. Josephson, *The Politicos*, 706; G. B. Gist, "Progressive Reform In A Rural Community: The Adams County Vote Fraud Case," *MVHR*, 60-78. On the Adams County case see also: "The Anti-Bribery Campaign," *American Review of Reviews*, XLIII (March 1911), 274; Albion Z. Blair, "Seventeen Hundred Rural Vote Sellers: How We Disenfranchised A Quarter Of The Voting Population Of Adams County, Ohio," *McClure's Magazine*, XXXVIII (November 1911), 28-40; George Creel and Sloane Gordon, "The Shame Of Ohio," *Cosmopolitan*, LI (October 1911), 599-610; Albert Shaw, "A National Lesson From Adams County," *American Review Of Reviews*, XLIII (February 1911), 171-180; "The Treason In Ohio," *Century Magazine*, LXXXI (March 1911), 792-793; and "Wholesale, Traditional Bribery And Fraud," *The Chautauguan*, LXII (March 1911), 10-11.

29. M. Josephson, *The Politicos*, 430 and 706.

30. Dudley's quote is in *Ibid.*, 431-432; R. Carlyle Buley, "The Campaign of 1888 In Indiana," *Indiana Magazine Of History,* X (June 1914), 30-53; and Stella C. Stimson, "The Terre Haute Election Trial," *National Municipal Review,* V (January 1916), 38-46. See also L. E. Fredman, *Australian Ballot,* 22; George Hoadly, "Methods Of Ballot Reform," *Forum,* VII (August 1889), 623-633; and Robert LaFollette, "The Adoption Of The Australian Ballot In Indiana," *Indiana Magazine Of History,* XXIV (June 1928), 105-120. On Michigan vote fraud see A. C. Millspaugh, *Party Organization And Machinery In Michigan Since 1890,* 157-165.

31. E. Merton Coulter, *The South During Reconstruction* (Baton Rouge, 1947), 132, 139, 357-358, 369-370; William A. Dunning, *Reconstruction, Political And Economic, 1865-1877* (New York, 1907), 268, 278-280, and 304; Paul Lewinson, *Race, Class, And Party: A History Of Negro Suffrage And White Politics In The South* (New York, 1932), 89-91; and C. Vann Woodward, *Origins Of The New South, 1877-1913* (Baton Rouge, 1951), 56-58, 209-210, 277, 288, and 326-327. See also Emily N. Blair, "Every Man His Own Campaign Manager," *Outlook,* XCVII, (February 25, 1911), 426-433; Charles J. Bonaparte, "Political Corruption In Maryland," *Forum,* XIII (March 1892), 1-19; "Bourbon For Votes?" *Newsweek,* LV (June 6, 1960), 42; David R. Castleman, "Louisville Election Frauds In Court And Out," *National Municipal Review,* XVI (December 1927), 761-769; W.E.B. DuBois, *Black Reconstruction: An Essay Toward A History Of The Part Which Black Folk Played In The Attempt To Reconstruct Democracy In America, 1860-1880* (New York, 1935), 372, 376, 681-690; B. L. Felknor, *Dirty Politics,* 158-160; John Hope Franklin, *Reconstruction: After The Civil War* (Chicago, 1961), 155-158, 165; John J. Ingalls, "A Fair Vote And An Honest Count," in John D. Long (ed.) *The Republican Party* (New York, 1888), 327; a Kentucky legislator, "How An Election Was Bought And Sold," *Harper's* CCXXI (October 1960), 33-38; Richard P. McCormick, *The Second American Party System: Party Formation In The Jackson Era* (Chapel Hill, 1966), 201; M. Josephson, *The Politicos,* 206; "Payola By The Pint," *Time,* LXX (June 6, 1960), 20; Kenneth M. Stampp, *The Era Of Reconstruction, 1865-1877* (New York, 1965), 201-204; Robert Small, "Election Methods In The South," *North American Review,* CLI (November 1890), 593-600; C. Van Devander, *The Big Bosses,* 168-188; and Sidney Warren, "Corruption In Politics," *Current History,* XXII (May 1952), 285-289.

32. Alfred Steinberg, *Sam Johnson's Boy: A Close-up Of The President From Texas* (New York, 1968), 258-266.

33. A. Chapman, "Colorado's Election Frauds. 1) The Revolt Against 'Big Mitt' Rule," *World Today,* VIII (March 1905), 290-297; J. P. Harris, *Registration Of Voters In The United States,* 12-13; Thoburn W. Hatten, "Urban And Rural Voting In Colorado, 1898-1916," M.A. thesis, University of Washington, 1948; and "The Calendar Of The Month," *World Today,* VIII (January 1905), 112, (February 1905), 227, (March 1905), 338-339, and (May 1905), 564.

34. G. B. Gist, "Progressive Reform In A Rural Community: The Adams County Vote-Fraud Case," *Mississippi Valley Historical Review,* XLVIII, 63; J. G. Speed, "Purchase of Votes. 2) How Votes Are Bought In New York State," *Harper's Weekly,* XLIX, 422; and G. Kennan, "Holding Up A State: The True Story of Addicks and Delaware," *Outlook,* LXXIII (February 14, 1903), 390. See also Jeremiah W. Jenks, "Money In Practical Politics," *Century,* XLIV (October 1892), 947.

35. J. J. McCook, "The Alarming Proportion of Venal Voters," *Forum,* XIV, 1-13.

36. Portions of the transcript of the investigation of "Boss" Tweed relevant to election fraud are reprinted in W. R. Werner, *Tammany Hall*, 130-151; and "Report And Proceedings Of The Senate Committee Appointed To Investigate The Police Department Of The City Of New York." The quotation is from J. W. Goff, Counsel To The Committee For The Prosecution Of Election Frauds, in "Juggling With The Ballot," *North American Review*, 204. D. H. Kurtzman, "Methods Of Controlling Votes In Philadelphia," 122-136 and 161-166; L. Overacker and V. J. West, *Money In Elections*, 38-40; and J. P. Harris, *Registration Of Voters In The United States*, 78-80 and 334-377. See also Illinois General Assembly, "Chicago. Voting Machine Investigation. Report Of The Legislative Committee," 1915.

37. Stephan Thernstrom and Peter R. Knights, "Men In Motion: Some Data And Speculations About Urban Population Mobility In Nineteenth Century America," *The Journal Of Interdisciplinary History*, I (Autumn, 1970), 23; Peter R. Knights, *The Plain People Of Boston, 1830-1860. A Study In City Growth* (New York, 1971), 48-77; and Edgar E. Robinson, *The Presidential Vote, 1896-1932* (Stanford, 1947), 312.

38. Jacob A. Riis, *How The Other Half Lives. Studies Among The Tenements Of New York* (New York, 1890), 10, 65, and 70; Blake McKelvey, *The Urbanization Of America, 1860-1915* (New Brunswick, 1963), 120-121; and Humbert Nelli, *Italians In Chicago, 1880-1930: A Study In Ethnic Mobility* (New York, 1970), 32-34. Allan H. Spear indicated that Chicago black slums were also crowded, although less so than other minority or ethnic groups. *Black Chicago: The Making Of A Negro Ghetto, 1890-1920* (Chicago, 1967), 24.

39. J. A. Riis, *How The Other Half Lives*, 67-68; P. R. Knights, *The Plain People Of Boston*, 61-62; Jacob S. Siegel, "Estimates Of Coverage Of The Population By Sex, Race, And Age In The 1970 Census," a paper presented at the annual meeting of the Population Association of America, New Orleans, April 26, 1973, 26; Jim Toedtman, "Many Blacks Are Missed In The Census," Philadelphia *Inquirer*, October 31, 1976. See also Bureau of the Census, "1980 Census Update," January, 1981, 1-4.

40. Samuel J. Eldersveld and Albert A. Applegate, *Michigan Recounts for Governor, 1950 and 1952: A Systematic Analysis of Election Error* (Ann Arbor, 1954), passim. An even lower level of error was found in Minnesota in 1962 than in Michigan. Ronald F. Stinnett and Charles H. Backstrom, *Recount* (Washington, D.C., 1964), 223-61. Another attempt to analyze election "error" systematically is David M. Maynard, "Fraud and Error in Chicago Referendum Returns," *National Municipal Review*, XIX (March 1930), 164-167. See also Charlotte Goodman Steeh, "Racial Discrimination in Alabama, 1870-1910," Ph.D. dissertation, University of Michigan, 1974, especially 142, 150, and 224.

41. Some observers of urban politics, of course, did express considerable understanding and sympathy for urban immigrants. See for example Jane Addams "Ethical Survivals in Municipal Corruption," *International Journal of Ethics VIII* (April 1898), 273-291; J. H. Fenton, *Politics In The Border States*, 132-134; S. Mandelbaum, *Boss Tweed's New York*, passim; Eric L. McKitrick, "The Study Of Corruption," *Political Science Quarterly*, LXXII (December 1957), 502-514; C. E. Merriam, *Chicago: A More Intimate View Of Urban Politics*, 134; C. E. Merriam and H. F. Gosnell, *The American Party System*, 173-174; John T. Salter, "Party Organization In Philadelphia," *American Political Science Review*, XXVII (August, 1933), 623-625; and Nancy J. Weiss, *Charles Francis Murphy, 1858-1924: Respectability And Responsibility In Tammany Politics* (Northampton, MA, 1965), passim.

42. J. Bryce, *American Commonwealth*, I, 613; and M. Ostrogorski, *Democracy*, II, 94-95.

43. " 'The Boss's' Dominions," *Nation*, XIII (October 12, 1871), 236-237.

44. T. Roosevelt, "Machine Politics In New York City," *Century*, XXXIII, 74-82; J. Addams, "Ethical Survivals In Municipal Corruption," *International Journal Of Ethics*, VIII, 275; and Edward A. Ross, "Immigrants In Politics. The Political Consequences Of Immigration," *Century*, LXXXVII (January 1914), 392-398. See also: R. C. Brooks, *Corruption In American Politics And Life*, 32-36; "The Cure For Municipal Corruption," *Century*, XLIX (March, 1895), 790-791; J. I. Davenport, *The Election And Naturalization Frauds In New York City, 1860-1870* (2nd ed.; New York, 1894), 9-10; E. L. Godkin, "Criminal Politics," *North American Review*, CL (June 1890), 706-723; J. B. Harrison, "The Sale Of Votes In New Hampshire," *Century*, XLVII, 149-150; S. Low, "An American View Of Municipal Government In The United States," in J. Bryce, *American Commonwealth*, I, 620-635; A. C. Millspaugh, *Party Organization And Machinery In Michigan Since 1890*, 160-162; Amyas S. Northcote, "The Utter Corruption In American Politics," *Nineteenth Century*, XXXV (April 1894), 692-700; J. G. Speed, "Purchase Of Votes. 1) How Votes Are Bought In New York City," *Harper's Weekly*, LXIX, 386-388; and H. Welsh, "The Degradation of Pennsylvania Politics," *Forum*, XII, 330.

45. S. P. Orth, *The Boss And The Machine*, 60-61; J. P. Harris, *Registration Of Voters In The United States*, 2, 336, 344, and 372; M. Josephson, *The Politicos*, 150; and M. Royko, *Boss. Richard J. Daley Of Chicago*, 77.

46. H. George, "Money In Elections," *North American Review*, CCCXVI, 210; T. Roosevelt, "Machine Politics In New York City," *Century*, XXXIII, 79; W. M. Ivins, *Machine Politics And Money In Elections In New York City*, 62; "The Money Power In Politics," *Nation*, XLIV, 180. The Anti-Saloon League leader is quoted in Andrew Sinclair, *Era Of Excess*, 9; and E. R. Sikes, *State and Federal Corrupt-Practices Legislation*, 20.

47. M. Ostrogorski, *Democracy*, II, 118 and 343; Kirk H. Porter, *A History Of Suffrage In The United States* (Chicago 1969), 191-192; C. Seymour and D. P. Frary, *How The World Votes. The Story Of Democratic Development In Elections*, I, 256-257; and J. Bryce, *Modern Democracies*, II, 51. See also: E. N. Blair, "Every Man His Own Campaign Manager," *Outlook*, XCVII (February 25, 1911), 427; R. C. Buley, "The Campaign Of 1888 In Indiana," *Indiana Magazine Of History*, X, 45; J. W. Goff, "Juggling With The Ballot," *North American Review* CLVIII, 207; H. F. Gosnell, *Negro Politicians: The Rise of Negro Politics In Chicago*, 115 and 145-146; G. Kennan, "Holding Up A State. The True Story Of Addicks And Delaware," *Outlook*, LXXIII, 386 and 390 and (February 21, 1903), 433-444; M. Josephson, *The Politicos*, 706; a Kentucky legislator, "How An Election Was Bought And Sold," *Harper's* CCXXI, 33-38; A. C. Millspaugh, *Party Organization And Machinery In Michigan Since 1890*, 161; J. G. Speed, "Purchase Of Votes. 1) How Votes Are Bought In New York City," *Harper's* XLIX, 386, 388 and "Purchase Of Votes. 2) The Use Of Money In Doubtful States," *Harper's* XLIX, 498, 500, and 513; and C. H. Wooddy, *The Chicago Primary Of 1926: A Study In Election Methods*, 143-144.

48. " 'The Boss's' Dominions," *Nation*, XIII (October 12, 1871), 236; and Gerald W. McFarland, *Mugwumps, Morals And Politics* (Amherst, 1975), 35-54 and 201-205. Studies of the Committee of Seventy in New York City which played a prominent role in bringing down "Boss" Tweed in the 1870s and of the Chicago Municipal Voters' League confirm McFarland's findings. Richard B. Calhoun, "The Dethronement Of Boss Tweed: Personalities, Policies And Practices Of The Committee Of Seventy, 1871," M.A. thesis, Columbia University, 1967, 10-32; and Joan S. Miller, "The Politics Of Municipal Reform in Chicago During the Progressive Era: The Municipal Voter's League As A Test Case, 1896-1920," M.A. thesis, Roosevelt

University, 1966, 37-43. Studies of the backgrounds of progressive reformers, as well as Democratic and Republican leaders, during the Progressive era also reveal that most reformers in these years were members of the middle and upper classes. See Alfred D. Chandler, Jr., "The Origins Of Progressive Leadership," in Elting E. Morison (ed.) *The Letters Of Theodore Roosevelt* (Cambridge, 1954), VIII, Appendix III, 1462-1465; Jerome M. Clubb, "Congressional Opponents Of Reform, 1901-1913," Ph.D. dissertation, University of Washington, 163, 211-227; Samuel P. Hays, "The Politics of Reform In Municipal Government In The Progressive Era," *Pacific Northwest Quarterly* LV (January 1964), 16-27; George E. Mowry, *The California Progressives* (Chicago, 1963), 86-88; George E. Mowry, *The Era Of Theodore Roosevelt: 1900-1912* (New York, 1958), 85-87; Larry M. Pearson, "Illinois Political Leadership In 1912 And The Status-Revolution Theory," M.A. thesis, Southern Illinois University, 1969; E. Daniel Potts, "The Progressive Profile In Iowa," *Mid-America*, XLVII (October 1965), 257-268; Richard B. Sherman, "The Status Revolution And Massachusetts Progressive Leadership," *Political Science Quarterly*, LXXXVIII (March 1963), 59-65; David P. Thelen, "Social Tensions And The Origins Of Progressivism," *The Journal Of American History*, LVI (September 1969), 323-341; Jack Tager, "Progressives, Conservatives, And The Theory Of The Status Revolution," *Mid-America*, XLVIII (July 1966), 162-175; and Norman M. Wilensky, *Conservatives In The Progressive Era: The Taft Republicans Of 1912* (Gainesville, 1965). See also Jerome M. Clubb and Howard W. Allen, "Collective Biography and the Progressive Movement: The 'Status Revolution' Revisited," *Social Science History*, I (Summer, 1977), 518-534.

49. Richard Hofstadter, *Anti-Intellectualism In American Life* (New York, 1966), 178. Hofstadter's analysis of the reformer's attitude toward the urban immigrant is still the most perceptive discussion available. See *The Age of Reform. From Bryan to F.D.R.* (New York, 1956) 173-184, but also consult John D. Buenker, *Urban Liberalism And Progressive Reform* (New York, 1973), especially 198-239 and Robert H. Wiebe, *The Segmented Society: An Introduction To The Meaning Of America* (New York, 1975), 144.

50. New York Legislature, Senate Committee on the Police Department of the City of New York, "Minority Report", 62-76.

51. W. Dorsett, *The Pendergast Machine*, 123; G. B. Gist, "Progressive Reform In A Rural Community: The Adams County Vote-Fraud Case," *Mississippi Valley Historical Review*, XLVIII, 60-78; R. J. Butler and J. Driscoll, *Dock Walloper: The Story Of "Big Dick" Butler*, 67-68; and Joel A. Tarr, *A Study In Boss Politics: William Lorimer Of Chicago*, 119-121. Rarely have politicians admitted to having committed vote fraud. George Washington Plunkitt's generally candid discussion of "practical politics" does not mention vote fraud, and Edward J. Flynn categorically denied knowledge of any vote bribery in New York City, although he did believe that votes were purchased in rural areas. William L. Riordon, *Plunkitt of Tammany Hall*, intr. Arthur Mann (New York, 1963), passim; and E. J. Flynn, *You're The Boss*, 113.

52. U.S. Congress. House. *A Historical And Legal Digest Of All The Contested Election Cases In The House Of Representatives Of The United States From The First To The Fifty-Sixth Congress, 1789-1901*, by Chester H. Rowell, Document No. 510, 56th Congress, 2nd Session (Washington, 1901), 37-613; and U.S. Congress. House. *A Historical And Legal Digest Of All The Contested Election Cases In The House Of Representatives Of The United States From The Fifty-Seventh To And Including The Sixty-Fourth Congress, 1901-1917*, by Merrill Moores, Document No. 2052, 64th Congress, 2nd Session (Washington, 1917), passim.

53. This information was compiled from the *Biographical Directory Of The American Congress, 1774-1961* (Washington, 1961), 319-450. George B. Galloway, *History Of The House Of Representatives* (New York, 1961), 31 concluded that there were 541 contested elections considered by the House of Representatives for *all* causes between 1789 and 1951.

54. C. Seymour and D. P. Frary, *How The World Votes*, I, 256; Frank R. Kent, *The Great Game Of Politics* (New York, 1928), 303; V. O. Key, Jr., *Southern Politics*, 62-63; and R. Jensen, *The Winning Of The Midwest*, 36; and Leo Hershkowitz, *Tweed's New York: Another Look* (Garden City, NY, 1977), xii-xx. See also: William D. Miller, *Mr. Crump Of Memphis* (Baton Rouge, 1964), especially 185-223; Geoffrey Parsons, Jr. and Robert M. Yoder, "Ward Boss," *Survey Graphic*, XXX (April 1941), 247-249 and 262-263; James K. Pollock, Jr., *Party Campaign Funds* (New York, 1926), 143-144; "The Press And The Profs," *Newsweek*, LVII (February 27, 1961), 63; G. M. Reynolds, *Machine Politics In New Orleans, 1897-1926*, 129-131; and James T. Shotwell, "Democracy And Political Morality," *Political Science Quarterly*, XXXVI (March 1921), 1-8.

55. S. P. Huntington, *Political Order In Changing Societies*, 61; D. W. Brogan, *Politics In America* (New York, 1960), 113, but see also Brogan's entire chapter on "Machines And Bosses," 104-148; William L. Riordon, *Plunkitt of Tammany Hall* (New York, 1963), 28. See also J. A. Tarr, *A Study In Boss Politics*, 65-88.

56. Croker's comments are quoted in M. L. Werner, *Tammany Hall*, 449-450. Vare's instructions are quoted in D. H. Kurtzman, "Methods Of Controlling Votes In Philadelphia," 32.

57. W. L. Riordon, *Plunkitt of Tammany Hall*, 28; G. Myers, "The Secrets of Tammany's Success," *Forum*, XXXI (June, 1901), 496; E. A. Ross, "Immigrants In Politics: The Political Consequences Of Immigration," *Century*, 396; C. E. Merriam, *Chicago: A More Intimate View Of Urban Politics*, 232-233; Johnny Powers's quotation is in A. F. Davis, *Spearheads For Reform*, 162; J. S. Bruner and S. J. Korchin, "The Boss And The Vote; A Case Study In City Politics," *Public Opinion Quarterly*, 4-11; and D. W. Brogan, *Politics In America*, 117.

58. R. Wiebe, *The Segmented Society: An Introduction To The Meaning of America*, 144.

59. This point is suggested by Richard Hofstadter in *The Age Of Reform*, 308.

PART III
ANALYZING QUANTITATIVE DATA
ON ELECTORAL BEHAVIOR

Previous sections have described the abundance of election returns available for study and discussed certain cautions in handling those data. This section turns to techniques of description and analysis that are applied to historical election data. The methods presented in the three following chapters are not all-purpose analytic tools or in any sense fundamental approaches to the study of human behavior. In some ways these techniques are not typical of social analysis.

The analysis of historical election data utilizes techniques that are: *quantitative,* since the character of the data allows precise calculations; *aggregative,* since almost all of the units of analysis are precincts or counties or states, units which aggregate the behavior of hundreds or thousands of individuals; *over time,* while much of electoral analysis examines a single election or a static cross-section of data, many opportunities exist for over time comparisons and for examining long time serial patterns.

For the most part, we emphasize the ready access to large volumes of data, but this should not lead to the expectation that the quantitative analysis of electoral units over time is practically trouble-free. There are the universal problems of converting ideas into indicators and translating statements of relationship into measures of association. In addition, there is a generous smattering of problems requiring special attention from electoral analysts.

The operationalizing of concepts in electoral history has received little attention from analysts, doubtless because the concepts and indicators seem so nearly identical. If pressed, some analysts might argue that the appropriate indicator of a concept like turnout or a candidate's percentage of the vote is whatever the official reports contain. It is difficult to imagine a more straightforward operationalization than this for turnout, and yet as Shortridge discussed in Chapter 5, the denominator in "official estimates" may be misleading and in Chapter 7 Flanigan and Zingale mention some hazards in the numerator. More abstract concepts like party strength may appear to be measured precisely, but it will not usually be self-evident that particular indicators capture the conceptual intent of the analyst.

Quite possibly there is a different reason for neglecting to raise these issues when operationalizing concepts in electoral history—we may not have too many possibilities from which to choose. If, for example, we hope to study the departure of presidential and gubernatorial voting from party strength and the only other race we have in our set of data is the vote for Congress, then the vote for Congress has just become the indicator of party strength. And for obvious reasons we may prefer not to discuss the nature of this choice.

In addition to the traditional questions of validity, the electoral analyst of historical data has other concerns. Even indicators with a high degree of validity at one time may not behave reliably over a long period. There are many forms of this problem, but for electoral analysts it has been particularly troublesome in deciding when to merge differing party labels over a series of elections. Needless to say, the solutions to these problems are not narrowly methodological but require rationalization in terms of the design of a given piece of research.

While the validity of electoral variables may be questioned from time to time, there is no doubt that these data enjoy a high degree of precision. Most of the variables that we will discuss have *interval* properties, i.e., standard units measure the differences between values. So we confidently compare 13 percent of the vote with 29 percent of the vote because the units, percentages of the vote in this example, provide a common standard from 0 to 100 percent. Actually these interval variables are usually *ratio scales* since the zero is meaningful and we can say that 29 percent is more than twice as great as 13 percent. Most readers will recognize that this level of interval measurement with most variables having ratio scale properties is extremely uncommon in much of social analysis. It is perhaps one of the few luxuries in the study of electoral history.

Some valuable variables for electoral analysis have only low levels of measurement but they are no less useful for that. A common *nominal* variable would be region, where states, districts, and so forth are located in the South, the East, or whatever. The nominal categories are distinct from one another but are unranked and form no scale.

The analysis of election returns has not utilized many *ordinal* variables—ranked categories without a standardized metric between the categories. We feel compelled to question an axiom of data analysis which states that analysts should always use the highest level of measurement available. It would at first appear difficult to quarrel with an axiom that calls for always using the highest quality data but there is a way in which following this axiom may mislead us. To illustrate, we might rank congressional districts as "safe," "somewhat competitive," and "highly competitive" to form an ordinal variable. And we might use an interval variable, winner's margin in the last election, to place districts in the appropriate categories. Should we not simply use the interval variable directly and discard the ordinal categories?

One answer to the question, and an answer that leads us to prefer the lower level of measurement to the higher level, depends on considering the translation of statements of relationship into measures of association, rather than merely the operationalizing of a concept into a high quality indicator. If we hypothesize that as competitiveness increases turnout increases in congressional·districts, we could express this as every degree of competitiveness being associated with some increase in turnout. Or we could say that safe districts have lower turnout than competitive districts but the pattern is lumpy. Safe districts, as a category, behave one way, highly competitive districts another, and moderately competitive districts are in-between. What might be called "ordinal conceptualizations" should be translated into ordinal measures of association because the pattern may be extremely weak in an interval sense and much stronger as an ordinal relationship.

To illustrate this point with one further example, suppose we hypothesize that state legislatures under Democratic control raise taxes substantially, Republican legislatures do not, and divided control falls in between. We could appropriately test this possibility with a three-category ordinal variable for control of the legislature. It would be a test of quite a different hypothesis if we were to generate an interval variable that measured the size of the controlling majorities in some way. With such an interval variable we would be assessing the extent to which each increment of Democratic or Republican control is reflected in tax policy. This may be an interesting hypothesis but a different one, and not to be considered more sophisticated or more significant theoretically because it depends on an interval variable.

Since most electoral variables have interval properties and appropriately reflect an interval conceptualization, the focus on translating statements of relationship among variables into measures of association becomes a problem of making choices among the considerable array of statistical techniques that depend on interval variables. In Chapter 8 the traditional statistical techniques that express an additive relationship among variables that is linear in form are emphasized.

We are so unaccustomed to having analysts include references to the linear and additive properties of their statistical models that it is somewhat jarring to interject these reminders. So if we report that the vote for Kennedy in 1960 was highly correlated with the Catholic composition of states, it is not likely that anyone will miss the information that this finding is based on a linear fit to the data. It is likely to remain acceptable style that strong relationships will be reported with "linear" taken for granted but once weak or nonexistent relationships are reported, the "linear" qualifier becomes more important. (Presumably we would not wish to report that no imaginable curve would fit the data.) But beyond this the failure to find linear relationships where we expect some relationship ought to immediately raise the prospect of finding that a nonlinear model fits the data, and indeed, suggest to us that our initial idea was nonlinear although we had failed to notice that.

As we introduce several explanatory variables into our analysis, the manner in which these explanatory variables influence one another and their impact on the dependent variable becomes important. The additive model is marvelously simple in assuming that the explanatory variables do not interact with one another, but it is not a particularly shrewd way to approach most forms of explanation of social behavior. Additivity is an acceptable way to begin analysis because of its attractive simplicity, but it is likely that even our most straightforward ideas about social behavior are more complicated than additive models imply. We almost invariably suppose (at least on second thought) that the impact of an explanatory variable is affected by the values of other explanatory variables.

There are, however, many dimensions in statements of relationship that must be correctly translated into measures of association. In addition to the form of relationship as linear or curved, as additive or interactive, we must be attentive to the units of analysis included in the statement of relationship as well as the level of measurement in the variables.

Another aspect of translating statements of relationship into measures of association raises the familiar distinction between correlation and causation. The analyst bears responsibility for determining the extent to which a relationship is causal. For the most part, the same statistical techniques are used for assessing causal and noncausal patterns; all the crucial distinctions are in the analyst's theorizing about the statements of relationship. If the analyst convincingly argues that X causes Y and finds that X and Y are related, the finding may be interpreted as a causal relationship. The burden of establishing causation is completely dependent on the analyst's making convincing argument that a relationship represents more than association and that one variable has a causal impact on another.

By any standards, the most common focus of critical attention in electoral history has been on errors or "fallacies" in interpreting measures of association by inferring that units of analysis of one type are evidence for relationships of another type. More specifically, the well-known "ecological fallacy" refers to evidence based on aggregate units interpreted as if they were individual data. But the ecological fallacy is only one of many possible fallacies based on inferences from one type of units of analysis to another.

An entire chapter by Gudmund Iversen is devoted to the problems of ecological inference. Once again the responsibility for solving the problems falls on the analyst. There is no magic in the statistical techniques. Iversen restores a degree of caution to the prospects of inferring individual behavior from aggregate data—a degree of caution not always present in the literature directed at analysts of electoral history.

The ecological fallacy deserves special attention here not because it is peculiar to electoral history, but because so many analysts of electoral history have been determined to commit the fallacy. Perhaps over forty years of survey research studies of individual vote choice have contributed to analysts' need to examine individual behavior under all electoral circumstances. It is fair to say that the major themes in electoral analysis of recent decades have focused on individual attitudes and behavior in both contemporary and historical settings.

Another source of inspiration for analysts eager to commit the ecological fallacy possibly has been a steady supply of methodological advice to go about it in increasingly complex ways. Most methodologists have realized that the techniques for making inferences about individual behavior from ecological data require assumptions by the analyst about the behavior of individuals that are not in evidence in the data. Too often analysts have felt free to ignore the cautions, to overlook the assumptions, and to dwell on the findings magically extracted from heretofore unyielding data.

A balanced rereading of the methodological literature on ecological inference would reveal ample warnings, most of which have gone unheeded. Perhaps the most widely cited works in the field are the articles by Leo Goodman which were early responses to the well-known piece by W. S. Robinson.[1] A significant aspect of Goodman's advice would have analysts compute the outer limits of possible individual relationships hidden within the grouped data. This step requires no risky assumptions by the analyst and is invariably a property of ecological patterns that one should be aware of. Very seldom is Goodman's advice followed in electoral analysis. During the subsequent two decades there has been a steady stream of advice that has ignored the various cautions that alert us to serious barriers to successful inference.[2]

To readers familiar with statistics texts designed to provide guidance on methods of social research it may seem odd that no attention is given here to significance testing and sampling theory. Statistics as a discipline is devoted mainly to aiding in the testing of hypotheses using sample data and in particular advising us on how much confidence to have in those tests. Of course, relatively little analysis of election returns is based on samples, so estimates of error that depend on sampling theory are not applicable. Testing the significance of sample estimates is an important activity in many areas of research, but it is a mistake to view these traditional concerns of statistics as the whole of quantitative analysis.

The work of John Tukey has advocated a perspective on quantitative analysis called "exploratory data analysis."[3] His argument is based on the premise that we should first concern ourselves with describing the relationships among variables before we worry about how much confidence to have in our account. Analysts of electoral history take limited sets of data very seriously and should use as wide a range of techniques for examining that data as possible. Chapter 7 and 8 attempt to offer such a range of techniques.

NOTES

1. Leo Goodman, "Ecological Regressions and the Behavior of Individuals," *American Sociological Review* 19 (1953), 663-4; "Some Alternatives to Ecological Correlation," *American Journal of Sociology* 64 (1959), 610-25; W. S. Robinson, "Ecological Correlation and the Behavior of Individuals," *American Sociological Review* 15 (1950), 351-7.

2. See, for example, John Hammond, "New Approaches to Aggregate Electoral Data," *Journal of Interdisciplinary History* 9 (1979), 473-92; Eric A. Hanushek, John E. Jackson, and John F. Kain, "Model Specification, Use of Aggregate Data and the Ecological Correlation Fallacy" *Political Methodology* 1 (1974), 87-106; Laura Irwin Langbein and Allen J. Lichtman, *Ecological Inference,* Sage University Paper Series on Quantitative Applications in the Social Sciences, Series 07-010. (Beverly Hills: Sage Publications, 1978)

3. John W. Tukey, *Exploratory Data Analysis* (Reading, MA: Addison-Wesley, 1977), v.

7

SUMMARIZING QUANTITATIVE DATA

William H. Flanigan
Nancy H. Zingale

In this chapter, we will present a variety of techniques for use in describing single variables. We start with these relatively simple descriptive techniques not because they are a necessary foundation for understanding the more complicated statistical formulations to be considered in the next chapter (although they are that), but rather because they are important tools of analysis in their own right. Indeed, our prejudice on this point is rather strong: Simple descriptive techniques should be a starting point in almost any analysis. Becoming familiar with the properties and peculiarities of one's data is important from a number of perspectives. First, an exploratory probing of the data can be a useful way of inductively generating ideas for further analysis. Second, being aware of the characteristics of the data is essential to avoid violating the assumptions of more sophisticated techniques which might be used further along in the analysis. Last, and certainly not least, these very simple techniques may be the most appropriate way for displaying results in a clear, direct, and persuasive manner.

Even a simple description of an election outcome will take us a long way into quantitative techniques of analysis. Suppose we are concerned with the popular vote for President in the 1968 election. What are the simplest questions we want answered? First, surely we want to know who won and by what percentage of the vote in the nation as a whole. What kind of a showing did the losers make? Did the success of the candidates vary from state to state? Did one or more candidates win big or lose big in particular states? Did the candidates do better or worse than expected?

Although we can see that these questions only begin to probe the characteristics of an election outcome which we might routinely investigate, there are enough questions here to introduce four methodological topics: measurement, central tendency, dispersion, and comparison. A methodological examination of these topics will force us to link more explicitly and carefully our concepts (and the words we use to explain those ideas) with the operations we carry out on the data. To become methodologically sophisticated in the handling of ideas and data is to understand precisely how faithful the translation is between concepts and operations.

CONSTRUCTING INDICATORS

The first task in describing election results, in this example the 1968 presidential election, is to convert raw votes into percentages. While this seems straightforward, there are actually several ways to percentage the vote. One obvious calculation is to percentage the vote for a candidate over the total vote cast for all candidates. (A slight variation of this percentage would include in the denominator those voters who did not cast a ballot for President; however, frequently this additional information is unavailable.) Using this percentage of total votes we can say that Nixon won the popular vote contest in 1968 with 43 percent of the vote—and Humphrey lost with 43 percent of the vote.[1] Immediately we might wish for more precision and note that Nixon had 43.4 percent and Humphrey 42.7 percent. The remainder of the popular vote is accounted for mainly by Wallace's 13.5 percent.

The presence of a substantial vote for Wallace makes a second form of percentaging appear less appropriate; that is the percentage for the two major party candidates as a percentage of the two-party vote. This calculation yields a percentage for Nixon of 50.4 and for Humphrey of 49.6 percent. Curiously, this form of percentaging has been used more often, perhaps, than the more complete and perfectly accurate percentages of the total vote. There would appear to be two reasons for the use of two-party percentages: First, the two-party percentage usually provides a clear indication of the winner which the total vote percentages may not. Merely knowing that Nixon received 43.4 percent of the total vote in 1968 may lead to the erroneous conclusion that he lost in a landslide. There are, however, simple ways of keeping track of who won election contests and it is not essential that this information also be available in the percentage of the vote. A second reason for using two-party percentages is more compelling; under some circumstances, particularly when unofficial sources are used, only the major party vote is reported. We might not prefer the two-party percentage but if that is all we have, that is what we use. Furthermore, in a series of data with some two-party percentages imposed on us, we would be forced to compute all percentages that way in order to maintain comparability.

Appendix A to this chapter contains a discussion of these and other indicators commonly used in election analysis, so at this point we want to move on to the discussion of other methodological considerations.

DISTRIBUTION OF A VARIABLE

Once we have decided on an appropriate form of measurement for a variable—notice this is a tentative decision that we may reconsider frequently in light of further analysis—we turn our attention to the distribution of values for the indicator. For the 1968 presidential election there are three variables of immediate interest, the percentage of the total vote for Nixon, for Humphrey, and for Wallace. We will examine the distribution of one candidate's votes and then consider several forms of comparison as simple means of interpreting these data, even though in practice these two activities would probably occur together.

First, we turn to the examination of the distributions of the popular votes for President from each of the fifty states. Usually such information comes to us in alphabetical order, a meaningful organization of the results and one that remains useful for reference purposes, but an arrangement that does not promote exploration of the data. The columns on the left in Table 7.1 show an alphabetical listing of the percentages of the vote for the three candidates and Figure 7.1 displays a simple conversion of the data on Nixon's 1968 vote into a display which retains the identity of the states but reorders them according to the percentage of the vote received by Nixon.

The frequency distribution of Nixon's popular vote displayed in Figure 7.1 is a straightforward rearrangement of the state percentages from their alphabetical order in Table 7.1 into an order from small to large percentages. There is no loss of information in this conversion since the state designations are used to create a visual image of the location of many or few states along the range of values. Whenever the units of analysis are meaningful, as states certainly are, it is valuable to retain the identity of the units, at least in these preliminary stages of analysis. (In other cases the units might be too numerous for such treatment, for example, all congres-

TABLE 7.1   Percentaged Distributions of Electoral Variables by States

| State | Popular Vote for | | | | Nixon 1968-1960 |
	Nixon	Humphrey	Wallace	Nixon Margin	
AL	14	19	66	−52	−28
AK	45	43	12	2	−6
AZ	55	35	10	20	−1
AR	31	30	39	−8	−12
CA	48	45	7	3	−2
CO	51	41	8	10	−4
CT	44	50	6	−6	−2
DE	45	42	13	3	−4
FL	41	31	29	10	−11
GA	30	27	43	−13	−7
HI	39	60	2	−21	−11
ID	57	31	13	26	3
IL	47	44	9	3	−3
IN	50	44	12	6	−5
IA	53	41	6	12	−4
KS	55	35	10	20	−6
KY	44	38	18	6	−10
LA	24	28	48	−24	−5
ME	43	55	2	−12	−14
MD	42	44	15	−2	−3
MA	33	63	4	−30	−7
MI	42	48	10	−6	−7
MN	42	54	4	−12	−7
MS	14	23	64	−50	−11
MO	45	44	11	1	−5
MT	51	42	7	9	0
NE	60	32	8	28	−2
NV	48	39	13	9	−1
NH	52	44	4	6	−1
NJ	46	44	9	2	−3
NM	52	40	8	12	3
NY	44	50	5	−6	−3
NC	40	29	31	9	−8
ND	56	38	6	18	1
OH	45	43	12	2	−8
OK	48	32	20	16	−14
OR	50	44	6	6	−3
PA	44	48	8	−4	−5
RI	32	64	4	−32	−4
SC	38	30	32	6	−11
SD	53	42	5	11	−5
TN	38	28	34	4	−15
TX	40	41	19	−1	−9

(Continued)

TABLE 7.1 continued

State	Popular Vote for			Nixon Margin	Nixon 1968-1960
	Nixon	Humphrey	Wallace		
UT	57	37	6	20	2
VT	53	44	3	9	−6
VA	43	33	24	10	−9
WA	45	47	7	−2	−6
WV	41	50	10	−9	−6
WI	48	44	8	4	−4
WY	56	36	9	20	1

sional districts, or the units might not be of interest, as would usually be true of sample data.)

From the distribution of Nixon's support by states we are able to make sense of some information directly available from the rearranged data. A few southern states provided very low levels of support for Nixon; at the other end of the display, a few prairie and mountain states represent his strongest showing. The main cluster of states, the center of the distribution, is around 44 or 45 percent. Most states fall between 38 percent and 57 percent but that is not a particularly discriminating characteristic since that range covers both landslide victories and landslide defeats.

Later in this chapter we will introduce several more precise formulations for describing a single distribution such as this one, but it would be a serious mistake to assume that extremely precise calculations for determining the center of the distribution or its pattern of dispersion are more informative or a firmer basis for analysis than the rearranged percentages in Figure 7.1. All the more precise statistical measures drop the identity of the units and their location in the distribution. The traditional formulations have the advantage of reducing a great deal of information to a single number which facilitates comparison with other distributions, especially comparisons with many distributions. But the more we want to examine a particular distribution and learn a lot about it, the better we are served by displays like Figure 7.1.

Of course, no analyst is likely to be content with a description of the percentage of the vote for a candidate. We want to know how Nixon fared against Humphrey and Wallace. Since the 1968 election was complicated by a third party candidate, we can only be certain from the information in Figure 7.1 that Nixon won the states where he had 50 percent or more of the vote. It is a simple matter, however, to return to Table 7.1 and

```
14  AL MS
15
16
17
18
19
20
21
22
23
24  LA
25
26
27
28
29
30  GA
31  AR
32  RI
33  MA
34
35
36
37
38  SC TN
39  HI
40  NC TX
41  FL WV
42  MD MI MN
43  ME VA
44  CT KY NY PA
45  AK DE MO OH WA
46  NJ
47  IL
48  CA NV OK WI
49
50  IN OR
51  CO MT
52  NH NM
53  IA SD VT
54
55  AZ KS
56  ND WY
57  ID UT
58
59
60  NE
```

Figure 7.1   Ordered Distribution of the Percentage of the Vote for Nixon in 1968 by States

generate a new variable which shows whether Nixon's percentage was larger or smaller than the percentage of his more popular opponent. This creates a variable that may be positive, as in Alaska with +2 where Nixon led Humphrey 45 to 43 percent, or negative, as in Alabama with −52 where Nixon trailed Wallace 14 to 66.

This new variable, which we have labeled "Nixon's margin," in the fourth column of Table 7.1, is displayed in Figure 7.2 and reveals a flatter distribution over a greater range of values. In order to see the shape of the distribution more clearly, we can group the values and produce a new distribution, shown in Figure 7.3, with only a modest loss of information. The collapsed data reveal more unambiguously that the center of the distribution is a narrow margin of victory for Nixon of between 1 and 6 percent. The outlying states where his margin of victory was greatest are the same states where his percentage of the vote was highest. His weakest showing was in Alabama and Mississippi where his percentage of the vote was very low. But his next two biggest defeats were in Rhode Island and Massachusetts, which did not stand out in the distribution of percentages in Figure 7.1.

Even a superficial examination of Nixon's 1968 vote would draw on comparisons with one or more estimates of an expected vote or some meaningful baseline. Perhaps in Nixon's case an obvious and uncomplicated comparison is with his percentage of the vote in 1960. We can see how much better or worse he did state by state through subtraction of his 1960 percentage from his 1968 percentage. This generates another new variable listed in the fifth column of Table 7.1 as "Nixon 1968-1960," and displayed in Figure 7.4. This variable is more tightly bunched around the center of the distribution between differences of −3 and −6 percent. Of course, Nixon had a smaller percentage of the vote almost everywhere in the three-candidate race of 1968 even though it netted him 80 additional electoral college votes. The few states in which Nixon actually improved over his earlier showing are all prairie and mountain states, while his substantially weaker showings are, with the exception of Maine and Hawaii, in southern states. The relatively tight distribution conveys an impression of consistency in voting patterns across the years even in the presence of a disruptive third-party candidate.

For comparison with Nixon's vote and to display data we will use below, the rearranged distributions of the votes for Humphrey and for Wallace are shown in Figures 7.5A and 7.5B. In comparison with Nixon's vote, Humphrey's percentages reveal a flatter distribution but with a clear middle value. The Wallace vote, on the other hand, is strikingly dissimilar from either Nixon's or Humphrey's, with a skewed distribution concen-

```
                         -52  AL
                         -51
                         -50  MS
                         -49
                          .
                          .
                          .
                         -33
                         -32  RI
                         -31
                         -30  MA
                         -29
                         -28
                         -27
                         -26
                         -25
                         -24  LA
                         -23
                         -22
                         -21  HI
                         -20
                         -19
                         -18
                         -17
                         -16
                         -15
                         -14
                         -13  GA
                         -12  ME MN
                         -11
                         -10
                          -9  WV
                          -8  AR
                          -7
                          -6  CT MI NY
                          -5
                          -4  PA
                          -3
                          -2  MD WA
                          -1  TX
                           0
                           1  MO
                           2  AK NJ OH
                           3  CA DE IL
                           4  TN WI
                           5
                           6  IN KY NH OR SC
                           7
                           8
                           9  MT NV NC VT
                          10  CO FL VA
                          11  SD
                          12  IA NM
                          13
                          14
                          15
                          16  OK
                          17
                          18  ND
                          19
                          20  AZ KS UT WY
                          21
                          22
                          23
                          24
                          25
                          26  ID
                          27
                          28  NE
```

Figure 7.2 Ordered Distribution of Nixon's Margin in 1968 by States[a]

a. The vote for Humphrey or Wallace, whichever was greater, was subtracted from the percentage for Nixon.

Range	States
−52 to −50	AL MS
−49 to −47	
.	
.	
−33 to −31	RI
−30 to −28	MA
−27 to −25	
−24 to −22	LA
−21 to −19	HI
−18 to −16	
−15 to −13	GA
−12 to −10	ME MN
−9 to −7	WV AR
−6 to −4	CT MI NY PA
−3 to −1	MD WA TX
0	
1 to 3	MO AK NJ OH CA DE IL
4 to 6	TN WI IN KY NH OR SC
7 to 9	MT NV NC VT
10 to 12	CO FL VA SD IA NM
13 to 15	
16 to 18	ND
19 to 21	AZ KS UT WY
22 to 24	
25 to 27	ID
28 to 30	NE

Figure 7.3 Collapsed, Ordered Distribution of Nixon's Margin in 1968 by States

trated at the low end of the scale and a long thin tail of values toward the higher percentages.

As long as we are committed to more and more intensive analysis of a limited set of data, these analytic devices, and extensions of them, serve us well. And in our view most electoral analysts would be better served doing more with "paper and pencil" analysis and less with computers. However, these techniques do not serve all purposes equally well. In particular they do not permit rapid analysis of large quantities of data and they do not yield simple summary statistics for presentation. Even if analysts work over their data exhaustively, they are unlikely to present more than a fraction of that work in published form. Regardless of how little or how

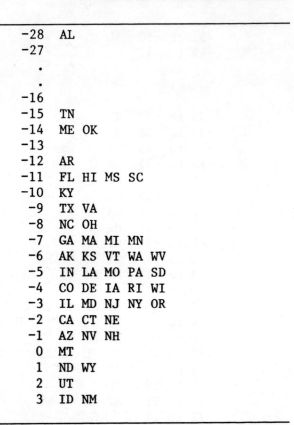

-28	AL			
-27				
.				
.				
-16				
-15	TN			
-14	ME	OK		
-13				
-12	AR			
-11	FL	HI	MS	SC
-10	KY			
-9	TX	VA		
-8	NC	OH		
-7	GA	MA	MI	MN
-6	AK	KS	VT	WA WV
-5	IN	LA	MO	PA SD
-4	CO	DE	IA	RI WI
-3	IL	MD	NJ	NY OR
-2	CA	CT	NE	
-1	AZ	NV	NH	
0	MT			
1	ND	WY		
2	UT			
3	ID	NM		

Figure 7.4 Ordered Distribution of the Difference between the Vote for Nixon in 1968 and 1960 by States[a]

a. The percentage of the total vote for Nixon in 1960 was subtracted from the percentage of the total vote for Nixon in 1968.

much exploratory data analysis goes on, the analyst eventually faces choices over which summary statistics to use to convey in print the information acquired, information probably acquired in a much more cumbersome fashion than published work reveals.

Methodological sophistication should lead to the selection of statistics for describing distributions that mislead neither the analyst nor the reader. In the remainder of the chapter we will discuss techniques for locating the middle of a distribution and techniques for describing the dispersion of values around the middle. We will propose bases for evaluating these various techniques and attempt to illustrate these choices sufficiently so that meaningful substantive considerations can dominate the evaluation.

A. Humphrey		B. Wallace	
19	AL	0	
20		1	
21		2	HI ME
22		3	VT
23	MS	4	MA MN NH RI
24		5	NY SD
25		6	CT IA ND OR UT
26		7	CA MT WA
27	GA	8	CO NE NM PA WI
28	LA TN	9	IL NJ WY
29	NC	10	AZ KS MI WV
30	AR SC	11	MO
31	FL ID	12	AK IN OH
32	NE OK	13	DE ID NV
33	VA	14	
34		15	MD
35	AZ KS	16	
36	WY	17	
37	UT	18	KY
38	KY ND	19	TX
39	NV	20	OK
40	NM	21	
41	CO IA TX	22	
42	DE MT SD	23	
43	AK OH	24	VA
44	IL IN MD MO NH NJ OR VT WI	25	
45	CA	26	
46		27	
47	WA	28	
48	MI PA	29	FL
49		30	
50	CT NY WV	31	NC
51		32	SC
52		33	
53		34	TN
54	MN	35	
55	ME	36	
56		37	
57		38	
58		39	AR
59		40	
60	HI	41	
61		42	
62		43	GA
63	MA	44	
64	RI	45	
		46	
		47	
		48	LA
		49	
		.	
		.	
		63	
		64	MS
		65	
		66	AL

Figure 7.5   Ordered Distribution of the Votes for Humphrey and Wallace in 1968 by States

TABLE 7.2   Frequency Table

Percentage of the Vote for Nixon	Number of States
14	2
⋮	
24	1
⋮	
30	1
31	1
32	1
33	1
34	0
35	0
36	0
37	0
38	2
39	1
40	2
41	2
42	3
43	2
44	4
45	5
46	1
47	1
48	4
49	0
50	2
51	2
52	2
53	3
54	0
55	2
56	2
57	2
58	0
59	0
60	1

We give as much attention as we do to traditional statistics not because these familiar measures are likely to serve all analytic purposes well, but rather because as consumers and critics of research we need to understand the commonly used statistics to assess their worth. Our overall intent is to help analysts to be as creative as possible in exploring their data and as conventional as is appropriate in presenting their results.

PRESENTATION OF FREQUENCY DISTRIBUTIONS

In the preceding pages we have displayed frequency distributions confident that their characteristics are easily understood. A *frequency distribution* is an array of data indicating the number of cases (the frequency) at each specified value of the variable. The rearranged data used above in Figures 7.1 to 7.5 presented a clear image of a frequency distribution and can be converted easily into more conventional forms: a frequency table, histogram, or frequency polygon.

The frequency table is an extremely common form of data presentation and is illustrated in Table 7.2 as a summary of the information on Nixon's percentage of the vote in 1968. The uncollapsed frequency table shows that four states gave Nixon 44 percent of the total vote—the same information discernible in the rearranged data from Figure 7.1, but the identity of the states is lost. As mentioned above, the loss of the units' identities would be of no concern with many data presentations.

The similarity between a frequency table and the histogram and frequency polygon can be illustrated by rotating the rearranged data display 90 degrees as shown in Figure 7.6A. A *histogram*, the second part of Figure 7.6, is formed by bars at each value indicating the frequency of units by their height. A *frequency polygon* is a line graph connecting points which represent the frequency of units at each value along the horizontal axis. All three displays in Figure 7.6 reveal the same shape in slightly different ways. We can change the shape of these frequency distributions by grouping values on the horizontal axis or spreading the values by making finer distinctions. In all of these presentations, including the frequency table, we sacrifice information on the distribution by using broader and broader categories. The increasingly fine distinctions become more and more cumbersome to handle.

These several forms of presenting frequency distributions have about the same informational value. The *frequency table* is the most compact form of presentation but lacks the visual image of variation in frequencies. The *histogram* is preferable for creating an impression of distinct categories. A *frequency polygon* creates an image of a continuous distribution of values. It would be curious to argue strongly for one form of frequency distribution over another; analysts should worry more about appropriate labels and an accurate presentation.

CENTRAL TENDENCY

We are almost always interested in the middle or center of a frequency distribution; sometimes we characterize the middle value as "typical" or

A. Ordered Distribution

```
                                                                 PA
                                                              NY    WA
                                                         TX  KY  OH  WI
                                                    TN   FL  MI  MO  OK
                                                    SC   NC  VA  DE  NV        VT
AL MS                      LA      GA RI       HI      KY  MD  AK  CA     OR MT NM  KS WY UT
                                   AR MA                    ME  CT  NJ  IL  IN CO NH IA SD AZ ND ID  NE

14 15 16 17 18 19 20 21 22 23 24 25 26 27 28 29 30 31 32 33 34 35 36 37 38 39 40 41 42 43 44 45 46 47 48 49 50 51 52 53 54 55 56 57 58 59 60
```

B. Histogram

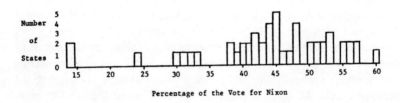

Number
of
States

Percentage of the Vote for Nixon

C. Frequency Polygon

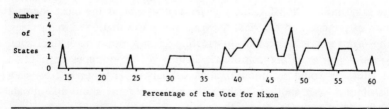

Number
of
States

Percentage of the Vote for Nixon

Figure 7.6   Frequency Distributions of the Nixon Vote in 1968 by States

"average." It is easy to estimate roughly from a frequency table or histogram where the center of the distribution is located, but there are numerous techniques for making estimates of central tendency much more precise. In addition to wanting to know the center value of a distribution for simple descriptive purposes, we may want to compare the central value of one distribution with the central value of other distributions, or we may wish to subtract the middle value from the observed values to examine how much above or below the middle they are. For these purposes some precision and consistency is required.

In practice, the various forms of calculating the center of a distribution do not usually lead to dissimilar estimates, so for examining our data convenience may dictate usage. However, for presenting results, some estimates will make more sense than others or be susceptible to fewer potential weaknesses. We will discuss two common measures of central tendency, the mean and the median, and one more unusual measure, the trimean, and evaluate their properties.

The *mean* or average. The most familiar measure of central tendency is probably the mean, the average value of a distribution, calculated by summing the values in the distribution and dividing by the total number of cases. Symbolically the mean of variable X, ($\bar{X}$), can be expressed as:

$$\bar{X} = \frac{\Sigma X_i}{N}$$

where X_i is the value of the ith unit on variable X and N is the total number of units.

The *median* or middle value. A second, easy-to-understand measure of central tendency is the median, the middle value of a distribution. If there is an odd number of cases, the median is defined as the middle value; if there is an even number of cases, the median is calculated as the mean of the two middle values.

Some discussions of central tendency include the *mode,* the value or category with the most cases, but it has no advantages over the mean or median for most purposes. The value with the greatest frequency may be far from the center of the distribution by any other standard, or a number of different values may be tied for the largest number of cases. For descriptive reasons it may be interesting to note that a particular value has the most cases, but this should not replace the need to find the middle of the distribution.

Both the mean and median have acceptable meanings and under many analytic circumstances we would not conceptualize our interests so precisely that we could confidently choose between the average and the middle value of a distribution. Furthermore, for many distributions there

TABLE 7.3   Measures of Central Tendency Using States

	1968 VOTE FOR:		
	Nixon	*Humphrey*	*Wallace*
Mean	44.3	40.6	14.9
Median	45.0	41.5	9.5
Trimean	45.5	40.0	10.75

is little or no difference between the values of the mean and the median. An examination of the means and medians calculated for the state percentages of the vote for Nixon, Humphrey, and Wallace and shown in Table 7.3 illustrates this similarity for both the Nixon and Humphrey distributions. For example, the mean of the 50 state percentages of the vote for Nixon is 44.3 percent and the median is 45 percent. The vote for Wallace in 1968, on the other hand, illustrates the possibility of noticeable divergence in the values with a mean of almost 15 percent and a median under 10 percent. In other words, the average state percentage for Wallace is higher by 5 percent than the percentage of the middle state.

The difference between the mean and median of the Wallace vote provides an example of the most basic distinction between the two measures. Every value in a distribution enters into the calculation of the mean and the few, extremely high percentages in the Wallace vote influence the mean. The median is not affected by the value of the outliers and takes its value from the center of the distribution. In any skewed distribution the median will be closer to the bulk of the cases than the mean.[2] This does not imply that the median is superior to the mean but that the two meanings of central tendency yield different values for some distributions.

It is possible, however, to summarize a set of considerations as a basis for evaluating the mean and median.

Advantages of the mean:

(1) The mean is easily understood because it corresponds to the commonsense meaning of average.
(2) The mean is fairly robust in that most minor changes in the data will not affect the value of the mean by a significant amount.
(3) The mean has useful statistical properties: the differences or deviations above and below the mean sum to zero, and the sum of these deviations squared is a minimum, a uniquely low sum which characterizes deviations from the mean.

Disadvantages of the mean:

(1) The mean is sensitive to extreme values. The mean can fluctuate considerably from one distribution to another even though the great bulk of the cases in the middle of the distributions are identical.

Advantages of the median:

(1) The median is easily understood as the middle value of a distribution.
(2) The median is quite robust in that it is unaffected by all changes in the data except those at the middle value.
(3) The median has an interesting statistical property in that the absolute value of the deviations around the median sum to the lowest possible value for any midpoint but it is not a unique value, i.e., deviations from other midpoints could sum to the same low value.

Disadvantages of the median:

(1) In a bimodal distribution a trivial change in the data can cause the median to fluctuate across a gap precisely at the middle of the distribution. (The most casual inspection of the shape of a distribution alerts us to this possibility.)

There is not much of a methodological basis for selecting the mean or the median for the presentation of results and, in fact, analysts might be guided in their choice by the customs established in prior research. For exploratory analysis, however, an analyst might prefer a more robust, if uncommon, measure to either the mean or the median. We will consider only one such measure, the *trimean,* borrowed from the work of John Tukey.[3] (An analyst could easily devise a personal measure with similar safeguards.) The trimean which is a sort of corrected median avoids sensitivity to extreme values without being dependent on the value of a single location like the median. The trimean is defined with this formula:

$$\text{Trimean} = \frac{2 \times \text{median} + \text{1st quartile} + \text{3rd quartile}}{4}$$

The trimean is a weighted average of the median and the quartiles of a distribution. (The 1st and 3rd quartiles are the values one-fourth and three-fourths of the way through a distribution, i.e., the 25th and 75th percentiles—the median is the 50th percentile or the 2nd quartile.) The trimean shown in Table 7.3 yields values close to the median for each candidate. The trimean has never been used in electoral analysis so far as we are aware but that ought not to dissuade analysts from using such measures in exploratory analysis.

MEASURES OF DISPERSION

While analysts must be attentive to the shape of a distribution and its central tendency, this does not exhaust interest in a variable. We are concerned with the amount of variation in a distribution, whether a variable is tightly packed around its center or widely dispersed. Some measures of dispersion yield good summary pictures for exploratory analysis of distributions, other measures provide a precise basis for comparison and a foundation for interpreting more advanced statistical analysis. The measures of dispersion do not provide as complete an image of the shape of a distribution as the histogram or polygon, but they do provide simple summary values.

The two simplest measures of dispersion we will discuss are not used too frequently. The first is the *range,* which is merely the difference between the lowest value in the distribution and the highest. The range is expressed in the metric of the variable and obviously is dependent on the location only of the two most extreme high and low values. The variation in the rest of the distribution does not influence the range.

The other simple measure is the *interquartile range,* the difference between the value of the 1st and 3rd quartiles. The interquartile range measures the distance from the lowest to highest values in the middle half of the overall distribution. It disregards the lowest fourth and the highest fourth of the observations.

Again using the state percentages of voting for President in 1968, we find similar ranges for Nixon and Humphrey but a greater range in Wallace's vote, reflecting the more extreme pattern of his support. Table 7.4 shows a range of 46 for Nixon, 45 for Humphrey and 64 for Wallace. The interquartile ranges are more reflective of the differences in the patterns of the bulk of the states' dispersion, with 12 for Nixon, 13 for Humphrey, and 13 for Wallace.

We now turn to three more traditional measures of dispersion, the average deviation, variance, and standard deviation, each of which uses deviations from the mean as the basic unit in their calculation. In addition, we will present the values of these measures for the distribution of the states' votes to allow comparison of these measures with those above.

The *average deviation* is a straightforward measure of variation in which the absolute differences between the value for each subunit and the mean of all subunits are calculated and then these absolute differences are

TABLE 7.4　Measures of Dispersion Using States for the 1968 Vote

	Range	Interquartile Range	Average Deviation	Standard Deviation	Variance
Nixon	46	12	7.1	9.8	95.7
Humphrey	45	13	7.4	9.5	90.9
Wallace	64	13	10.9	14.9	221.9

averaged. To calculate the average deviation in Humphrey's vote in 1968, we would first find the mean of his vote across the states, then subtract this mean from each state's vote. The resulting deviations are then summed, ignoring signs, and the mean of this sum is taken. We interpret this to mean the average deviation of states around the mean is 7.4 percent.

$$\text{Average deviation} = \frac{\Sigma |X_i - \overline{X}|}{N}$$

The *standard deviation* and the *variance* are the most commonly used measures of disperson. The variance is similar to the average deviation except that the deviations from the mean are squared before they are summed and averaged. The standard deviation is simply the square root of the variance. The simplest interpretation of these results is, for the variance, that the average value of the deviations squared is 90.90 where the units are "squared percentages." For the standard deviation, the square root of the sum of the squared deviations is 9.5 percent.

$$\text{Variance} = \frac{\Sigma (X_i - \overline{X})^2}{N} \qquad \text{Standard deviation} = \sqrt{\frac{\Sigma (X_i - \overline{X})^2}{N}}$$

We can now use these measures to compare the variability of Nixon's vote with Humphrey's vote and Wallace's vote in the states. The coefficients shown in Table 7.4 suggest that there are roughly similar amounts of variation in Humphrey's and in Nixon's vote. The larger coefficients for Wallace correctly create the impression that there was more variation in his votes across the states, i.e., Wallace had strong support in several states very far from his mean vote.

Like all summary measures, these statistics have the disadvantage of losing, or not using, a good deal of information which is contained in the full set of data. Most notably, they tell us nothing about the shape of the distribution. For example, the Nixon and Humphrey vote percentages have quite similar values on these measures of dispersion, yet we made somewhat different observations about the Nixon and Humphrey vote distributions on the basis of the frequency distributions. The Nixon vote had a flat distribution with fewer extreme values; Humphrey's votes were peaked but with more extreme values in both directions.

Advantages of the average deviation:

(1) The average deviation has a straightforward interpretation as the average size of the variation around the mean.
(2) The average deviation is expressed in the units of the original variable.

Disadvantages of the average deviation:

(1) The average deviation is not commonly used and may be unfamiliar to readers.

Advantages of the standard deviation:

(1) The standard deviation is expressed in the units of the original variable.

Disadvantages of the standard deviation:

(1) In calculating the standard deviation the deviations are squared, which gives extreme values greater weight than those close to the mean. (There is no general substantive reason for overweighting extreme values any more than for underweighting them, although it is sometimes justified as cautious. The squaring of values is more properly viewed as a long-standing device for getting rid of the signs.)
(2) The standard deviation has no simple commonsense interpretation.

Advantages of the variance:

(1) The variance is used extensively in more advanced statistics.

Disadvantages of the variance:

(1) In calculating the variance the deviations are squared, which gives extreme values greater weight than those close to the mean.
(2) The variance has no simple commonsense interpretation and is expressed in no readily interpretable units.

This evaluation establishes a ranking that is contrary to current research practice; perhaps the best explanation is that both the variance and standard deviation have significance in other areas of statistics. Again there is not much to choose among the several measures of dispersion, and for the presentation of results there is no great hazard in following tradition.

We need to pay attention to variation for another reason. In the next chapter we will devote most of our attention to explaining the variation in a set of values. If there is very little variation in a variable, there is very little to explain. Analysts must decide that the amount of variation in a variable is of interest and worth explaining.

OVER TIME ELECTORAL DATA

So far we have focused our attention on the characteristics of one variable with observations from many units for a single interval of time. Now we need to ask what difference it makes if the variable is observed over many time intervals for a single unit. Often, of course, we are interested in series of elections and such variables as turnout or party strength. At one level this is merely a problem of data presentation—arraying a set of data points in a time-ordered fashion so that long-term trends as well as changes from one point to the next can be examined.

We are not likely to be concerned with data displays simpler than the one in Figure 7.7, which shows the percentages of the vote for President from 1828 to 1980. This is obviously a different form of distribution than discussed above but still understandable in a straightforward fashion. The percentages reveal eras of Democratic dominance as from 1932 to 1944 and eras of Republican dominance as from 1896 to 1908. The display in Figure 7.7 also shows the elections in which third parties made substantial inroads into the major party votes such as 1912 or 1968.

We could convert these data to a simple frequency distribution but then we would lose track of the time order. For the electoral analyst and certainly for the political historian, time order is often the primary interest. If we are totally indifferent to time order, then the data presumably would be treated as those above.

TREND ANALYSIS

It is customary in the examination of time series to focus on two elements, the overall trend in the data and the deviations from that trend. This can be seen as analogous to the central tendency and dispersion, but it is not the same.

First, we need to estimate the trend. Unfortunately, not much guidance exists in the substantive literature on appropriate methods to use. A simple but quite arbitrary method for estimating the trend is a *moving average* or a *moving median*. A moving average or a moving median is formed by calculating the mean or the median for a set of values, say, the three elections from 1828 to 1836, and then moving forward one election and

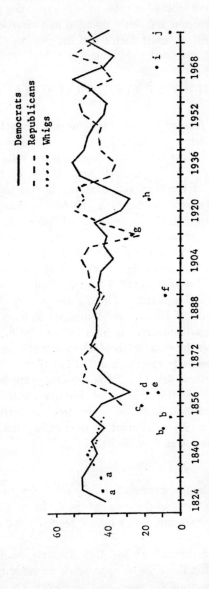

Figure 7.7 Presidential Vote in the United States, 1824-1980

Other parties gaining at least 5 percent of the vote: a. National Republican; b. Free Soil; c. American; d. Southern Democratic; e. Constitutional Union; f. People's; g. Bull Moose; h. Progressive; i. American Independent; j. Independent.

calculating a second mean or median, and so on. The choice of how many elections to use in the moving set is arbitrary but a choice of three, four, or five is usually appropriate.

It is more common in social science literature to find time series data smoothed with moving averages rather than moving medians and several texts offer guidance in the use of moving averages.[4] We decided to use a moving median in our illustration because the medians do a slightly better job of responding to lasting shifts in a series and ignore the occasional, isolated deviant observation. In these series and many others, the choice between mean and median will matter little in estimating either the trend or the deviations from the trend.

The smoothed data, the values of the moving median, are shown in Figure 7.8 for the Democratic percentage of the vote with the smoothed values connected by the solid line and the actual percentages left unconnected. The smoothed series reveals a century-long trend of declining Democratic vote for President followed by the dramatic increase in Democratic strength associated with the New Deal. The recent decades appear more erratic even with smoothed data, but once again there is a trend of declining Democratic support.

The large deviations from the smoothed trend in Figure 7.8 offer no surprises. Two deviating elections above the trend are the Democratic landslides of 1932 and 1964. The biggest deviation below the trend line was the Douglas vote in 1860, with the 1920 election the next largest deviating loss.

The more observations used in computing moving medians or moving averages, the smoother the resulting values will be and the larger the deviations from the smoothed line. It is important to view the deviations as a function of the particular trend line we have utilized. Our substantive interest in the deviations around a trend must be justified in terms of the meaning of the values of the trend. In Figure 7.8 we have left relatively few rough edges around the smoothed line by comparing each election with a median calculated from a set including the immediately adjacent elections plus the election itself. This accomplishes a high degree of smoothing which is appropriate if we intend to focus our attention on the smoothed line. These data and the differences between the medians and the actual percentages are shown in the first three columns of Table 7.5.

Sometimes for other substantive reasons we might focus our attention on deviations and use the same basic data for different purposes. We could inquire of these data which elections in the series depart dramatically from the elections both before and after. We would then compare each election with the smoothed values before it and after it as shown in the last two columns of Table 7.5. The elections of 1860, 1916, and 1964, with the

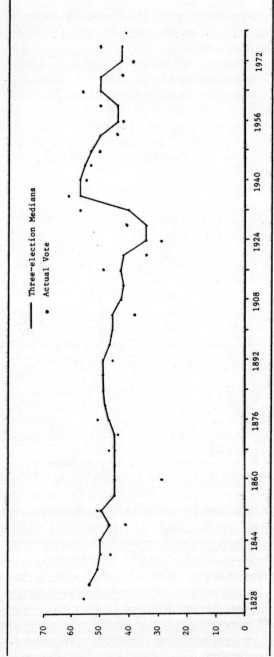

Figure 7.8 Democratic Vote for President and Three-Election Medians in the United States, 1828-1980.

TABLE 7.5   Democratic Vote for President, Three-Election Medians,
            and Deviations from the Medians, 1828-1980.

Year	Democratic Vote For President	Three Election Median with Adjacent Elections	Deviations from medians based on		
			two adjacent elections	three prior elections	three subsequent elections
1828	56				+5
1832	54	54	0		+4
1836	51	51	0		+4
1840	47	50	−3	−7	−3
1844	50	47	+3	−1	+5
1848	42	50	−8	−8	−3
1852	51	45	+6	+4	+6
1856	45	45	0	−5	0
1860	29	45	-16	−16	−16
1864	45	45	0	0	−2
1868	47	45	+2	+2	−1
1872	44	47	−3	−1	−5
1876	51	48	+3	+6	+2
1880	48	49	−1	+1	−1
1884	49	49	0	+1	+2
1888	49	49	0	0	+3
1892	46	47	−1	−3	0
1896	47	46	+1	−2	+4
1900	46	46	0	−1	+4
1904	38	43	−5	−8	−5
1908	43	42	+1	−3	+1
1912	42	43	−1	−1	+8
1916	49	42	+7	+7	+15
1920	34	34	0	−9	−7
1924	29	34	−5	−13	−28
1928	41	41	0	+7	−16
1932	57	57	0	+23	+2
1936	61	57	+4	+20	+8
1940	55	55	0	−2	+5
1944	53	53	0	−4	+9
1948	50	50	0	−5	+6
1952	44	44	0	−9	−6
1956	42	44	−2	−8	−8
1960	50	50	0	+6	+7
1964	61	50	+11	+17	+18
1968	43	43	0	−7	+2
1972	38	43	−5	−12	
1976	50	41	+9	+7	
1980	41	•		−2	

values circled show marked departures in the Democratic vote from the surrounding elections. These elections, of course, are familiar as "deviating elections" from Democratic voting patterns.[5] (A somewhat different set of elections would emerge from analysis of the Republican vote.)

The large shift in the electorate during the New Deal realignment can be seen in these last two columns of data in Table 7.5. The elections of 1932 and 1936 differ dramatically from the earlier elections, the boxed data in column five, just as 1924 and 1928 differ substantially from the subsequent elections as shown in the last column.

If smoothing data and examining the deviations focuses attention on the central tendency of a series, we can explore the dispersion of sets of observations over time as well. Using state data for the Democratic percentage of the presidential vote from 1828 to 1976, we can examine how concentrated or dispersed these state percentages were over the years. We might, for example, be interested in the amount of polarization in the behavior of state electorates at different points in the nation's history. In this illustration we make the calculations of the median, quartiles, minimum and maximum values for each election and plot the results in an over time graph as shown in Figure 7.9. The medians are connected by a solid line from election to election. The vertical distance between the first and third quartiles, also a solid line, represents the interquartile range. The minimum and maximum percentages for the Democratic presidential candidate are unconnected points. This plot not only reveals the amount of dispersion in state behavior at each election, it indicates at what level of Democratic support these patterns occur.

The state election data (with the exception of the Civil War era) show stable voting through the end of the nineteenth century, with most elections characterized by a rather high degree of concentration around the median. After the turn of the century, levels of Democratic support vary more and quite a few elections have larger interquartile ranges, i.e., vertical bars. In the 1920s, for example, the bulk of the states were more dissimilar from one another than they were in the 1950s.

The insensitivity of the maximum value, and to a considerable degree the range, can be seen in Figure 7.9. Because of the "solid south," Democratic percentages in the most Democratic state hovered just under 100 percent from 1900 to 1944. Clearly, the greatest decreases in the range occurred in those years when the southern states deserted the national Democratic Party. The range is, of course, determined by the maximum and minimum values and as such is affected by extreme values— even a single extreme case as Mississippi's 13 percent in 1964. For this reason, the interquartile range may be regarded as a more stable and valid estimate of the degree of dispersion of the states. On the basis of this

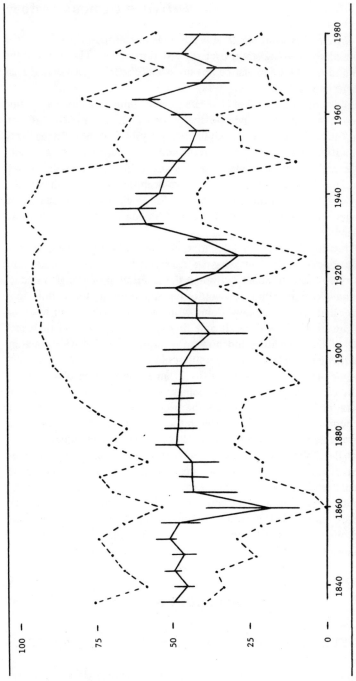

Figure 7.9 Democratic Vote for President in the United States with Medians, Quartiles, Minimum and Maximum Values, 1836-1980

measure, there has been remarkably little change in the dispersion in the Democratic vote among states over the last thirty years. The values of the median and quartiles have varied but the size of the interquartile range has stayed pretty much the same.

These examples by no means exhaust the techniques for exploring time series data, but they do indicate the types of simple displays that can become the basis for further analysis. No analyst of election data is likely to be indifferent to over time patterns and characteristics. The generally available methodological guidance in this area of analysis must be viewed with caution because most methods have been designed to eliminate the "underlying trends and interdependencies." The electoral analyst may be most interested in precisely what the methodologist is trained to remove from view.

The methodological principles of sound quantitative analysis are disarmingly simple: understand what we are trying to do and appreciate how close we have come to doing it. Even in the description of a single variable, this creates opportunities for confusion and error in the connections between what we are actually doing with the data analysis and what we say we are doing. It is difficult and tiresome to keep in mind the exact meaning of our indicators and how to interpret their behavior precisely given particular calculations based on that indicator.

It would not be foolish to argue that from primitive levels of analysis to the most complex our traditional training has reflected the "language of interpretation" while emphasizing the techniques of analysis. Unfortunately, perhaps, the training we offer in the language of interpretation is to focus ever more carefully on the characteristics of the techniques. Quantitative analysis, however, poses a double translation problem. We must constantly reassure ourselves that we are correctly translating concepts and statements about those concepts into indicators and calculations using those indicators, as well as correctly translating the results of the calculations back into verbal statements. Long before we have mastered the analysis of single variables, we move into the much more treacherous area of relationships among variables.

APPENDIX A

CONSTRUCTING INDICATORS WITH ELECTION DATA

In comparison with many areas of political history, election analysis yields variables that are easy to understand and have high levels of measurement. The main choices facing analysis are substantive, i.e., deciding precisely what meaning the analysis should have by deciding what to include. Relatively few compromises are forced on analysis because of missing or inadequate data, and no significant weapons of statistical analysis are denied us because of weaknesses in the measurement of our central variables.

We will attempt throughout to emphasize the substantive meaning of indicators in the belief that analysts should routinely make choices of indicators and their interpretation on substantive grounds. Our bias on this point is simple in principle: Technical criteria should come into play only after the substantive choices are made. In practice, however, this is a rule frequently surrounded by ambiguity. Analysts may not always recognize substantive implications in making technical choices.

The following presentation focuses on indicators of turnout and partisan strength since these are central to most election analysis and they are the components of more complex variables.

Turnout. The general meaning of turnout is clear enough: it is the number of voters in an election. Turnout almost always is expressed as a percentage of the eligible electorate, or

$$\text{Turnout} = \frac{\text{Number of voters}}{\text{Eligible electorate}}$$

The difficulties in estimating both the numerator and the denominator are such that we have devoted Chapter 5 by Ray Shortridge to them.

There is some uncertainty over precisely what information is desired for the numerator, although the range of numbers at stake is likely to be quite small. The "number of voters" could be the total number of voters who went to the polls on a given election day, or the number who actually voted in a particular race, usually the race with the largest number of votes cast. Given a choice we would almost certainly prefer the former, and almost always settle for the latter. Either value is bound to be an acceptable numerator for most analytic purposes. Analysts must be alert to the possibility that the highest vote total is in a race other than the top of the ticket.

Surely the problems in estimating total votes are slight in comparison with the problems confronted in estimating the eligible electorate. There are several unsatisfactory estimates usually available for the denominator. One is an official figure on registered voters which may either over- or underestimate the eligible electorate. Generally if the registration lists are regularly purged, they underestimate the eligible electorate. If the lists are not purged frequently, either because of legal requirements or lax administration, they can greatly overestimate the eligible electorate. Another alternative estimate is based on census data which can usually be manipulated to take into account most eligibility requirements with the exception of residence. But even with census data, some basic information is missing, such as citizenship status in the 1970 census.

For turnout estimates in elections close together in time these problems are not likely to be too troublesome, since the biases and errors should be fairly constant for short time periods.

Drop-Off. Another indicator based on turnout is designed to capture the decline in turnout in off-year elections. Actually the form of calculation used for drop-off could be applied to other comparisons, but its limited use in published research focuses on the net decline in turnout in off-year congressional elections compared with presidential elections. The definition is

$$\text{Drop-off} = \frac{\text{Number of voters in election 2}}{\text{Number of voters in election 1}}$$

where by convention election 1 would be the presidential and election 2 the congressional, usually generating a value below 100 percent. The formula used by W. Dean Burnham takes the reciprocal of the percentage.[6]

$$\text{Drop-off} = 1 - \frac{\text{Number of voters in election 2}}{\text{Number of voters in election 1}}$$

This has the effect of calibrating drop-off so that zero means no difference in turnout in the two elections, a small positive number means a slight decline in turnout and a large positive number means a big decline. If turnout in the following election increases over the first election, drop-off is negative.

Roll-Off. This index is based on the difference between the number of votes at the top of the ticket and the number of votes somewhere down the ticket at a single election. Roll-off is intended to assess the tendency the electorate to vote for the most important offices but fail to cast votes for lesser offices.[7] The calculation is uncomplicated.

$$\text{Roll-off} = \frac{\text{Number of votes for the top office - number of votes for the office receiving fewest votes}}{\text{Number of votes for the top office}}$$

There are some potential problems with this index that an analyst would need to clarify in order to interpret data correctly. One might want to exclude uncontested races from consideration. If the focus is on "voter fatigue," then one might decide to take the race at the bottom of the ticket regardless of its total vote. Selecting the race with lowest total vote maximizes the value of the index.

The top race on the ticket is not invariably the race with the largest total vote and an analyst could revise the index to take the difference between the largest and smallest vote wherever they occur. It should be noted, also, that this index captures *net* roll-off; if some voters fail to vote for the top office but do cast a vote for the race with the lowest vote total, they are lost in the aggregation of the data.

Candidate's Percentage of the Vote. This most common of all electoral variables is relatively free of problems. We indicated in the text our preference for a percentage based on the total vote in a race:

$$\frac{\text{Percentage for}}{\text{Candidate A}} = \frac{\text{Number of votes for Candidate A}}{\text{Total number of votes for all candidates}}$$

over a calculation based on only two candidates:

$$\frac{\text{Percentage for}}{\text{Candidate A}} = \frac{\text{Number of votes for Candidate A}}{\text{Number of votes for Candidates A and B}}$$

In many elections the percentages would be so similar that it would be difficult to distinguish them. When there are noticeable differences because of other candidates, the total vote percentage is preferred as it accurately reflects the relative strength of all the candidates.

Margin of Victory. This measure may be used simply to describe how close an election outcome was or as an indicator of electoral competition more generally. As a measure of the margin of victory it is clear enough.

$$\text{Margin of Victory} = \begin{array}{c}\text{Percentage of the Total Vote}\\\text{for the Winning Candidate}\end{array} - \begin{array}{c}\text{Percentage of the}\\\text{Total Vote for the}\\\text{Second Place Candi-}\\\text{date}\end{array}$$

Notice the two percentages are of the total vote so the margin of victory is expressed as a percentage of the total vote.

As an index of competition the margin of victory in one election is far from ideal. No simple electoral variable is likely to be a good indicator of either party activity or candidates' perceptions of the likely margin, two main bases of the conceptualization of competition in electoral analysis.[8]

Aggregate Ticket-Splitting. This measure is based on the difference between the largest and smallest percentage for a party in a set of races at one election. The formula should be calculated with percentages based on total vote.

$$\begin{array}{c}\text{Aggregate ticket-splitting}\\\text{for Party A}\end{array} = \begin{array}{c}\text{Larest percentage}\\\text{for Party A in election 1}\end{array} - \begin{array}{c}\text{Smallest}\\\text{percentage for}\\\text{Party A in elec-}\\\text{tion 1}\end{array}$$

A valid objection has been raised by Cowart to the index of aggregate ticket-splitting.[9] The index may seriously misrepresent individual-level voting behavior. Aggregate ticket-splitting measures *net* change and, of course, there may be considerable compensating change at the individual level that goes undetected in the aggregate data. Worse, there is no reason to suppose that the size of net change and the amount of total change vary together, so aggregate ticket-splitting cannot be interpreted as even a poor indicator of individual-level ticket-splitting. As long as analysts keep the meaning and limitations of aggregate ticket-splitting in mind, however, it is a usable index of net shifting in support within an election.

Party Strength (at one election). Analysts frequently require an estimate of party strength, usually making it a base of comparison for individual candidates. All aggregate indicators of party strength from the simple to the complex are to a degree unsatisfactory, especially if we conceptualize the variable in terms of individual partisan loyalty or party identification.[10]

One simple indicator of party strength is the vote for a *single candidate* from a race where in the judgment of the analyst, the race was decided purely, or nearly so, on the basis of party attachment. Usually this would be a race between unknown candidates for an unimportant office, but the key is that an argument can be made that party alone determined the vote choices. There are no special technical problems with this index but on substantive grounds we would usually doubt that any race was decided solely on partisan grounds. Because of clues provided by names, or mistakes in casting the vote, or whatever, some voters can be expected to vote for the "wrong" candidate from a partisan perspective. We must assume that these departures from expected party behavior cancel out.

More use is made of indices of *average party strength* drawing on the percentages for the party from several races.[11] The value in using the average of several percentages lies in the expectation that the deviant and idiosyncratic features of the several races will cancel out. This may be an unrealistic expectation, but it relieves the analyst of the burden of justifying a single election.

As long as the analyst does not take the average party strength too seriously it is a safe enough measure. It is an acceptable indicator of average party voting in a particular election, if not a persuasive assessment of underlying partisan loyalties. As a measure of party voting it can be used for comparison with the performance of a candidate of the party in that election and in general for assessments of relative party strength.

Party Strength (over time). A number of substantive interests lead analysts to seek over time indicators of party strength. The level of party support at each election can be based on a single race or the average from a set of races, simple assessments use moving averages of these values, or moving medians as illustrated previously. These provide fairly robust and easy to understand measures of party strength over time. Again there is an expectation that deviations will cancel out over the years. A most troublesome aspect of such over time indicators is coping with the variety of party labels and the changes in them to retain comparability in the series.

There are several more complex methods of assessing party strength but they go beyond the simple measurement and definitional considerations discussed here.[12]

NOTES

1. The data used in this chapter and the next were made available by the Historical Archive of the Inter-university Consortium for Political and Social Research.

2. A common measure of skewness takes advantage of this property.

$$\text{Skewness} = \frac{3(\text{Mean-Median})}{\text{Standard Deviation}}$$

3. For this particular measure, see John W. Tukey, *Exploratory Data Analysis* (Reading, MA: Addison-Wesley, 1977), 46. With a little imagination (and a computer), an analyst could devise endless variations of the trimean that would be more and more resistant to trivial changes in the data.

4. For more illustrations of smoothing with medians, see John W. Tukey, *Exploratory Data Analysis,* Ch. 7, 8. For more traditional treatments see Bruce L. Bowerman and Richard T. O'Connell, *Forecasting and Time Series* (Belmont, CA: Duxbury Press, 1979); Robert G. Brown, *Smoothing, Forecasting and Prediction of Discrete Time Series* (Englewood Cliffs, NJ: Prentice-Hall, 1962).

5. Many different techniques have been used to assess the shifts in electoral patterns. See, for example, Jerome M. Clubb, William H. Flanigan, and Nancy H. Zingale, *Partisan Realignment* (Beverly Hills: Sage Publications, 1980) Ch. 2, 3; Gerald Pomper, "Classification of Presidential Elections," *Journal of Politics* 29 (1967), 535-61; Walter Dean Burnham, *Critical Elections and the Mainsprings of American Politics* (New York: Norton, 1979); Lee Benson, Joel H. Silbey, and Phyllis F. Field, "Toward a Theory of Stability and Change in American Voting Patterns: New York State, 1792-1970," in Joel H. Silbey, Allan G. Bogue, and William H. Flanigan (eds.) *The History of American Electoral Behavior* (Princeton: Princeton University Press, 1978), 78-105.

6. Walter Dean Burnham, "The Changing Shape of the American Political Universe," *American Political Science Review* 59 (1965), 7-28.

7. *Ibid.*

8. William H. Flanigan and Nancy H. Zingale, "Measures of Electoral Competition," *Political Methodology* 1, 4 (Fall 1974), 31-60.

9. Andrew T. Cowart, "A Cautionary Note on Aggregate Indicators of Split-Ticket Voting," *Political Methodology* 1 (Winter 1974), 109-130; Burnham, "The Changing Shape of the American Political Universe."

10. If the goal of the aggregate analysis is to duplicate Converse's "normal vote," then the analyst is in trouble. If the conceptualization is closer to average party voting, then aggregate indicators are appropriate. For this contrast, see Philip E. Converse, "The Concept of a Normal Vote" in Angus Campbell, Philip E. Converse, Warren E. Miller, and Donald E. Stokes (eds.) *Elections and the Political Order* (New York: John Wiley, 1966), 9-39.

11. For a compendium of party strength estimates, see Paul T. David, *Party Strength in the United States, 1872-1970* (Charlottesville: University Press of Virginia, 1972).

12. See the references in note 5.

8

RELATIONSHIPS AMONG VARIABLES

William H. Flanigan
Nancy H. Zingale

Chapter 7 concentrated on the measurement and description of single variables. This chapter shifts the emphasis from the central tendency and distribution of one variable to the joint distribution or co-variation of two or more variables. Often we state this simply as wanting to know how much of the variation in one variable is explained by the variation in another variable.

In the previous chapter we found it impossible to describe the state patterns of presidential voting in 1968 without mentioning region, a second variable. We naturally think of states as located in regions, we see in the overall distribution a cluster of states from one region, and we begin to blur the neat distinction between describing the distribution of one variable and explaining the distribution of one variable in terms of a second variable.

We can pursue this line of analysis through several steps to assess more systematically the extent to which the regions of the nation account for the variation in the 1968 vote for Nixon across the states. Figure 8.1 displays the percentage of the vote for Nixon with each of the fifty states assigned to one of eight regions. Obviously some differences associated with the regions appear. The cluster of states in the South, for example, is collectively on the low side of the scale, while the prairie and mountain states are on the high side of the scale. Seeing all the states arrayed within

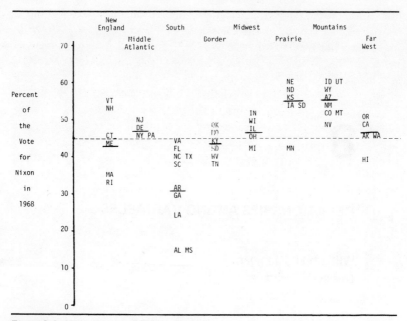

Figure 8.1 Nixon Vote in 1968 by Regions

regions may temper the impression created by one or two deviant states, for example, as in New England, where the low support for Nixon by Rhode Island and Massachusetts is balanced by Vermont and New Hampshire.

Although the image presented by Figure 8.1 is informative, we are not limited in our analysis to visual impressions. We can, in addition to examining the graphic display, pursue more precise quantitative assessment of the extent to which regional differences account for the dispersion of states around the national mean.

Within the arrays of states in Figure 8.1 there are dark lines representing the regional means and a dotted line for the national mean. If we were to ignore regions and simply calculate the deviation of each state from the national mean, square that deviation, and sum the squared deviations for all the states, $\Sigma (X_i - \bar{X})^2$, we have a measure of the national variation in the 1968 Nixon vote. This total national sum of squares is shown in Table 8.1 as 4734, and it is this overall variation in state behavior that we are trying to account for with the regional groupings.

The amount of the total variation that is attributed to regional differences is measured by another set of squared deviations, but in this calculation the deviation of a regional mean from the national mean is squared. The elements of the calculations for each region are shown in Table 8.1 with the regional mean, $\bar{X}_R$, the difference between the regional mean and the national mean, $(\bar{X}_R - \bar{X})$, the difference squared, $(\bar{X}_R - \bar{X})^2$, and then the multiplication of that term by the number of states in that particular region, $n_R(\bar{X}_R - \bar{X})^2$. The last column displays the contribution of each region to the overall capacity of the regions collectively to account for the variation of the states around the national mean. Obviously the South makes the major contribution to the explained sum of squares. Of the particular regional groupings used here, the South has the largest deviation and the most states.

The proportion of the total variation accounted for by the regions is

$$\frac{\text{explained sum of squares}}{\text{total sum of squares}} = \frac{\Sigma n_R(\bar{X}_R - \bar{X})^2}{\Sigma(X_i - \bar{X})^2} \quad \text{or} \quad \frac{2822}{4734} \quad \text{or 60 percent}$$

Notice that if each state were exactly on the regional mean, region would account for all the variation.

Another element of the total variation not shown in this analysis is the amount of variation remaining within the regions, the unexplained variation, $\Sigma n_R(X_i - \bar{X}_R)^2$ which is necessarily the difference between 4,734 and 2,822, or 1,913. To state these points differently, the overall variation is partitioned into two mutually exclusive elements, the "between group" variation and the "within group" variation. When handled in this way, all the variation is accounted for by two terms.

In this example using Nixon's vote in 1968, the capacity of the regions to account for so much of the state variation is associated with the rather distinctly different behavior of the southern, prairie, and mountain states. The other five regions have means quite close to the national mean as well as quite a bit of within-region variation. This examination of 1968 presidential voting illustrates "one-way analysis of variance" and introduces the idea of explaining or accounting for the variation in one variable with a second variable. This form of analysis assumes very little about the explanatory variable. All the analyst has to be able to do is assign the cases to one of the groups or categories—in this case assign each state to one (and only one) region. The regions are in no particular order and the calculations are not influenced in the least by the order in which the regions are handled. Since there is no order entailed in the analysis, the interpretation of the results must not incorporate any notions of order either.[1]

It is common for electoral analysts to utilize methods for explaining variation that make greater demands on the data but also yield much more

TABLE 8.1   Analysis of Nixon's 1968 Vote by Region.

Regions	Regional Mean $\overline{X}_R$	Regional Deviation $(\overline{X}_R - \overline{X})$	Deviations Squared $(\overline{X}_R - \overline{X})^2$	Number of States n	Sum of Squares $n_R(\overline{X}_R - \overline{X})^2$
New England	42.83	−1.45	2.10	6	12.62
Middle Atlantic	44.75	.47	.22	4	.88
South	31.50	−12.78	163.33	10	1633.28
Border	43.00	−1.28	1.64	6	9.83
Midwest	46.40	2.12	4.49	5	22.47
Prairie	53.17	8.89	79.03	6	474.19
Mountain	53.38	9.10	82.81	8	662.48
Far West	45.40	1.12	1.25	5	6.27

Explained Sum of Squares $= \Sigma_{n_R}(X_R - \overline{X})^2$ 2822.02

National Mean = 44.28

Total Sum of Squares $= \Sigma(\text{State \%} - \overline{X})^2 = 4734.04$

$$\frac{\text{Explained Sum of Squares}}{\text{Total Sum of Squares}} = \frac{2822.02}{4734.04} = .60 = \begin{array}{l}\text{60 percent of the total} \\ \text{variation is accounted} \\ \text{for by region.}\end{array}$$

informative interpretations. Actually, when analysts move beyond the simplicity of one-way analysis of variance to the use of correlation and regression analysis, they make some rather heroic assumptions about their data and the substantive nature of the behavior they hope to explain.

For the most part, this chapter deals with correlation and regression analysis as the major technique available for assessing relationships among variables. We will give most attention to this approach because (1) it is widely used, (2) it is relatively complicated, and (3) it leads to more advanced techniques and models. Most analysts will find correlation and regression a usable tool, since aggregate election data generally meet the requirements of this form of analysis and large amounts of computation can be readily performed by high speed data processing facilities.

LINEAR REGRESSION ANALYSIS WITH TWO VARIABLES

In order to present linear regression analysis we must reemphasize some points introduced previously. First, the variables used in regression analysis are expected to have *interval* properties, i.e., since we will perform arithmetic calculations on the values, presumably we believe the numerical values are meaningful and the differences between values are meaningful. Election data ordinarily satisfy this criterion. We take for granted that 46 percent of the vote for a candidate is meaningful and that 46 percent is 5 percent more than 41 percent or 12 percent less than 58 percent. (We have even greater confidence in this level of measurement in that we have no trouble agreeing that 46 percent is twice as big as 23 percent and half as much as 92 percent. Measures which allow such multiplication and division are referred to as *ratio* scales.) Recall that the regional categories had neither numerical values nor an order among them, thus representing a lower level of measurement. For the variables used in the following examples and for much of electoral analysis, measurement does not pose barriers to the use of quantitative techniques.

Second, we are assuming initially that it is appropriate to examine the pattern of relationship between two variables as if it were a straight line. Therefore, we refer to the analysis as *linear* regression. (We might soften this language somewhat and say that because linear analysis is easier to do and easier to interpret, we merely start with a straight line because we really do not know what to expect and we assume nothing. There is much truth in that, but since we rarely go further, it is awkward to characterize most linear regression analysis of electoral history as a first step to anything. Typically it is the last step.)

Third, linear regression analysis and the calculations used to generate summary measures for describing a pattern of relationship is only one way—but the almost universal way—of fitting a straight line to a set of data. A great advantage with linear regression analysis, an advantage that sometimes justifies serious violations of the rules for using the technique, is the widespread understanding of the linear equation and the coefficients calculated with it. Furthermore, as an analyst gains experience with linear regression analysis, it becomes more and more informative to violate rules in exploratory data analysis. We will confine our discussion to more conservative illustrations and applications. This is an area of work where it has never been necessary to teach bad habits.

Regression analysis provides precise information about crucial aspects of the relationship between two interval variables. Fitting a linear regression model to data reveals whether high or low values on one variable are associated with high or low values on the other and how uniform this pattern of variation is over the whole range of observed values. We can take advantage of these basic properties to describe patterns of variation in data with quite dissimilar substantive characteristics.

A common and not very demanding expectation about two variables is that one is a good predictor of another; if we know the value of one variable, we can make a prediction about the other. In electoral analysis, we might ask: Was the vote for Roosevelt in 1932 a good predictor of his vote in 1936? Is the vote for Governor a good predictor of the vote for U.S. Senator? Was Whig voting in the 1840s a good predictor of Republican voting after the Civil War? These questions are simple and straightforward in that the analyst has not committed himself to the existence of a causal connection among the variables. There is no change in the statistics of a relationship when the analyst asks "Does X cause Y?" as opposed to "Does X predict Y?" or "Is X associated with Y?" The difference is the analyst's imputing causation to the relationship between X and Y. The following examples could be viewed as mere association, but the analyst could extend the interpretation to include causal implications. Does a high level of competition cause a high level of turnout? Does the level of Democratic voting increase with unemployment and poverty? Does the vote for a popular candidate at the top of a ticket lead to increased support for unknown candidates down the ticket?

The same statistical calculations can be viewed in still another way by asking how much impact one variable has on another. Usually we are interested in this information when we suspect a causal relationship, but interpretation of the data is meaningful without assuming causal patterns. For example, regression analysis can reveal how much of an increase in the vote for Kennedy is associated with a 1 percent increase in the proportion of Catholics in a state. We can examine this relationship without being able to specify any precise causal patterns, and we might explicitly entertain the possibility that "percentage Catholic" stands for quite dissimilar causes that happen to be correlated with our explanatory variable. Even less of a connection between variables would be assumed in examining the co-variation of the percentage Catholic in the states and the level of unemployment. In such instances no direction of impact or influence is suggested but we still might be interested in their joint association.

To take another example, suppose we are examining the relationship between voter registration and turnout for a set of units. In the regression analysis, turnout would be the dependent variable and registration the explanatory variable. We do not, however, postulate that registration "causes" turnout, and yet there is an asymmetry in the relationship that goes beyond an interest in their joint association. We might call this relationship "partial dependence" or "conditional," but it is somewhere between joint association and causal impact.

Without being cavalier about the problems connected with causal theorizing and the causal implications in analysis, we should be aware that

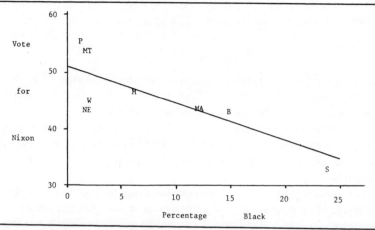

Figure 8.2 Scatterplot and Regression Slope for Regional Medians of Percentage Black in 1970 and the Vote for Nixon in 1968

regression analysis neither magically solves these problems nor contributes particularly to their complexity.

LINEAR REGRESSION EQUATION

The example of regression analysis that we will use to illustrate the calculation and interpretation of coefficients is the relationship between Nixon's vote in 1968 and the percentage black of the total population in 1970. These data will be smoothed to regional medians in order to simplify the display. The analysis takes the form of asking: Is racial composition a good predictor of the Nixon vote in 1968? Or, How much impact did racial composition have on Nixon's support? The regional medians for the two variables are shown in Figure 8.2, along with the elements we will use to discuss regression analysis.

Any straight line can be expressed by this equation

$$Y = a + b X$$

> where a, called the *intercept,* is the value of Y when
> X equals zero, and b is the *slope* of the line expressed
> as the amount of change in Y associated with a one
> unit change in X.

In Figure 8.2 the intercept, a, on the Y axis is 50.47 percent and the slope, b, is negative, −.61, which means the line slopes downward from the intercept. The regression equation for the straight line fitted to these data is, then,

$$Y = 50.47 - .61\ X$$

So for any value of X there is a corresponding expected value of Y which can be calculated from the intercept and the slope. In the regression equation the slope, b, is called the *regression coefficient*.

It is these *expected values* of Y which form a straight line, not the actual regional medians of Nixon's vote. Only if the linear fit were perfect would the observed values coincide exactly with the expected values on a straight line.

The deviations of the *actual* values of the dependent variable from these expected values measure the amount of error in our ability to predict the dependent variable and indicate the extent to which the data depart from a perfect linear relationship. If the actual observations fell exactly on the line of expected values, we could precisely predict or account for the vote for Nixon of each region knowing its racial composition; there would be no error and we could say in this case there was a perfect linear relationship between Nixon's vote and racial composition.

The constants in the regression equation, a and b, are solved for the straight line that is "best fitting" in a "least squares" sense. This best fitting straight line is the line which minimizes the sum of squared deviations, i.e., the squared errors in predicting the actual observations with the line. We can change the equation slightly to accommodate the errors, the over- and underestimates of expected values of Y

$$Y_i = a + b\ X_i + e_i$$

> Where e_i is an error term (or residual or deviation)
> that expresses the difference between the expected
> value, $\hat{Y}_i$, and the observed value, Y_i.

We can also introduce the symbol for an expected value, $\hat{Y}_i$, and revise the equation

$$\hat{Y}_i = a + b\ X_i$$

> Where $\hat{Y}_i$ is the expected value of Y for a particular
> X_i (and all $\hat{Y}_i$'s fall on the regression line).

In Figure 8.3 we have enlarged the upper left portion of Figure 8.2 to illustrate the terms in these equations. For New England there is a median

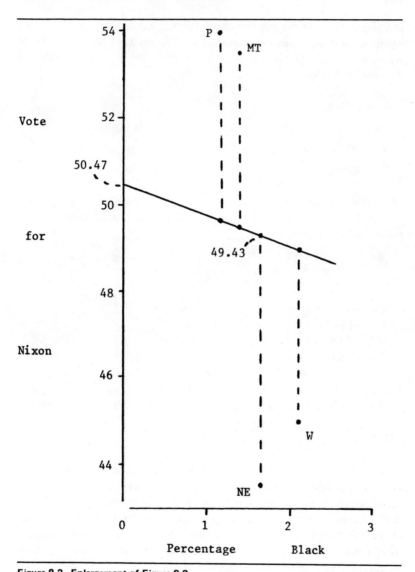

Figure 8.3 Enlargement of Figure 8.2

percentage black in the population of 1.7, the explanatory variable in the equation, and a median percentage of 43.5 in the vote for Nixon. These values enter the equations in these ways. First, for an expected value of the vote for Nixon

$\hat{Y}_i = a + b X_i$

$\hat{Y}_i = 50.47 - .61 \ (1.7)$ (where i is New England)

$\hat{Y}_i = 50.47 - 1.04$

$\hat{Y}_i = 49.43$

The linear regression equation generates an expected Nixon vote of 49.43 percent for New England, which is greater than the observed vote. We can express this error several ways.

$Y_i = a + b X_i + e_i$

or

$43.5 - (a + b X_i) + e_i$

$43.5 = (49.43) + e_i$

$43.5 - 49.43 = e_i$

$- 5.93 = e_i$

The actual vote is 5.93 percent below the expected value. More simply, the error is the difference between the expected and the observed values.

$e_i = Y_i - \hat{Y}_i$

Now to repeat a point, it is the error term for each observation which is squared in finding a best fitting line in a "least squares" sense. The line is found which minimizes the sum of squared error terms. This property is analogous to the sum of squared deviations around a mean mentioned in Chapter 7. We will leave to text books in statistics the conversion of formal criteria into calculating formulas because we propose to concentrate on interpretation of the results of regression analysis.

To review the two coefficients introduced so far, a, the intercept, and b, the regression coefficient, can be interpreted with the data displayed in Figure 8.2. In this example the intercept is not particularly interesting, but we can interpret it to mean that in the absence of blacks in a region (i.e., zero on the X variable) and given the behavior of these eight regions, we would expect Nixon to receive 50.47 percent of the vote. Since there are no such regions, there is no obvious substantive use to make of this estimate. (We could also find that if a region were 100 percent black, Nixon could be expected to receive a -10.53 percent of the vote.)

The regression coefficient, $-.61$, expresses the impact of the racial composition variable on the Nixon vote, and the negative slope of this line means that as the percentage of blacks in the population increased, Nixon's share of the vote declined. More precisely, with a 1 percent increase in the percentage black in the population, there was a .6 percent decline in the Nixon vote. Or similarly, a 10 percent increase in the black percentage in a region was accompanied by a 6 percent decline in the Nixon vote.

In order to exploit the opportunities in regression analysis fully we need to introduce several additional coefficients and discuss their interpretation. The extent to which the explanatory variable is successful in predicting the values of the dependent variable is evaluated by the *coefficient of determination,* r^2. In impressionistic terms, r^2 measures the amount of dispersion of the data points around the least squares line. The greater the dispersion, the smaller the value of r^2. More formally, the coefficient of determination represents the proportion of variation in the dependent variable accounted for by the explanatory variable and is calculated by dividing the "explained variation" in Y by the "total variation" in Y. The explained variation, or the explained sum of squares, can be thought of as the improvement in prediction provided by the expected values based on the regression equation. The explained sum of squares measures the dispersion of the expected values, $\hat{Y}_i$, around the mean, $\overline{Y}$,

$$\Sigma(\hat{Y}_i - \overline{Y})^2$$

Without the prediction of Y based on the regression equation, our "best guess" or expected value of each Y_i would be the mean of Y. The explained sum of squares goes beyond this and describes the amount of the variation in Y that can be explained by knowing the values of the explanatory variable. This amount explained is calculated as a proportion of the total variation in Y.

$$r^2 = \frac{\Sigma(\hat{Y}_i - \overline{Y})^2}{\Sigma(Y_i - \overline{Y})^2} = \frac{\text{Explained sum of squares}}{\text{Total sum of squares}}$$

r^2 is thus the proportion of the total variation in Y accounted for by the explanatory variable. In our example, the coefficient of determination is .66, which means that 66 percent of the regional variation in Nixon's vote in 1968 is accounted for by racial composition. The total sum of squares is 270.88 and the explained sum of squares is 178.78.

$$r^2 = \frac{\Sigma(\hat{Y}_i - \overline{Y})^2}{\Sigma(Y_i - \overline{Y})^2}$$

$$= \frac{178.78}{270.88}$$

$$= .66$$

In addition to allowing the "direction of impact" interpretation offered above, r^2 is one measure of joint association between two variables. And r^2 has the same value regardless of which variable is viewed as explaining the other.[2]

The *correlation coefficient*, r, is the square root of r^2, obviously, but is usually defined by a different formula,

$$r = \frac{\Sigma(X_i - \overline{X})(Y_i - \overline{Y})}{\sqrt{\Sigma(X_i - \overline{X})^2\,\Sigma(Y_i - \overline{Y})^2}} \text{ or } \frac{\Sigma(X_i - \overline{X})(Y_i - \overline{Y})}{N\,S.D._X\,S.D._Y}$$

where N is the number of observations and $S.D._X$ and $S.D._Y$ are standard deviations.

This formulation has no simple verbal interpretation which is an awkward feature of the correlation coefficient. So r is usually interpreted with the word "correlation" and in the illustration above we might say that the 1968 vote for Nixon and the percent black are negatively correlated at $-.81$.

Either r, the correlation coefficient, or r^2, the coefficient of determination, captures joint association between two variables, but tradition favors using the correlation coefficient. Besides comparability with earlier analysis, there is a further advantage with r in that it can indicate a negative relationship. Analysts are almost always interested in an inverse relationship between two variables, not just the magnitude of association.

Finally, in addition to the obvious connection between r and r^2, there are equivalences among the whole set of coefficients, and displaying them gives us an opportunity to begin to add subscripts to coefficients. For example, b_{YX} indicates that X is the explanatory variable while b_{XY} would indicate that Y is the explanatory variable. It is always possible to compute a second regression coefficient, b_{XY}, if it is possible to compute the first one, b_{YX}.

The product of two regression coefficients, b_{YX} and b_{XY}, equals the coefficient of determination which can be shown as either r^2_{YX} or r^2_{XY}.

$$r^2_{YX} = r^2_{XY} = b_{YX} \cdot b_{XY}$$

Both r and r^2 can be seen as measures of joint association between two variables because they are functions of the products of the two directional measures of impact.[3]

SUMMARY EVALUATION OF REGRESSION COEFFICIENT, CORRELATION COEFFICIENT, AND COEFFICIENT OF DETERMINATION

Before considering the advantages and disadvantages of the coefficients separately, we should review the characteristics of simple linear regression. The *least squares regression* line which is basic to all three coefficients has some of the statistical properties of a mean as noted above in Chapter 7: the deviations from the line measured in units of the dependent variable sum to zero, and the deviations squared sum to a minimum. A least squares fit has a tendency to be oversensitive to extreme values (because the deviations are squared) which may mean that the slope is deflected by a few outlying cases or a few cases can contribute most of the error. Visual inspection of the scatterplot alerts the analyst to these problems. On the basis of that inspection, the analyst can decide whether it is preferable to have the most deviant cases influence results or if they should on substantive grounds be excluded from the analysis.

Regression Coefficient (b_{YX}). The regression coefficient gives a numerical value to the slope of the regression line which is expressed as a change in units of the dependent variable associated with a change of one unit in the explanatory variable.

Advantages of a regression coefficient:

(1) The regression coefficient has a directional, causal interpretation once the analyst assumes one variable influences the other.
(2) The coefficient may be either positive or negative indicating the direction of relationship.
(3) When the dependent variable has a small variance in comparison with the explanatory variable, a regression coefficient takes on a small value regardless of how well the observations fit the line because very little change in the dependent variable is involved. This is a simple advantage of a regression coefficient over the other coefficients in that the analyst is warned not to take a relationship

seriously—even though it is strong—because not much variation is there to explain in the first place.

Disadvantages of a regression coefficient:

(1) Since a regression coefficient is based on the units in which the variables are measured, the size of the coefficient is not limited in range as the other coefficients are.

(2) A related disadvantage is the vulnerability of the regression coefficient to a change in scale of either variable.

(3) The regression coefficient must not be used as an indicator of joint association and the regression coefficient, b_{YX}, must not be assumed to express the other bivariate relationship, b_{XY}.

Correlation Coefficient (r_{YX}). The correlation coefficient gives a numerical value to the joint association between two variables. Basically, it describes how closely the data fit a straight line.

Advantages of a correlation coefficient:

(1) The correlation coefficient is an indicator of joint association.

(2) The value of a correlation coefficient may be positive or negative indicating the direction of relationship.

(3) The value of a correlation coefficient varies within a fixed range between +1.0 and −1.0 which is attractive for comparative purposes.

(4) The correlation coefficient is not affected by changing the scale of either or both variables.

(5) The correlation coefficient is the most commonly used measure of association in the analysis of aggregate political data.

Disadvantages of a correlation coefficient:

(1) The correlation coefficient has no simple, verbal interpretation.

(2) The correlation coefficient measures joint variation regardless of the amount of variation in the variables so it is possible for "uninteresting" patterns to yield a large coefficient.

Coefficient of Determination (r^2_{YX}). The coefficient of determination gives a numerical value for the joint association between two variables as well as a numerical value which has a directional interpretation. Like the correlation coefficient, it basically describes how well the observations fit a straight line.

Advantages of a coefficient of determination:

(1) The coefficient of determination is an indicator of joint association.

(2) The numerical value of the coefficient of determination is interpretable as the percentage of variation in one variable accounted for by the other, and this interpretation is applicable to the variables either way, since $r^2_{YX} = r^2_{XY}$.

(3) The coefficient of determination varies within a fixed range between +1.0 and 0.0.

(4) The value of the coefficient of determination is not affected by the changing scale of either or both variables.

Disadvantages of a coefficient of determination:

(1) The coefficient of determination does not indicate the direction of relationship since it is always positive. (This is not so serious in practice as it might appear since we can always discover the direction of relationship in other ways and we almost always know the direction anyway if we are familiar with the data.)

(2) Like the correlation coefficient, the coefficient of determination measures joint association regardless of the variation in the variables so it is possible for an "uninteresting" pattern to yield a large coefficient.

MULTIPLE LINEAR REGRESSION

Many different topics naturally follow promptly upon the presentation of simple linear regression but we will deal with only a few in the remaining pages: multiple regression analysis, dummy variables, joint effects, and curvilinear regression. The linear regression equation can be extended to two explanatory variables so that we can inquire how well racial composition and income together account for the vote for Nixon. Beyond assuming the patterns are linear as in two variable analysis, the multiple regression equation specifies a particular relationship between the explanatory variables. Many forms of interrelationship among explanatory variables are imaginable but we will concentrate on a simple, conventional version, the *additive* equation

$$Y_i = a + b_{YZ.X} Z + b_{YX.Z} X + e_i$$

or for the expected value of the dependent variable

$$\hat{Y}_i = a + b_{YZ.X} Z + b_{YX.Z} X$$

And as in the simple case, the error term, e_i, or the residual, is the difference between the actual and expected value

$$e_i = Y_i - \hat{Y}_i$$

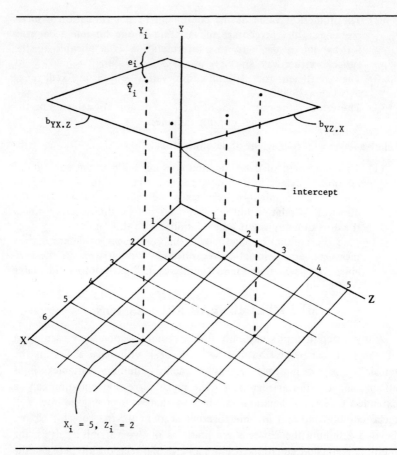

Figure 8.4 Graphical Representation of Multiple Regression Analysis

Customarily the multiple regression equation with two variables is presented graphically as a plane in a three-dimensional space as shown in Figure 8.4. The multiple regression equation is solved for a least squares, best fitting plane for two explanatory variables by minimizing the sum of squared errors. Once there are more variables the calculations are still straightforward, but there are no graphical presentations for four dimensional space and beyond.

The partial regression slopes, $b_{YZ.X}$ and $b_{YX.Z}$, illustrated in Figure 8.4 as the edges of the plane, are usually expressed as "the amount of change in Y associated with a change of one unit in Z controlling for X." We might equally appropriately say "the linear influence of Z on Y controlling for the linear influence of X." The various expressions of this and other coefficients leave out one or more characteristics of the equation since it would be extremely awkward stylistically to make full reference to all of the properties of which we need to be aware. For example, the additive nature of the equation can be emphasized by saying "the impact of Z on Y at (or for) each value of X," or "the impact of Z on Y holding X constant."

A *partial correlation coefficient,* e.g., $r_{YZ.X}$, expresses "the joint association between Y and Z controlling for X." The partial correlation coefficient is a standardized restatement of the relationship expressed by the partial regression coefficient

$$r_{YZ.X} = b_{YZ.X} \cdot \frac{S.D._{Z.X}}{S.D._{Y.X}}$$

where S.D. $_{Z.X}$ and S.D.$_{Y.X}$ are standard deviations of the variables Z and Y controlled by X.

The *coefficient of partial determination,* $r^2_{YZ.X}$ or $r^2_{YX.Z}$, has two interpretations. Obviously, as the square of the partial correlation, the coefficient of partial determination is a measure of joint association. There is a second interpretation that is more unidirectional and can be seen in this alternative formulation

$$r^2_{YZ.X} = \frac{R^2_{Y.ZX} - r^2_{YX}}{1 - r^2_{YX}}$$

where $R^2_{Y.ZX}$ is the coefficient of multiple determination describing the amount of variation in Y explained by Z and X jointly.

In this view the coefficient of partial determination, $r^2_{YX.Z}$ can be described as the "proportion of remaining variation in Y not accounted for by X that is explained by the addition of Z." The coefficient describes a proportion of the *remaining* variation, it should be noted, not of the total variation in Y—that value is captured by the numerator alone and curiously is not usually analyzed.

In addition to a coefficient of partial determination for each explanatory variable, there is a *coefficient of multiple determination,* R^2, for the entire equation expressing the percentage of variation in Y accounted for by the linear, additive influence of all the explanatory variables together. The formula for the coefficient of multiple determination is the same as in the two-variable case but, of course, the expected values, $\hat{Y}_i$, are computed differently. In our illustration

$$R^2{}_{Y.XZ} = \frac{\Sigma(\hat{Y}_i - \overline{Y})^2}{\Sigma(Y_i - \hat{Y})^2} = \frac{\text{explained sum of squares}}{\text{total sum of squares}}$$

Two variables, racial composition and income, explain 69 percent of the variation in the 1968 Nixon vote, $R^2{}_{Y.XZ} = .69$.

The coefficient of multiple correlation, $R_{Y.XZ}$, is the square root of the coefficient of multiple determination, obviously, and has a value of .82. Unlike other correlation coefficients the multiple correlation cannot take on a negative value, but varies only from 0 to +1.0. It is also correct to interpret the multiple correlation coefficient as the simple correlation between the actual and expected values.

$$R_{Y.XZ} = r_{\hat{Y}Y}$$

One more general topic under multiple regression analysis will be discussed—the use of *standardized variables* in the equation. It is possible to generate regression coefficients that are not affected by the scale or the dispersion of the variables. When we enter standardized variables in regression equations, we call the resulting coefficients *standardized regression coefficients*. There are many types of transformation; the one discussed here is usually called a "Z-score" or a "standard score." The process of transforming a variable is straightforward.[4]

$$\text{"Z"}_{Yi} = \frac{(Y_i - \overline{Y})}{S.D._Y}$$

A variable standardized as z-scores has both positive and negative values, the new scores sum to zero, so the mean is zero and the standard deviation of the new variable necessarily has a value of one.

When we compute a regression equation with variables transformed to z-scores, the standardized regression coefficients are called "beta coefficients." The impact of the variables can be assessed in a comparable way, in terms of each variable's standard deviation. In our example, one explanatory variable is measured in dollars and the other in percentage black. Assessing impact on the vote in terms of unit change in dollars or percentage black makes direct comparison of the two variables meaningless. The transformation provides one form of comparability: each variable is standardized so that values are expressed in standard deviation units over or under the mean. The beta coefficients can be directly calculated from regression coefficients and the standard deviations.

$$\beta_{YZ.X} = b_{YZ.X} \frac{S.D._Z}{S.D._Y}$$

$$\beta_{YX.Z} = b_{YX.Z} \frac{S.D._X}{S.D._Y}$$

In our example, the unstandardized partial regression coefficient for income was $-.002$ which, of course, is scaled to a unit change of one dollar but becomes a beta coefficient of $-.19$. The two coefficients for racial composition change much less, from $-.68$ to a beta coefficient of $-.90$. Beta coefficients have values and interpretations close to partial correlation coefficients and they can be represented with similar formulas

$$\beta_{YZ.X} = b_{YZ.X} \frac{S.D._Z}{S.D._Y}$$

$$r_{YZ.X} = b_{YZ.X} \frac{S.D._{Z.X}}{S.D._{Y.X}}$$

The difference is the standard deviations on the right, one set is for plain variables and the other for residualized variables. Usually $\frac{S.D._Z}{S.D._{Z.X}}$ does not equal $\frac{S.D._{Y.X}}{S.D._Y}$ so $\beta_{YZ.X}$ will not equal $r_{YZ.X}$. In our example $\beta_{YZ.X}$ equals .19 and $r_{YZ.X}$ equals .28 where Y is the Nixon vote in 1968, Z is income, and X is racial composition. Standardized regression coefficients and partial correlation coefficients rarely have precisely the same values, but they reflect the same overall pattern in relation to one another.

SUMMARY EVALUATION OF
MULTIPLE REGRESSION ANALYSIS

The main coefficients presented in connection with multiple regression analysis based on the simple additive model can be summarized and evaluated as follows:

Coefficient of Multiple Correlation $(R_{Y.XZ})$. The coefficient of multiple correlation describes with a numerical value the association between Y and the joint linear impact of X and Z. Basically, it describes how well the data fit a plane or a higher order shape.

Advantages of a coefficient of multiple correlation:

(1) The value of the coefficient varies within a fixed range between 0 and +1.0 which is attractive for comparative purposes.
(2) The coefficient is not affected by a change in scale of any of the variables.

Disadvantages of a coefficient of multiple correlation:

(1) The coefficient has no simple, verbal interpretation.
(2) The coefficient measures the association with the dependent variable regardless of the amount of variation in that variable so "uninteresting" patterns may yield large coefficients.

Coefficient of Multiple Determination ($R^2_{Y.XZ}$). The coefficient of multiple determination describes the proportion of variation in Y accounted for by the linear, additive impact of the explanatory variables.

Advantages of a coefficient of multiple determination:

(1) The coefficient has a straightforward interpretation as the percentage of the variation in the dependent variable accounted for by the equation.
(2) The coefficient varies within a fixed range between 0 and +1.0 which allows comparison with other equations.
(3) The value of the coefficient is not affected by a change in scale of any of the variables.

Disadvantages of a coefficient of multiple determination:

(1) Like the multiple correlation coefficient, this coefficient measures explained variation regardless of how much variation there is to explain, so it is possible for an "uninteresting" pattern to yield a large coefficient.

Partial regression coefficient ($b_{YX.Z}$). The partial regression coefficient gives a numerical value for the amount of change in Y associated with a unit change in X controlling for Z (or all the other variables in the equation). The coefficient assesses the partial regression slope controlling for all the other variables and the coefficient is usually interpreted as describing the unique impact of one variable in the presence of the other variables.

Advantages of a partial regression coefficient.

(1) The coefficient has a directional, causal interpretation once the analyst assumes one variable influences the other.

(2) The coefficient may be either positive or negative indicating the direction of the controlled relationship.

(3) The impact of the explanatory variable is expressed in readily interpretable units.

(4) When the dependent variable has a small variance left to explain, the partial regression coefficient takes on a small value regardless of the strength of relationship.

Disadvantages of a partial regression coefficient:

(1) The coefficient is influenced by the units of analysis of both variables, so comparison is hazardous with other coefficients and equations.

(2) The coefficient is not bounded in value, so comparisons are difficult.

Standardized regression coefficient ($\beta_{YX.Z}$). The standardized regression coefficient, or beta coefficient, assesses the impact of X on Y controlling for Z and normalized for the distributional properties of Y and X. The standardized regression coefficient is basically a measure of association.

Advantages of a standardized regression coefficient:

(1) The coefficient has a directional interpretation and may be either positive or negative in value.

(2) The coefficient is bounded in value between +1.0 and −1.0.

Disadvantages of a standardized regression coefficient:

(1) The coefficient has no simple verbal interpretation.

(2) Since both variables are normed for their distributional characteristics, the coefficient does not reflect amount of impact so much as strength of association.

Coefficient of Partial Correlation ($r_{YX.Z}$). The partial correlation coefficient measures the joint association between Y and X controlling for the other variables.

Advantages of a coefficient of partial correlation:

(1) The value may be either positive or negative indicating the direction of relationship.

(2) The coefficient is bounded in range between +1.0 and −1.0.

(3) The coefficient is not affected by a change in scale of either variable.

Disadvantages of a coefficient of partial correlation:

(1) The coefficient has no simple interpretation.

(2) The coefficient measures joint association regardless of the amount of variation involved, so it is possible for "uninteresting" patterns to yield large values.

Coefficient of Partial Determination ($r^2_{YX.Z}$). The coefficient measures the proportion of variation in Y not accounted for by Z (or all the other variables) that is explained by the addition of X. It is the proportion of remaining variation in Y accounted for uniquely by the addition of X.

Advantages of a coefficient of partial determination:

(1) The coefficient is a measure of joint association.
(2) The coefficient has a directional interpretation as the percentage of remaining variation in Y accounted for by X after the other variables have accounted for all the variation they can.
(3) The coefficient varies between 0 and +1.0.
(4) The coefficient is not affected by changes in scale of any of the variables.

Disadvantages of a coefficient of partial determination:

(1) The coefficient expresses the amount of remaining variation explained regardless of how much variation remains, so it may describe a high precentage of a small amount of variation.

Obviously the partial coefficients have different strengths and weaknesses and potentially would serve different substantive purposes. In order to clarify and distinguish the substantive interpretation of each coefficient we will present them by way of summary.

$b_{YZ.X}$ = the amount of change in Y (expressed in units of Y) associated with a one unit change in Z controlling for X.

$\beta_{YZ.X}$ = the change in Y associated with a change in Z (expressed in standardized units of dispersion) controlling for X.

$r_{YZ.X}$ = the joint association between Y and Z controlling for X.

$r^2_{YZ.X}$ = the joint association between Y and Z controlling for X, and the proportion of the remaining variation in Y accounted for by Z controlling for X.

COMMENTS ON MULTIPLE REGRESSION ANALYSIS

The main substantive use of regression analysis with two or more explanatory variables has been to control for "all other factors," i.e., the intent has been to isolate the unique contribution of each explanatory variable in the presence of all other variables. The estimate of the unique effect of a particular variable is not a highly valuable one unless the analyst can argue that all the other appropriate variables have been controlled in the analysis. If important variables are omitted from this analysis (because data are unavailable or because the analyst has conceptualized the problem inadequately or whatever), the impact of these missing factors may be erroneously attributed to the variables included in the equation. So, it is easy for us to exaggerate the unique contribution of variables.

It is also possible for us to control excessively the impact of a variable by including in the analysis several variables which to some degree measure the same thing. As two or more explanatory variables become more highly interrelated, they control away each others' variation—they reduce their explanatory potential. The analyst's desire to include "all other factors" in the analysis may lead to the inclusion of overlapping and redundant variables, with the consequence that no one variable appears to have much impact because of the presence of the others. This may be viewed as a measurement problem or conceptual confusion, but it will create under-estimations of the unique contributions of factors to the explanation of the behavior of the dependent variable.

In its most extreme form, the interrelationship of two explanatory variables prevents solution of the regression equation. When two explanatory variables are perfectly related or when one explanatory variable is perfectly related to any combination of other explanatory variables in the equation, we have perfect "multicollinearity" and the equation cannot be solved.

These difficulties are associated with the efforts to discover unique effects for particular explanatory variables; the coefficients of multiple correlation and determination are not distorted by over- or undercon-trolling an explanatory variable. The emphasis on unique contributions to an explanation controlled for all other variables is not appropriate for all conceptualizations. We may believe our explanatory variables *interact* with one another, that they have a varying impact on the dependent variable depending on the value of another variable. The additive multiple regres-sion equation yields a best-fitting solution assuming that the impact of each explanatory variable is constant across all values of all the other variables. The great bulk of electoral analysis has retained the familiar additive model and not ventured into the practically limitless domain of nonadditive variations of the model. We may theorize about nonadditive relationships but we fit data to additive models. Once we consider the possibility of departing from the additive model, we need more analytic guidance from our theories, because there are so many nonadditive oppor-tunities that trial-and-error is not feasible. The additive model is a safe choice that initially gets by with little in the way of justification, and most analysts will question it only when expected relationships fail to material-ize.

Closely connected with doubts about additivity is a second major departure from the conventional regression model—abandoning linearity.

Once again, we need theoretical guidance for this step because there are endless nonlinear variations of the data that might be tried. Just as we specify the linear form of the relationship in the traditional model, we must specify the precise nonlinear form in order to solve the equation and to interpret the results. Furthermore, as we allow our curvilinear models to become more and more complex, the indicators of overall fit, the coefficients of correlation and determination, cannot decline in value. The coefficients will either get larger, signaling a better fit, or remain unchanged because they have reached a maximum value. On the other hand, most departures from linearity become difficult, if not impossible, to describe in words that remain faithful to the actual form of the relationship.

Analysts, not to mention their readers, are much more comfortable with the additive, linear model. Even when analysts depart from the basic model, they do not always modify their interpretative language to reflect the change in meaning that their model implies. In the final section of this chapter we will draw attention to several simple departures from the conventional model, but these are merely illustrative and readers must consult other texts for a full treatment of these topics.

APPLICATIONS OF REGRESSION ANALYSIS

We have selected three modifications of basic regression analysis to illustrate the types of applications that can be developed for electoral analysis. In each case, these adaptations address a weakness in the traditional approach.

All of the complications in the assessment of the relationship between Y and X when controlling for Z arise because there is usually some relationship between the explanatory variable, X, and the control variable, Z. If there is no relationship between the explanatory variable and the control variable, then the control variable does not affect the relationship between the explanatory variable and the dependent variable. In other words, the control has no impact. Typically, explanatory variables are related to some degree, hence, the control makes a difference—and causes complications. The more highly interrelated two explanatory variables are, the more difficult it is to estimate confidently their separate effects. When the explanatory variables are highly interrelated, the condition is referred to as *multicollinearity* but problems exist at all levels of interrelationship.[5]

FLIP-FLOP REGRESSION

When two explanatory variables are related, it is possible for an analyst to take a substantive interest in their *combined effects* as well as their separate effects. Multiple coefficients assess overall relationships between the dependent variable and all the explanatory variables without attention to their unique contributions to that relationship. Traditional use of partial coefficients gives estimates of unique effects associated with variables without any assignment to joint or combined effects.[6] But the more highly interrelated we find the explanatory variables, the more uneasy we should be with the complete decomposition of the relationship into unique effects for each explanatory variable. Another method for assigning effects, with the unpromising name of "flip-flop regression," conservatively assigns much of the explanation of the dependent variable to joint effects, an impact shared by two or more explanatory variables.

The technique is uncomplicated but somewhat inefficient with computer processing when more than three variables are involved. If we treat the coefficient of multiple determination as an estimate of overall explanatory power for two variables X and Z, we can subtract the simple coefficients of determination for each variable from the multiple coefficient.

$$R^2_{Y.XZ} - r^2_{YX} = Z^* = \text{additional impact of Z}$$

$$R^2_{Y.XZ} - r^2_{YZ} = X^* = \text{additional impact of X}$$

Z^* and X^* can be described as the additional amount of variation in Y accounted for by the addition of each variable to the explanation. If X and Z are related to any extent, Z^* plus X^* will be less than $R^2_{Y.XZ}$. The difference between Z^* plus X^* and $R^2_{Y.XZ}$ is the joint impact of X and Z.

$$R^2_{Y.XZ} - (Z^* + X^*) = \text{joint impact of X and Z.}$$

If X and Z are highly related, there will be small unique effects and most of the overall effect will be joint.

Notice that the flip-flop regression values sum to the coefficient of multiple determination. These estimates of joint and separate effects derived from "flip-flop regression" have, so far as we are aware, been utilized only once in aggregate analysis of elections, but they offer an attractive alternative to traditional methods which ignore joint effects.[7]

Flip-flop regression minimizes the estimates of unique effects and leaves the maximum amount of the explanation as shared impact. For some explanatory variables joint effects may not be meaningful, but for much of electoral analysis leaving variables entangled may display appropriate caution. Analysts can decide whether to include estimates that perhaps exaggerate shared effects along with estimates that rule out shared effects altogether.

Dummy Variables. Under many circumstances analysts employ concepts and indicators that are merely categories, i.e., nominal variables rather than interval. It is, of course, desirable for the analyst to remain faithful to the nominal character of a conceptualization and translate the statements of relationship into nominal form when appropriate. Dummy variables afford that opportunity. Perhaps dummy variable analysis offers the simplest and most promising expansion in the use of multiple regression analysis introduced in recent years. A dummy variable is simplicity itself although it is quite a modification of an ordinary interval variable. A dummy variable has only two values, by convention 0 and 1, which code the presence or absence of a characteristic. For example, a dummy variable for region could score the South as 1 and the non-South as 0. Such a variable can be used without complication in simple regression analysis as an explanatory variable.

We can return to the illustration presented at the beginning of this chapter and utilize state data with the 1968 vote for Nixon as the dependent variable and the regional dummy variable as the explanatory variable. Using those data we get the following values:

$$Y = 47.5 - 16.0 \, X$$

We can say that region has an impact of 16 percentage points on Nixon's vote or, alternatively, that the difference between the regions is 16 percent. (The usual interpretation of the regression coefficient as the change in Y associated with a unit change in X is stated differently, since with a dummy variable all the change in X is captured with two categories.) It can be noted that the intercept, a, is the average value for the non-South (when X equals 0) and that a + b equals the average for the South. For this equation the r^2 is .43. Actually, this regression analysis with one dummy variable is equivalent to one-way analysis of variance with two categories in which 43 percent of the variance is explained by the two categories.

Usually we are interested in more than two categories for our explanatory efforts. To continue the illustration with regional analysis of the

Nixon vote in 1968, a set of dummy variables can be generated to represent the eight regions in Figure 8.1. The variables could be scored for the states as follows:

Variable 1, New England = 1, all other states = 0.

Variable 2, Middle Atlantic = 1, all other states = 0.

Variable 3, South = 1, all other states = 0.

Variable 4, Border = 1, all other states = 0.

Variable 5, Midwest = 1, all other states = 0.

Variable 6, Prairie = 1, all other states = 0.

Variable 7, Mountain = 1, all other states = 0.

These dummy variables fully score the regions, and it is important to remember to eliminate one variable before entering the set into regression analysis. If all eight variables were used, there would be perfect multicollinearity and the regression equation could not be solved. In order to assess the overall impact of the eight regions collectively, it does not matter which one of the dummy variables is eliminated. The coefficient of multiple determination for this set of regional dummy variables with the 1968 Nixon vote is .60, which corresponds precisely with the percentage of explained variation found in the example at the beginning of this chapter.

While regression analysis with dummy variables does not cause us to abandon the additive, linear equations, it makes it possible to extend the interpretations to nonadditive patterns in a rather simple fashion. We will not pursue the many possibilities for combining variables that permit nonadditive explanations, but it should be noted that many of our ideas about relationships among factors influencing electoral behavior should be translated into nonadditive patterns.[8]

NONLINEAR REGRESSION ANALYSIS

It is important to understand what happens when we abandon the assumption of linearity in nonlinear regression analysis. It should be emphasized that there is a basic hazard in abandoning straight line fits. Increasingly complex curves cannot provide a worse fit to the data and usually improve the fit; yet curves are more difficult to interpret than straight lines. Therefore as the fit improves, the interpretation becomes less straightforward.

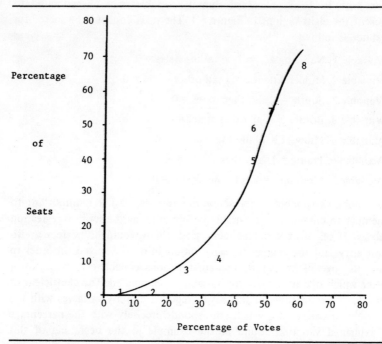

Figure 8.5 Scatterplot of Hypothetical Election Data Showing the Percentages of Seats and Votes for a Party

There are not as many familiar illustrations of curvilinear models in electoral analysis as perhaps there should be, and this reflects the relatively undeveloped nature of both theory and analysis in electoral history. A fairly simple example of nonlinear analysis is provided by the expected relationship between a party's percentage of the vote for Congress and the percentage of the seats won by the party.[9] The expectations are quite straightforward. With a set of winner-take-all, single-member constituencies, we expect that a party with a small share of the vote will win no or very few seats. Furthermore, an increase in popular support from 5 percent to 10 percent may yield no additional seats in the legislature. On the other hand a 5 percent difference between 45 and 50 percent could be expected to yield much more than 5 percent of the seats. Finally if a party were to garner around 90 percent of the popular vote, they would already have so many of the seats that it would be difficult to match a gain in votes with a gain in seats.

These several expectations about the relationship between votes and seats is not at all linear. If we plot this expected pattern, it will look more or less like the solid curved line in Figure 8.5. We do not suppose real data

TABLE 8.2   Hypothetical Data Representing the Percentage of Votes and Seats Received by a Party in a Series of Elections.

Elections	Percentage of Votes	Percentage of Seats	Natural Logarithms of Percentages Votes	Natural Logarithms of Percentages Seats
1	5	1	1.6	0
2	15	2	2.7	.7
3	25	8	3.2	2.1
4	35	12	3.6	2.5
5	45	40	3.8	3.7
6	45	50	3.8	3.9
7	50	55	3.9	4.0
8	60	70	4.1	4.2

$$r^2 = .90$$

$$\log_{seats} = -3.5 + 1.84 \log_{votes}$$

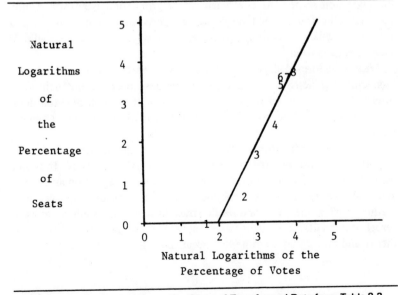

Figure 8.6   Scatterplot and Regression Slope of Transformed Data from Table 8.2

will fall exactly on the curved line anymore than we did with the linear model but we are interested in how good the fit of the data to the line is. We have added some hypothetical data around the curved line in Figure 8.5.

In order to assess how strong the relationship is we convert the data from an expected curvilinear pattern into an expected linear pattern. In order to change a curve like the one in Figure 8.5 into an expected straight line we take the log of the values on both the dependent and explanatory variables. Whereas with the original data we expected a perfect relationship to form a curve, with the transformed data we expect a perfect relationship to form a straight line.

By *transforming* the two ratios by their natural logs a curvilinear form of relationship has been translated into a linear form. Typically we handle curvilinear relationships in this way; they are reexpressed as linear equations which we solve by least squares. However, the meaning of the transformed equation is basically curvilinear and the interpretation of the results should be in terms of the curvilinear form of the relationship.

As can be seen in Table 8.2, the transformation of the values for election 4 converts the value of votes from 35 percent to 3.6, and the value of seats from 12 percent to 2.5. An ordinary linear regression analysis is carried out with the transformed values. The scatterplot of the transformed values in Figure 8.6 reveals a tight fit around the solid line, the regression slope. The coefficient of determination is .90 which indicates that the transformed variables are tightly fit to a straight line *and* that the original expectation that the variables were related in a curvilinear manner is supported.[10]

With transformed data, we are not always interested in the value of regression coefficients or the intercept because they are not helpful in interpreting the original variables. The coefficient of determination does, however, indicate how well the original data conform to the curvilinear pattern.

These topics constitute only a beginning in the appreciation of the opportunities and hazards in the use of regression analysis. It is not inconsistent to tell readers that most applications of regression analysis to electoral history have been misguided in some respects, and yet urge further applications. The failures illustrate mistaken translations between verbal statements and quantitative analysis; these have been failures of theory and interpretation more than weaknesses in the techniques.

NOTES

1. There is potential for "overinterpreting" results here. Suppose we use a set of categories in an analysis of variance design that has an obvious order, say groupings from high income to low income. We must not interpret our results as if the obvious ordering produced an explanation based on order–only that the grouping produced the results. The order may or may not have been reflected in the capacity of the set of categories to account for variation. This caution also applies to dummy variables discussed below.

2. The common formulas for r^2 do not lend themselves to the revelation that r^2_{YX} must equal r^2_{XY} although it is clear enough from the formula for r. The coefficient of determination can also be defined in terms of the failure to predict Y

$$r^2 = 1 - \frac{\Sigma(Y_i - \hat{Y}_i)^2}{\Sigma(Y_i - \overline{Y})^2} = 1 - \frac{\text{unexplained sum of squares}}{\text{total sum of squares}}$$

3. This can be seen in these equivalences:

$$r_{YX} = b_{YX} \; \frac{\text{S.D.}_X}{\text{S.D.}_Y} = b_{XY} \; \frac{\text{S.D.}_Y}{\text{S.D.}_X}$$

The correlation coefficient is standardized for the metric and the dispersion of each variable. Although it is conventionally ignored, in the two-variable case the correlation coefficient is equal to the beta coefficient to be discussed below.

4. Below we discuss transforming variables in order to analyze nonlinear patterns, which is quite different from standardizing variables.

5. In most areas of statistics severe cautions abound, but the hazards of multicollinearity have been deemphasized. Most simple treatments of the subject do not draw attention to the high degree of multicollinearity that can result from the interrelationships among several variables. It is not adequate to examine the simple relationships among explanatory variables, the appropriate test is rather the multiple correlation between each explanatory variable and all the others.

6. A widely neglected source of information on equations with numerous explanatory variables is the "multiple partial" coefficients where $r_{Y.XZ.WV}$ shows the joint association between Y and X plus Z controlling for W and V. All kinds of interesting relationships could be examined in this way, but unfortunately it is moderately inconvenient to compute these coefficients with standard computer packages.

7. See Jae-on Kim, John R. Petrocik, and Stephen N. Enoksen, "Voter Turnout Among the American States", *American Political Science Review* 69 (March 1975), 107-23. For a discussion of the technique under the label "commonality analysis," see Fred N. Kerlinger and Elazar J. Pedhazur, *Multiple Regression in Behavioral Research* (New York: Holt, Rinehart & Winston, 1973), 297-305.

8. The existing literature on dummy variables does not emphasize the utility of grouping sets of dummy variables such as regions in regression analysis, but it is a straightforward use of the technique. The prospect of using several sets of dummy variables in regression equations may seem troublesome, but cumbersome data processing ought not to inhibit sound analysis. The odd feature associated with handling sets of dummy variables is that for most purposes the sets must be kept

intact. A set of dummy variables, for example representing regions, may be used as a control or as an explanatory set. There are no technical reasons not to imagine $r_{YX.ZW}^2$ as representing sets of dummy variables for X, Z, and W so the full notation might by $r_{Y(X1,X2,X3) \cdot (Z1,Z2)(W1,W2,W3)}^2$ where the symbols within parentheses represent sets of dummy variables.

There are several applications of dummy variables, beyond the illustrations in the text. If two dummy variables, say South, non-South and industrial, nonindustrial, for state analysis were used, the results would be identical with "two-way analysis of variance." If in addition we created a third dummy variable, for example industrial South, representing the interaction of the other two, the model would be equivalent to "two-way analysis of variance with interaction."

Beyond this, dummy variables may be mixed with ordinary interval variables in several ways. The usual illustration in textbooks shows one dummy variable and one interval variable, in which case the analyst is solving for a model in which it is expected that the regression slope will be the same for both categories of the dummy variable but that the intercepts may vary.

If the analyst wants to allow for the possibility that the regression slopes as well as the intercepts may differ, then it is necessary to add another variable to the equation which represents the interaction of the dummy variable and the interval variable. This is accomplished by multiplying the two to generate a new interactive variable. For a good discussion of these possibilities, see Jan Kmenta, *Elements of Econometrics* (New York: Macmillan, 1971), 409-425.

9. The best introductory discussion we are aware of is found in Edward R. Tufte, *Data Analysis for Politics and Policy* (Englewood Cliffs, NJ: Prentice-Hall, 1974), 65-8, 91-101, 121-124; see also James G. March, "Party Representation as a Function of Election Results," *Public Opinion Quarterly* 11 (Winter 1957-58), 521-542.

10. We are not concerned that the relationship is also quite strong with a linear fit with the untransformed data. If our conceptualization calls for a nonlinear relationship, then that is what we should analyze. Another aspect of these transformations is more troublesome. The least squares fit is to the logged values, which has the effect of treating the errors surrounding larger values (in the original data) as less important since they are depressed, relatively, by this transformation. It would be extraordinary to justify this bias on substantive grounds, even though it captures the curvilinear pattern appropriately enough.

9

GROUP DATA AND INDIVIDUAL BEHAVIOR

Gudmund R. Iversen

INTRODUCTION

All study of humans attempts to find order and structure in some chaotic set of behavior. This is as true in fields such as literature, history, and anthropology as it is in political science, sociology, psychology, and economics. The methods may differ, and not all actions are of equal interest, but there is a common search for principles that can explain the observed behavior.

In most cases, this search involves simplifications in order to reach the necessary generalizations. It may also be that quantification is needed in order to simplify and make sense of the large mass of available information. At this point, statistical methods usually enter to aid in the analysis of the data.

On the most general level, the problem discussed in this chapter consists of how we go about reasoning from the results of a statistical analysis back to the substantive problem under study. For an example involving one variable, suppose we examine aspects of economic activity in several cities at a given point in time. One quantification could be annual income as reported in the tax records, where we are faced with columns and columns of numbers. To make sense of all these numbers, it is necessary that they be condensed in some way. Statisticians tell us that one way to condense the numbers would be to compute the mean income for each city. Or, if the distribution of incomes is skewed, the median income may be a more representative measure of the income level.

Such an average for a city, be it the mean or the median, describes the income level in the city. We realize that a given individual in the particular city would not be expected to have exactly this income, but the average gives a characteristic of the whole group of people that make up the city. The average can be used to compare the cities and thereby give an indication of the differences in economic activities between the cities. Thus, an average is computed from a set of units on one level, often that of the individual, and it gives a characteristic of a higher level unit, the group made up of the individuals.

Translating the results of a statistical analysis into substantive conclusions about human behavior becomes considerably more complicated when we are dealing with the relationship between two variables rather than dealing with properties of only one variable at a time. In particular, the question of whether the conclusions refer to groups or individuals becomes crucial. More specifically, then, this chapter deals with the study of relationships between variables and the problem of group-level versus individual-level relationships.

To illustrate and be more specific about what is meant by a relationship on the group level as well as on the individual level, let us consider an example. First, the relationship between two variables on the level of the group can be examined the following way. Assume it has been observed that the higher the percentage of Catholics in a ward, the higher the percentage of Democratic vote. With data on religious affiliation and vote for several wards, it is possible to present these data in a scatterplot. The variable along the horizontal axis is percentage Catholic, and the variable along the vertical axis is percentage Democratic vote. Each dot in the scatterplot represents one ward. A set of hypothetical data is shown in Figure 9.1.

The relationship between the two variables can be analyzed using standard statistical techniques. Regression analysis enables us to replace the scatter of points with a straight line that describes the form of the relationship. Correlation analysis can be used to measure the strength of the relationship, i.e., how close the points in the scatter are to the line.

The main difficulty with such a statistical analysis comes when the statistical results have to be translated back to throw light on the substantive problem about the relationship between religion and vote. Suppose the correlation coefficient between the two variables equals .75. Thus, there is a strong relationship between the variables, and the relationship is positive in the sense that the higher the percentage Catholic in a ward, the

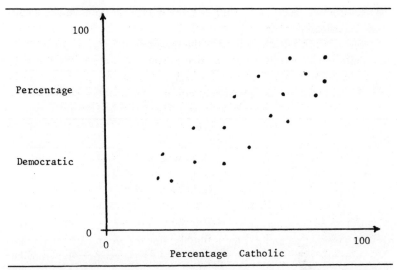

Figure 9.1 Hypothetical Data Showing Percentage Catholic and Democratic Vote in a Set of Wards

higher is the percentage Democratic vote. Slightly reformulated, this says that the more Catholics there are in a ward the more people vote Democratic. Or, carried one step further, Catholics tend to vote for the Democratic party.

Maybe. It may also be that the translation above was carried too far. The unit in the statistical analysis was the ward, and the proper translation should only go back to the unit used in the analysis. Thus, it is only possible to translate back to the wards and not all the way back to individual voters. The correlation of .75 is a property of the groups in this study, and any conclusions based on such a correlation coefficient apply only to groups.

Turning to the relationship between the two variables, religion and vote, on the individual level, Catholic versus non-Catholic and Democrat versus Republican are properties of individuals. If we want to study the relationship between these characteristics on the individual level, this has to be done with data where the individual is the unit of analysis. To see if there is a relationship between the two characteristics for the city whose wards were analyzed above, we need a table like Table 9.1. This is a table for the entire city, where the entries are obtained by adding across similar tables for each of the wards, assuming that the four cell frequencies were available in each ward. Here the unit of analysis is the individual, and conclusions from the statistical analysis therefore apply to individuals.

TABLE 9.1   Religious Affiliation and Party Vote for the City as a Whole,
            in Percent

	Democratic	Non-Democratic	Total
Catholic	15	35	50
Non-Catholic	45	5	50
Total	60	40	100%

The correlation between two categorical variables can be measured many ways; for these data the correlation coefficient $\phi = -.61$. From this coefficient, and the table itself, it can be seen that the relationship is quite strong. But the correlation is negative and it is the non-Catholics that tend to vote Democratic and not the Catholics. For the group data the relationship went the other way, and we would have been completely wrong had we concluded that the group correlation coefficient applied to the individuals.

From this example we see it is not possible to use the group data to infer about the behavior of individuals. When the group is the unit in the analysis, the conclusions apply to the groups; when the individual is the unit, the conclusions apply to the individuals. The fallacy of using group data to describe the behavior of individuals is known as the ecological fallacy.

The reason the group-level relationship can be so different from the individual-level relationship is that the two correlation coefficients tap different parts of the data. Basically, the data consist of a table like Table 9.1 for each ward in the city. The scatterplot in Figure 9.1 was obtained by taking the percentages Catholic and Democratic from the margins of each table. This scatterplot leads to the correlation coefficient where the ward is the unit. On the other hand, the individual-level correlation coefficient was computed from the four interior cell percentages in Table 9.1. These percentages were obtained by adding up the corresponding interior cell frequencies in all the wards. Thus, the group correlation comes from the margins of the tables, and the individual correlation comes from the cells in the overall table.

Since these two aspects of the data have very little to do with each other, the two relationships are conceptually and numerically different. For any given group correlation coefficient it is possible to have many different individual correlation coefficients, and from the group relationship alone there is no way of determining the individual relationship.

This is because there are so many possible configurations of cell frequencies that add up to the same marginal frequencies. It also follows that a comparison between two, or more, group-level correlation coefficients tells us nothing about how the corresponding individual-level coefficients compare. Finally, the group level depends upon how the individual-level data are aggregated. In this example the ward was the group unit, but clearly we could have used other levels, for example precinct or county.

The obvious conclusion is that if the individual is the unit in one's study, relationships should be examined from data that have the individual as the unit on which measurements are taken. Similarly, if the group is the unit in one's study, relationships should be examined from data that have the group as the unit on which measurements are taken. This problem would not be very difficult if it were only a matter of choosing the right data for our analysis. The difficulty arises when the individual-level data are not available. The group data, i.e. the margins of the tables, can always be constructed from the individual-level data, i.e. the cell entries. But it is not easy to reconstruct the interior cell entries from the margins.

The reason group-level data are more readily available than individual-level data, both for electoral and other types of research, is that the group data are obtained from two one-dimensional distributions, while the individual-level data are obtained from one two-dimensional, joint distribution. The world is full of single variable distributions, but joint distributions are not as common. Quite often the single variable distributions are matters of public record, while the corresponding joint distributions are not even recorded. Take voting as an example. For any pair of elections we can construct a table like Table 9.2 for each election district; where, for the sake of simplicity, we assume everyone voted in both elections.

The percentage votes for each of the parties at the two elections can be found from public election records, but the four cell entries in the table by law are not even recorded. The only way this joint distribution could be found would be to follow each voter into the booth and observe how the person voted in each of the two elections. Then it would be known how many people voted each of the four combinations Dem-Dem, Dem-Rep, Rep-Dem and Rep-Rep. Based on these frequencies, we could compute a correlation coefficient for each ward, measuring the relationship between the votes at the two elections. This correlation has the individual person as the unit. We could also add the cell frequencies for all the wards and get the so-called turnover table for some larger unit, say city, and compute an individual-level correlation for the whole city.

Such turnover tables show how many people voted the same party at both elections and how many changed from one party to another. The known totals from the two elections can be used to find the net change of

TABLE 9.2   Votes for Two Parties at Two Elections, in Percent

		Election 2		
		Dem	Rep	Total
Election	Dem	Unknown	Unknown	Known
1	Rep	Unknown	Unknown	Known
	Total	Known	Known	100

votes, and only the complete turnover table gives the full information about the change. It is this change of votes that is of interest in most electoral research and represents the information we need to know if we are to begin to understand the ebb and flow of political parties.

Since there are so many possible combinations of the unknown cell entries that add up to the known margins, there is supposedly no way we can recover the cell entries in a table from the margins of that table. As seen later in this chapter, it may be possible to estimate the cell entries with some additional data and some formal assumptions, but for the moment the cell frequencies are unknown and the margins are known. Thus, the only possible analysis that can be done is the analysis of the relationship between the votes at the two elections based on the group as the unit of analysis. While this relationship is not to be confused with the relationship between the variables with the individual as the unit, it may also be that the group relationship is of interest in itself.

It was Robinson who revived the issue of group- and individual-level relationships for the sociological profession.[1] He presented the formal relationship between the two correlation coefficients and warned against using the group correlation coefficient as a substitute for the individual-level correlation coefficient. The response to his paper took two different directions. One was that we should not necessarily stop studying relationships between two or more variables on the level of the group, because there clearly are cases where the group is the natural unit. Thus, as long as we know that the group is the unit, it is appropriate to use the group as the unit of analysis. The second and more serious direction consisted of showing that under certain circumstances it is possible to recover the missing cell entries from the margins of a set of tables. The pioneering work was done by Goodman.[2] Papers in this area have also been written by, among others, Madansky; Telser; Lee, Judge, and Zellner; Stokes; and Iversen.[3]

The relationship between the group- and individual-level correlation coefficients is discussed further in the next section, and possible ways of recovering the individual-level data are discussed in the following three sections.

GROUP- AND INDIVIDUAL-LEVEL CORRELATION COEFFICIENTS

In this section, we examine more closely why the correlation coefficient computed from data where the group is the unit is not necessarily equal to the correlation coefficient computed from data where the individual is the unit of analysis. While the discussion here is in terms of the product-moment correlation coefficient between the two variables, the same problem arises when the relationship between the two variables is studied using regression analysis. Just as for the correlation coefficients, the regression slope based on group-level data will usually differ from the same slope based on individual-level data. With several variables and the use of multiple regression analysis, the problem of using data from the appropriate levels becomes even more pronounced and hard to deal with.

It is possible to give an equation that contains both r_I and r_G, where the r's are the correlation coefficients computed from individual and group data, respectively. This is the equation Robinson first brought to the sociological profession, and it is derived in Appendix 1.[4] Such an equation gives the formal relationship between the two correlation coefficients. The equation can be used to gain a better understanding of why the two coefficients usually are different, and it can be used to find conditions under which they are the same.

The example in the first section deals with the two nominal level variables, party and religion, each having two categories. In the following we consider the more general case where the two variables are interval level variables. By using 0 and 1 as scores for the two categories of each of the nominal level variables, the product-moment correlation coefficient, r, for interval level variables reduces to the phi-coefficient for the 2x2 table defined by the two nominal level variables, and the mean for each variable reduces to the proportion of people in the category scored 1. Turning to interval level variables, therefore, enables us to deal with a slightly more general case without losing sight of the case first considered.

Appendix 1 shows that one way to have the two coefficients equal is to have the groups completely homogeneous for each of the variables. For our original example with the two nominal level variables, this requirement

TABLE 9.3   Example of a Group Where There is No Variation in the
             Scores on Either Variable

	Dem	Non-Dem	Total
Cath			100%
Non-Cath			0
Total	0%	100	100%

means that each group has to be of the same kind as shown in Table 9.3, where all the people are in only one category on the party variable and only one category on the religious variable. In this particular table everyone is Catholic on one variable and non-Democrat on the other. When all the tables are homogeneous like this we have $r_I = r_G$, and the group data can therefore be used to find the individual-level correlation between the two variables. However, from the margins in Table 9.3 it is possible to recover the true cell frequencies directly; all the people have to be in the Catholic non-Democrat cell of the table from the way the margins are distributed. Since we can find the cell frequencies for all the tables in this case, it is also possible to compute r_I directly from the cell frequencies as well.

A more general case under which the two coefficients are equal exists when the ratios of the variation between the groups to the total variation of the scores are the same for each of the variables and their cross products. This is a more difficult condition to understand intuitively. The condition arises from considering various sums of squares and sums of cross products, and it is explained more fully in Appendix 1. Finally, both cases mentioned above are special cases of the rule that says that the group and individual correlations are equal when $p_{xy} = \sqrt{p_x p_y}$. Here p_{xy} is the ratio of the between group sum of cross products to the total sum of cross products, and p_x and p_y are the same ratios for the sums of squares for the two variables. This condition is also derived and discussed further in Appendix 1.

The main point here is that the two correlation coefficients are equal only under very specific conditions, and most often the conditions are not satisfied. Thus, we have to look elsewhere if we want to infer about the individual-level relationship between two variables when only group data are available.

TABLE 9.4   Minimum and Maximun Values of the Cell Frequency in the
Upper Left Corner of a Table

	Minimum			Maximum	
(1)	3	4	(4)	0	4
6	0	6	3	3	6
7	3	10	7	3	10

ESTIMATING INDIVIDUAL DATA FROM GROUP DATA

Duncan and Davis took the following approach in an attempt to infer from group data to the individual data.[5] They noted that the margins of a two-way table present certain restrictions on the range of possible values of the cell frequencies. A simple example is presented in Table 9.4 for the case of a two-by-two table. When the margins are given, there is one degree of freedom in such a table, meaning that the four cell frequencies are all determined as soon as one of them is known. Focusing on the frequency in the upper left hand corner of the table, the smallest possible value is 1 and the largest possible value is 4. Such a range can be determined for each table, resulting in two sets of tables with filled-in frequencies. For each set of tables we can add up the cell frequencies and compute the individual-level correlation coefficient for the resulting overall table. The true r_I must then lie somewhere in the range between the two coefficients obtained this way. We do not know where, but it may be that this procedure limits the range of possible values to something less than from -1 to $+1$. A shortcut procedure for finding these bounds is given by Goodman.[6]

The usefulness of this approach depends upon how much we are able to reduce the range of possible values for the individual-level correlation coefficient. From the outset, we know that the value has to lie between minus one and plus one. If the Duncan-Davis method leaves us with a possible range, say from -0.40 to 0.60, we have cut the range in half. More important, however, is that we still do not really know much about the value of r_I. The range is still too large to be of much use, and this is a conclusion at which one often arrives from using this method.

Another, and perhaps more profitable direction to follow consists of actually trying to recover the missing cell entries directly from the margins. In principle this is an impossible task, since there are so many different configurations of cell entries that can add up to the observed marginal frequencies in each table. But it may be possible to estimate the cell entries with the aid of some model that specifies how the cell entries are related to the margins or some other variables. A few of the more commonly used models are discussed in this section.

Finally, the recovery of the individual-level data may be possible if certain kinds of additional data are available. For example, we may have the margins for each of the states and, in addition, a national survey that gives estimates of the cell entries for the nation as a whole. From these data and an appropriate model, it may be possible to estimate the cell entries for each state. A few situations of this kind are discussed in the next section.

The first attempt to estimate missing cell entries from margins seems to be that of Miller.[7] He observed the distribution of a set of elements at several points in time, and at each point an element could fall in one of two categories. Thus, he knew the marginal distributions of the table showing the pattern of change from one point in time to the next. But he did not have the cell entires showing how many elements changed and how many did not change categories. He assumed that this time series was governed by a Markov chain. Thus, his model consisted of assuming constant transition probabilities across the points in time. He was thereby able to estimate the transition probabilities, and the cell frequencies, by what amounts to a regression analysis.

In two sociological journals, Goodman takes up estimation of missing cell entries.[8] The first paper is mainly a comment on Robinson's paper, where Goodman introduces the least squares method for the estimation of transition probabilities, this time using tables from geographic subdivisions rather than time series data.[9] A much more extensive treatment of this estimation problem is given in Goodman's second paper. After again introducing the regression method for the estimation, he gives the standard formulas for the variances of the various estimators and discusses some of the conditions under which the regression analysis is appropriate. In addition to the model assuming the same transition probabilities in all the tables, Goodman proposes three other models for the estimation of the missing cell entries. Some special cases of these models are introduced below, arising from a somewhat different perspective discussed more extensively by Iversen.[10]

Some of the notation needed for the models for recovery of missing cell entries is introduced here in Tables 9.5 and 9.6 and some in Appendix 2.

TABLE 9.5   Notation for Marginal Proportions in the kth Table

	Dem	Non-Dem	Total
Catholic			$p_{1.k}$
Non-Catholic			$p_{2.k} = 1 - p_{1.k}$
Total	$p_{.1k}$	$p_{.2k}$	1

TABLE 9.6   Notations for Proportions in Each Row in the kth Table

	Dem	Non-Dem	Total
Catholic	r_{11k}	$1 - r_{11k}$	1
Non-Catholic	r_{21k}	$1 - r_{21k}$	1

In the same appendix it is shown how the marginal proportions and the row proportions are related according to the equation

$$p_{.1k} = r_{21k} + (r_{11k} - r_{21k}) p_{1.k}$$

This is the row equation that forms the basis for most of the attempts at recovering the missing cell entries. Introducing the mean of the r_{11}'s as α and the mean of the r_{21}'s as γ, the equation can be written

$$p_{.1k} = \gamma + (\alpha - \gamma) p_{1.k} + e_k$$

where e_k is a residual term defined in Appendix 2.

Now we have arrived at something which very much resembles a simple regression model. The equation above shows that the kth observation of the independent variable equals p_{1k} and for the dependent variable it equals $p_{.1k}$. The unknown intercept equals γ and the unknown slope equals $(\alpha - \gamma)$. By minimizing the sum Σe_k^2 with respect to the two unknown parameters, perhaps using weights to compensate for having the residual depending on the independent variable, we can get estimates of the parameters α and γ. The estimates of α and γ can be taken as estimates of the missing row proportions r_{11k} and r_{21k} in the kth table. From the estimated proportions it is possible to estimate the missing cell entries in the various tables.

The question immediately arises whether the estimated cell frequencies are close to the true but unknown frequencies. It can be shown that only when the true values of the row proportions in Table 9.6 are close to the mean proportions are the estimates close to the true values. Thus, the proportion Democrats among the Catholics (r_{11k}) has to be about the same in all the groups, and the proportion Democrats among the non-Catholics (r_{21k}) has to be about the same in all the groups. Furthermore, the same requirement of only small variations in the r's is needed in order for the estimates of α and γ to be close to the means of the r_{11}'s and r_{21}'s, respectively. This point cannot be stressed hard enough; regressing the column proportions on the row proportions the way it is done above will always result in estimates of the means of the proportions, but these estimates can only be used when the r's do not vary much from group to group. The conditional row proportions are unknown, however, and we have no way of checking whether they vary much or not. Since α and γ are mean proportions, their values have to lie in the range from zero to one. If the estimates are outside this range, we have a good indication that the assumption of small variations is wrong, and that we should not use this model for the estimation of the missing cell entries. But when the estimates fall within the admissable range, we need additional evidence to justify the use of this model.

Such evidence could possibly come from substantive theory underlying the phenomenon we are studying. One possibility may be that there are notions in the substantive theory of different kinds of effects. In particular, it may be that the theory can contribute to the question of whether there are individual- or group-level effects of the independent variable that influence the dependent variable. The sociological literature, as exemplified by Davis, Spaeth, and Huson, has noted that a dependent variable Y (vote) may be determined by two aspects of an independent variable X (religion).[11] First, there may be an effect of X on Y from an individual's score on X. This individual level effect can be contrasted with the effect on Y for an individual from the level of X in the group to which the individual belongs. This is the effect of X on the group level. For our example, one may vote Democratic because one is a Catholic (individual effect), or one may vote Democratic because there is a high percentage of Catholics in the group one belongs to (group effect). There may also be a third effect present, resulting from an interaction of the group- and individual-level effects. Davis, Spaeth, and Huson develop a classification scheme using these effects, and this scheme permits us to specify other models for the estimation of the missing cell entries.[12]

In order to better understand the estimation model used above, assume for a moment that the cell entries are known and that we can make a

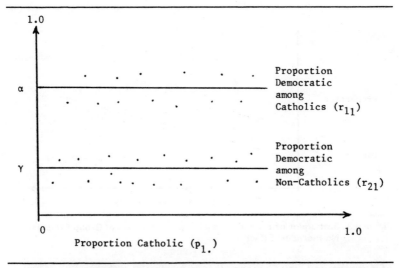

Figure 9.2 Scatterplot of the Conditional Proportions r_{11} and r_{21} against the Marginal Proportion $p_{1.}$ when the Conditional Proportions Do Not Vary Much from Table to Table (Individual Effect Only)

scatterplot of the r_{11}'s and the r_{21}'s against $p_{1.}$, the proportion Catholic the group. Such a scatterplot is shown in Figure 9.2. The plot shows that the r_{11}'s are all about the same, the r_{21}'s are all about the same, and the r_{11}'s differ from the r_{21}'s. Interpreting r_{11} as the probability of a non-Catholic voting Democratic, the figure shows that the only thing influencing the probability of a person voting Democratic is whether the person is a Catholic or not. The composition of the group to which the person belongs, in the sense of whether the group has a low or high proportion of Catholics ($p_{1.}$), has no effect on the probability of voting Democratic. Thus, the estimation model we examine in some detail above is the model assuming the presence of an individual effect and no group effect. If we have a substantive theory which says that religion affects voting only through the individual level and not the group level, the model above is the one that should be tried for the estimation of the missing cell entries.

The case of group effect and no individual effect occurs when the probability of voting Democratic is the same for Catholics and non-Catholics in a group, and this common probability depends on the proportion Catholics in the group. In this case the individual characteristic

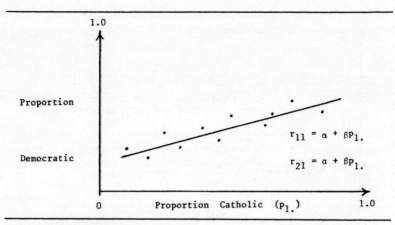

Figure 9.3 Scatterplot of r_{11} and r_{21} against $p_{1.}$ in the Case of Group Effect but No No Individual Effect

of Catholic and non-Catholic does not affect the probability of voting Democratic, only the group characteristic affects the probability.

With only the group effect present, the scatterplot of r_{11} and r_{21} against $p_{1.}$ would look like the scatterplot in Figure 9.3. The lines for r_{11} and r_{21} overlap here, and because of the positive slope, the probability of voting Democratic increases with the proportion Catholic in the group.

Since equal row proportions in a table implies no relationship between the two variables for that table, we have independence between the two variables in each of the tables when only the group effect is present. Independence in each table implies that $r_W = 0$ for the tables, where r_W is the average correlation between the two variables within the groups, as defined in Appendix 1. But we do not necessarily have $r_I = 0$, meaning that we may still have a relationship between the two variables in the overall table. It is unlikely that there is only a group effect present in our example, since electoral research has established that voting and religion are not independent, no matter on what level the data are aggregated.

If there is a group effect only, the basic row equation leads to the equation

$$p_{.1k} = a + \beta \, p_{1.k} + e_k$$

where α and β are the intercept and slope of the line in Figure 9.3, respectively. This equation can be used to estimate the missing cell entries, as discussed in Appendix 2.

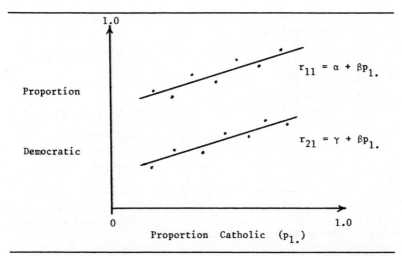

Figure 9.4 Scatterplot of r_{11} and r_{21} against $p_{1.}$ in the Presence of Both Individual and Group Effects

It is also possible to have both individual and group effects present in a set of tables. Then the scatterplot of r_{11} and r_{21} against $p_{1.}$ would look like the scatterplot in Figure 9.4. The figure shows that for any group (any value of $p_{1.}$) the probability of voting Democratic is higher for Catholics than non-Catholics. That signals the presence of the individual-level effect. The two lines also have a common slope different from zero. The presence of the positive slope means that the probability of voting Democratic increases with the proportion Catholic in the group to which people belong. Because of this dependence on the group characteristic, as measured by $p_{1.}$, there is also a group effect present in this example.

Under the assumption of the presence of both group and individual effects, the basic row equation becomes

$$p_{.1k} = \gamma + (\alpha + \beta - \gamma)\, p_{1.k} + e_k$$

as shown in Appendix 2. The four parameters in this model are the same as the slope and intercept parameters for the lines in Figure 9.4. Without additional information, however, this model cannot be used for the estimation of the missing cell entries, because it has too many parameters.

There is still a fourth case to be considered, but before doing that we can observe that there is no way in which the available data can be used to distinguish between the three cases above. The available data consist, in all

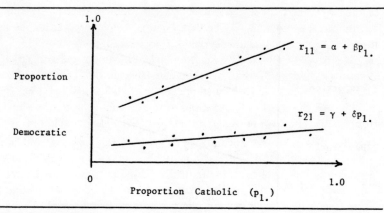

Figure 9.5 Scatterplot of r_{11} and r_{21} against $p_{1.}$ in the Presence of Individual, Group, and Interaction Effects

the cases, of the marginal proportions $p_{1.}$ and $p_{.1}$ from each of the tables; in our example the proportions Catholic and Democrat in each ward. The three cases above all require us to fit a line to the scatterplot of $p_{1.}$ and $p_{.1}$. But each of the three cases specifies a linear relationship between $p_{1.}$ and $p_{.1}$, and from an observed linear relationship alone there is no way of distinguishing between the three models. Without additional data, we therefore need some strong substantive theory in order to choose the model that could have generated our data.

The fourth case occurs when the lines for r_{11} and r_{21} have different slopes as well as different intercepts. The scatterplot of r_{11} and r_{21} against $p_{1.}$ for this case could look like the scatterplot in Figure 9.5. There is an individual effect present because Catholics and non-Catholics in the same group have different probabilities of voting Democratic, and there is a group effect present because the group composition, as measured by $p_{1.}$, affects the voting probabilities for both religious categories. But, in addition, the difference in voting probabilities for the religious categories varies with $p_{1.}$. Thus, there is another effect present, over and beyond the separate individual and group effects. This is an effect resulting from an interaction between the individual and group effects, and this effect is therefore labeled the interaction effect.

The basic row equation for this model becomes

$$p_{.1k} = \gamma + (\alpha - \gamma + \delta)p_{1.k} + (\beta - \delta)p_{1.k}^2 + e_k$$

Because of the presence of the term $p_{1.k}^2$ in this equation, the relationship between $p_{1.}$ and $p_{.1}$ is no longer linear and can therefore not be represented by a line. If a scatterplot of $p_{.1}$ against $p_{1.}$ suggests a curvilinear relationship, it very well may be that the data have been generated by this model. And because of the curvilinear nature of the relationship, it is possible to distinguish this case from the other three cases above. The equation is discussed further by Goodman; Duncan, Cuzzort, and Duncan; Boudon; and Boyd and Iversen, among others.[13]

The three parameter combinations γ, $\alpha-\gamma+\delta$ and $\beta-\delta$ can be estimated from the equation above using multiple regression analysis with $p_{.1}$ as the dependent variable and $p_{1.}$ and $p_{1.}^2$ as independent variables. But again there are difficulties. There are four parameters to be estimated and the regression analysis yields estimates of only three quantities, the intercept, the coefficient for $p_{1.}$ and the coefficient for $p_{1.}^2$. Thus, without additional information of some kind, the missing cell entries cannot be recovered under this model.

Summing up this section, we see how the presence of individual, group, and interaction effects leads to models for the recovery of missing cell entries in a set of 2x2 tables. Since the available data cannot tell us much about which is the correct model to use, we usually need a good substantive theory and, for some of the models, additional data in order to successfully recover the missing cell entries. The case with additional data is taken up in the next section, and an additional section considers ways in which these models generalize to tables with more than two rows and two columns.

This line of thinking can also be generalized to the case where the two variables are not categorical variables, like vote and religion, but interval variables X and Y. The three kinds of effects can be studied in the equation

$$y_{ik} = \beta_0 + \beta_1 x_{ik} + \beta_2 \bar{x}_k + \beta_3 x_{ik} \bar{x}_k + e_{ik}$$

Here y_{ik} and x_{ik} are the values of Y and X for the ith individual in the kth group and $\bar{x}_k$ is the mean of X in the kth group. The coefficients β_1, β_2 and β_3 are measures of individual, group, and interaction effects, respectively.

By aggregating the model we get the following equation for the relationship between the group means

$$\bar{y}_k = \beta_0 + (\beta_1 + \beta_2) \bar{x}_k + \beta_3 \bar{x}_k^2 + \bar{e}_k$$

This is the same equation as the one relating $p_{.1}$, $p_{1.}$ and $p_{1.}^2$ given earlier. With group data only it is not possible to separately measure individual and group effects, since we cannot estimate β_1 and β_2, only their sum. This model is discussed extensively by Boyd and Iversen.[14]

ESTIMATING INDIVIDUAL DATA FROM GROUP DATA AND PARTIAL INDIVIDUAL DATA

The point is frequently made in the previous sections that estimation of the missing cell entries may only be possible if additional data are available. These data can be of different types, and in this section we consider estimation procedures that can be used with some types of data.

Certain of these procedures may be of particular interest to historians, because the procedures may help unlock the unknown past by combining known, historical group data with present day survey data on individuals. Take presidential voting returns for the two major parties as an example. Any pair of consecutive elections defines a two-by-two table where the marginal percentages are all known, but the four cell percentages giving the turnover table are not known. It is possible, however, to use survey data for the elections after World War II to get very good estimates of the cell percentages for those pairs of elections. If we take the one hundred year period from 1880 to 1980, we get 25 two-by-two tables where the cell percentages are available for the last 8 tables but not for the first 17. The question then arises whether it is possible to use these two sets of tables together and recover the cell percentages for the first 17 pairs of elections. The answer is that it is possible to estimate the missing cell percentages with additional data of this kind. The additional survey data make it possible to estimate all the parameters in the most general model above, and from the estimated parameters it is possible to estimate the cell percentages in the tables for pairs of elections prior to 1948.

It has to be understood, however, that even if it is possible to estimate all the parameters in our model and thereby estimate all the missing cell percentages, we still have no guarantee that the estimates are close to the actual, but missing, values in those tables. What we do is to find estimates that are consistent with all the available data and the model being used. If the missing data do not follow the model, the estimates could be quite far from the true values. We are dealing with a complicated estimation problem here, and we do not have estimation in the usual statistical sense of having data from a sample where we could use the sample mean, for example, as an estimate of the corresponding population mean. The parameters in the models used here are further removed from the observed data, and it is this latency of the parameters that makes the estimation process more difficult. But still, what justifies working on an estimation problem of this kind is that when these models are applied to data with known cell entries, it has been possible to recover the known cell entries from the margins and thereby show that the models actually work. One such example, Iversen, deals with tables created by urban or rural residency and membership or not in the labor force.[15]

Finally, for this particular example of voting percentages, we proceed as if there were no changes in the electorate from one election to the next from nonvoting, reaching the voting age, and death. Instead, by working with percentages, it is as if we are following the paths of one hundred people through a century of elections.

There are several ways of estimating the parameters with additional data of the kind discussed above, and two of those are suggested in Appendix 3. It is not quite clear on what basis one chooses between alternative ways of estimating the parameters. Conventional statistical criteria for good estimating procedures are only of limited help in making this choice, since they are mostly concerned with estimating population parameters from sample data.

It is possible to have other data configurations. For example, we could have data on the margins for each of the 50 states and cell entries for the country as a whole from some nationwide sample survey. Additional data, as represented by this table for the entire country, can be used together with the data on the margins to estimate all four parameters in the most general model. Another possibility would be to have the marginal frequencies for each state and the internal cell frequencies for one state. These and other cases are considered more extensively in Boyd and Iversen.[16]

GENERALIZATIONS

The discussion above is limited to data consisting of tables with two rows and two columns. It is simpler to present most of the main ideas using small tables, and many of the models are not well developed for larger tables.

Generalizations are pursued in two directions here. The first consists of having tables with more than two rows and columns; that is, the variables have more than two categories. For the second generalization we turn from nominal level (categorical) variables and consider interval level variables; that is, variables that have a meaningful unit of measurement.

With only two categories, like Catholic and non-Catholic, the marginal proportion in the first row gives a measure of the group composition with respect to the religious variable. But with more categories, e.g. the four categories Catholic, Protestant, Jewish, and others, we need three proportions to describe the composition of any group. The general approach above is to set the conditional row proportions (r's) as functions of the marginal proportions. Doing this with larger tables results in two difficulties. First, the resulting models are more difficult to interpret in terms of group and individual level effects. Second, even fairly simple models often lead to situations where we end up with a model that has more parameters than we can estimate.

There is one model, however, that generalizes directly and that is the model which assumes the existence of an individual level effect only. Equations for this model are written out in Appendix 4, and the main requirement is that the conditional proportion in a given cell does not vary much from table to table. This, of course, is the same requirement as we had for two-by-two tables. Stokes discusses this case in some greater detail.[17]

The other case considered in this section deals with interval level variables. As pointed out by Boyd it is possible to use much of the material developed for the two-by-two table case in a fairly direct fashion.[18] In each group we know the distribution of the variable X, say age, as well as the distribution of the variable Y, say income. That is, we know how many people there are in each age category and how many are in each income category. But the joint distribution of the two variables is missing and it is not known how many people are in each age-income category. Without these data, it is not possible to study the relationship between the two variables in each group or for all the groups, with the individual as the unit of analysis.

If the bivariate data were known, the relationship between age and income in the kth group could be studied using a regression line with equation

$$Y = a_k + b_k X$$

where a_k is the intercept and b_k the slope of the regression line. But without such data we cannot directly find the intercept and slope, as well as the correlation coefficient.

In Appendix 5 it is shown in more detail how it is possible to introduce individual, group, and interaction effects and then use the resulting models to estimate the intercepts and slopes based on the means of X and Y from the groups. Just as for nominal level variables, most of the models require additional data of some kind of order to fully estimate all the parameters. With only an individual effect present, the intercepts and slopes are the same in all the groups. As far as income is concerned, it therefore makes no difference what group one is in. It only makes a difference what age one has, where age is an individual characteristic. With only a group effect present, the regression line in each group has slope equal to zero; that is, a person's income is not related to the person's age. But the intercept may depend on the mean of X in the group, so that the income level is determined by the average age in the group, which is a group characteristic.

With both individual and group effects present, we get a combination of the two cases above. The regression lines for the various groups have the same nonzero slopes, but the intercepts differ as a function of the mean age. Thus, a person's income is determined by the person's age as well as the mean age in the group to which the person belongs. Finally, with the presence of an interaction effect as well, the relationship between age and income is characterized by different regression lines in the various groups, and both slopes and intercepts depend on the group means. The various equations for these cases are given in Appendix 5.

With complete data on the individuals in each group, we now have a way of examining the data for the presence of the various effects. But here we are more concerned with the case when the individual data, the joint distributions, are not available. In Appendix 5 it is shown that when only the individual effect or only the group effect is present, we can estimate the slopes and intercepts, and therefore also the individual-level correlation coefficients, from the group means. But more commonly, we would expect to have two, or perhaps all three effects present. In that case we need additional data of one kind or another in order to estimate all the parameters. The case of interval variables is discussed more fully by Boyd and Iversen.[19]

Finally, the choice of rows representing the independent variable and columns representing the dependent variable in the various estimation equations is somewhat arbitrary. This choice corresponds to the independent and dependent variables in the example relating religion and vote, and it enabled us to develop the presence of individual, group, and interaction effects. But, in a more general sense, what these effects stand for are certain regularities among the quantities that make up the tables. Above, we consider such possible regularities for the conditional row proportions. The estimation procedures would work equally well, however, if there were these same kinds of regularities for the column conditional proportions. It does not make as much sense substantively to be talking about the individual effect of vote on religion. But if the conditional column proportions are constant across the tables, it is equally possible to estimate the cell entries. Thus, the models above really stand for two sets of models. One set consists of the models as they are expressed here, and the other set is obtained by interchanging rows and columns. There is often little reason to expect that one set of models should work better than the other set. Practically speaking, this means that after we have analyzed a set of tables as outlined above, we should transpose all the tables by changing the rows to columns and do the analysis all over again. Usually it is clear from the results which analysis is the more appropriate. For example, if one analysis fits the data well and gives estimated proportions within the range from zero to one, then the other analysis will give estimates that are less than zero and larger than one, and vice versa. For a further discussion of this point, see Iversen.[20]

CONCLUSIONS

In this chapter, we have shown that we may not have to be restricted to group-level data and run the risk of committing the ecological fallacy. Perhaps it is possible to recover missing cell entries and thereby individual-level relationships even though these data may not be available initially. By using the idea of individual- and group-level effects, we may gain a better understanding of some of the issues involved in estimating the missing cell entries. Estimating individual data is difficult, but the more we know about the underlying process that generated the tables and the more additional data we have, the more feasible it is to solve this problem.

APPENDIX 1

CONDITIONS UNDER WHICH $r_G = r_I$ AND AN EQUATION RELATING r_G AND r_I

Let the two variables be denoted X and Y, and assume that we have observations on the two variables for people, or some similar element, belonging to K different groups. Furthermore, let the ith person in the kth group have scores x_{ik} and y_{ik} on the two variables. Two subscripts are needed for each observation in order to keep track of both people and groups.

The correlation between X and Y, using the individual as the unit, is found by adding up the various squares and cross products over all the individuals. Thus,

$$r_I = \frac{\sum_i \sum_k (x_{ik} - \bar{x})(y_{ik} - \bar{y})}{\sqrt{\sum_i \sum_k (x_{ik} - \bar{x})^2 \sum_i \sum_k (y_{ik} - \bar{y})^2}}$$

The group correlation r_G is computed from the group means $\bar{x}_k$ and $\bar{y}_k$. With each square and cross product in the expression for the correlation coefficient weighted by n_k, the number of individuals in the corresponding group, r_G becomes

$$r_G = \frac{\sum_k n_k (\bar{x}_k - \bar{x})(\bar{y}_k - \bar{y})}{\sqrt{\sum_k n_k (\bar{x}_k - \bar{x})^2 \sum_k n_k (\bar{y}_k - \bar{y})^2}}$$

In order to show how the two correlation coefficients are related we need the following three equalities,

$$\sum_i \sum_k (x_{ik} - \bar{x})^2 = \sum_i \sum_k (x_{ik} - \bar{x}_k)^2 + \sum_k n_k (\bar{x}_k - \bar{x})^2$$

$$\sum_i \sum_k (y_{ik} - \bar{y})^2 = \sum_i \sum_k (y_{ik} - \bar{y}_k)^2 + \sum_k n_k (\bar{y}_k - \bar{y})^2$$

These two equalities are the same as those found in analysis of variance, where each term on the left is called the total sum of squares and the terms on the right are called the within group sum of squares and the between group sum of squares, respectively. The third equality states a similar relationship for the cross products,

$$\sum_i \sum_k (x_{ik} - \bar{x})(y_{ik} - \bar{y}) = \sum_i \sum_k (x_{ik} - \bar{x}_k)(y_{ik} - \bar{y}_k) + \sum_k n_k (\bar{x}_k - \bar{x})(\bar{y}_k - \bar{y}).$$

Let T stand for total, W for within, B for between, SS for sum of squares, and SCP for sum of cross products. Including x and y to show for which variable the symbol applies, the three equalities can be written

TSSx = WSSx + BSSx
TSSy = WSSy + BSSy
TSCPxy = WSCPxy + BSCPxy

With this notation it is possible to write the two correlation coefficients as

$$r_I = \frac{TSCPxy}{\sqrt{TSSx\, TSSy}} \qquad\qquad r_G = \frac{BSCPxy}{\sqrt{BSSx\, BSSy}}$$

These two correlation coefficients make use of the total and between sums of squares and cross products. It is also possible to define a similar coefficient using the within sums of squares and cross products. Let us define a new coefficient r_W, where

$$r_W = \frac{WSCPxy}{\sqrt{WSSx\ WSSy}}$$

The coefficient r_W can be seen as an average correlation coefficient of X and Y within the groups. It is a special kind of average, however. One way to see this better is to write out the correlation coefficient between X and Y in the kth group. Let the numerator be denoted $SCPxy_k$ and the sums of squares for X and Y SSx_k and SSy_k, respectively. Then the correlation coefficient between X and Y in the kth group can be written

$$r_k = \frac{SCPxy_k}{\sqrt{SSx_k\ SSy_k}}$$

With this notation the average within group correlation coefficient r_W becomes

$$r_W = \frac{SCPxy_1 + SCPxy_2 + \ldots + SCPxy_K}{\sqrt{(SSx_1 + SSx_2 + \ldots + SSx_K)(SSy_1 + SSy_2 + \ldots + SSy_K)}}$$

Thus, r_W is an average within group correlation in the sense that the numerators of the coefficients for each group are added up separately and each of the terms in the denominators are added up separately.

It is now possible to investigate conditions under which $r_I = r_G$. Going back to the three equalities and the definitions of the two correlation coefficients, we see that one way for r_I to equal r_G is to have

$$WSSx = WSSy = WSCPxy = 0$$

because then the total sums of squares and cross products equal the corresponding between groups sums. That is, the two correlation coefficients are equal when all the X-scores in each group are equal to each other and all the Y-scores in each group are equal to each other. Thus, if all the groups are completely homogeneous when it comes to the scores on both variables, then r_I and r_G are equal.

This can be seen as a special case of a more general case. For the more general case, assume that the between sums are the same proportion p of the total sums of squares for X, Y, and for the cross products. This assumption can be expressed

$$BSSx/TSSx = p$$
$$BSSy/TSSy = p$$
$$BSCPxy/TSCPxy = p$$

In the special case above we have $p = 1$. The three equalities relating the total, within and between sums, can then be written

$$TSSx = (1 - p)TSSx + (p)TSSx$$
$$TSSy = (1 - p)TSSy + (p)TSSy$$
$$TSCPxy = (1 - p)TSCPxy + (p)TSCPxy$$

The individual correlation coefficient r_I is not changed by this. But the group correlation coefficient becomes

$$r_G = \frac{(p)TSCPxy}{\sqrt{(p)TSSx\,(p)TSSy}} = \frac{TSCPxy}{\sqrt{TSSx\,TSSy}} = r_I$$

The three p's cancel and the last expression is the one we have for r_I. We therefore have r_I equal to r_G when the three ratios of between to total sums are the same. It also turns out that the within group correlation coefficient r_W is equal to r_G for this case.

A still more general condition exists for the quality of r_I and r_G when the proportions for the between and total sums are different, i.e.,

$$BSSx/TSSx = p_x$$
$$BSSy/TSSy = p_y$$
$$BSCPxy/TSCPxy = p_{xy}$$

Using these proportions, the group correlation coefficient can be written

$$r_G = \frac{p_{xy}\,TSCPxy}{\sqrt{p_x\,TSSx\,p_y\,TSSy}} = \frac{p_{xy}}{\sqrt{p_x p_y}}\,r_I$$

From this we see that the two correlation coefficients are equal when

$$p_{xy} = \sqrt{p_x p_y}$$

Thus, $r_G = r_I$ when the proportion for the sums of cross products is equal to the geometric mean of the proportions for the sums of squares for X and Y.

The following shows the type of conclusion that can be reached from this discussion. The equation relating the two correlation coefficients can be rewritten

$$r_I = (\sqrt{p_x p_y}/p_{xy})\,r_G$$

The two proportions p_x and p_y as well as the coefficient r_G are all known from the marginal distributions, but p_{xy} and r_I are unknown. The largest value of the proportion p_{xy} is 1.00. Therefore, if the three sums of cross products are all positive, the smallest possible value of r_I is equal to $\sqrt{p_x p_y}\,r_G$. But two of the sums of cross products are unknown if we only have the marginal distributions. A typical term in the total sum of cross products is

$$(x_{ik} - \bar{x})(y_{ik} - \bar{y})$$

For this individual, who is the ith person in the kth group, we need the product of the X-deviation and the Y-deviation from the means. But it is exactly this information that is missing; we do not have the joint distribution of the individuals on the two variables. The between group sum of cross products is known from the margins, but the total sum of cross products is not known. Thus, conditions such as those developed above have only a limited practical value.

Finally, the equation relating the various correlation coefficients can be found from the equality

$$TSCPxy = WSCPxy + BSCPxy$$

These three sums are all numerators in the corresponding correlation coefficients. Using that fact the equality can be written

$$r_I \sqrt{TSSx\ TSSy} = r_W \sqrt{WSSx\ WSSy} + r_G \sqrt{BSSx\ BSSy}$$

Dividing by the square root on the left side we get

$$r_I = r_W \sqrt{\frac{WSSx\ WSSy}{TSSx\ .TSSy}} + r_G \sqrt{\frac{BSSx\ BSSy}{TSSx\ TSSy}}$$

We can leave the equation this way, or we can use the fact that the within group sums plus the between group sums equal the total sums, and write the equation as

$$r_I = r_W \sqrt{(1 - \frac{BSSx}{TSSx})(1 - \frac{BSSy}{TSSy})} + r_G \sqrt{\frac{BSSx\ BSSy}{TSSx\ TSSy}}$$

It is from this equation Robinson develops his argument that r_I usually differs from r_G, and that the latter therefore cannot be used as a substitute for the former.[21]

APPENDIX 2

MODELS FOR THE ESTIMATION OF MISSING CELL ENTRIES

In addition to the notation introduced in the text we need notation for the frequencies in the kth table, as shown below.

TABLE 9.A   NOTATION FOR FREQUENCIES IN THE kth TABLE

	Dem.	Non-Dem	Total
Cath.	n_{11k}	n_{12k}	$n_{1 \cdot k}$
Non-Cath.	n_{21k}	n_{22k}	$n_{2 \cdot k}$
Total	$n_{\cdot 1k}$	$n_{\cdot 2k}$	n_k

The various proportions in Tables 9.5 and 9.6 are obtained from the frequencies above according to the expressions

$$r_{11k} = n_{11k}/n_{1 \cdot k} \qquad\qquad r_{21k} = n_{21k}/n_{2 \cdot k}$$

$$p_{1 \cdot k} = n_{1 \cdot k}/n_k \qquad\qquad p_{\cdot 1k} = n_{\cdot 1k}/n_k$$

In Tables 9.5, 9.6, and 9.A only the marginal frequencies and proportions are known. It is now possible to present what amounts to the model with constant transition probabilities for the recovery of the missing cell entries in all the tables. For the Democrats in the first column in Table 9.A the sum of the two cell frequencies equals the total number of Democrats. This can be expressed in the equation

$$n_{\cdot 1k} = n_{11k} + n_{21k}$$

Each of the cell frequencies can be expressed as a product of the corresponding row totals and row proportions. That way the equation above can be written

$$n_{\cdot 1k} = r_{11k} \, n_{1 \cdot k} + r_{21k} \, n_{2 \cdot k}$$

If both sides of this equation are divided by the total frequency n_k, we can replace the marginal frequencies by the corresponding proportions; i.e.,

$$p_{\cdot 1k} = r_{11k} \, p_{1 \cdot k} + r_{21k} \, (1 - p_{1 \cdot k})$$

Rearranging the terms the equation can be written

$$p_{.1k} = r_{21k} + (r_{11k} - r_{21k})p_{1.k}$$

This is the basic row equation, given in the text, relating the conditional row proportions and the two marginal proportions. This equation forms the basis for most of the development in this chapter.

The equation can be rewritten some more. Let the mean of the r_{11}'s be denoted α and let the difference between r_{11k} and the mean be denoted e_{1k}. Similarly, let the mean of the r_{21}'s be denoted γ and the difference between r_{21k} and the mean be denoted e_{2k}.

These relationships can be expressed in the equations

$$r_{11k} = \alpha + e_{1k} \qquad\qquad\qquad r_{21k} = \gamma + e_{2k}$$

Substituting the equations for r_{11k} and r_{21k} in the basic row equation above we get

$$p_{.1k} = \gamma + (\alpha - \gamma)p_{1.k} = + e_k$$

where the residual term e_k equals $e_{2k} + (e_{1k} - e_{2k})p_{1.k}$. Ordinary methods of estimation from simple regression can be used to estimate the intercept γ and slope $\alpha - \gamma$. The resulting estimates $\hat{\alpha}$ and $\hat{\gamma}$ can be used to estimate the proportions in each table. These estimated proportions, r_{11k} and r_{21k}, can be found from the equations

$$r_{11k} = \hat{\alpha} \qquad\qquad\qquad r_{21k} = \hat{\gamma}$$

Finally, the estimated proportions can be used to estimate the missing cell frequencies from the equations,

$$\hat{n}_{11k} = n_{1.k}\,\hat{r}_{11k} \qquad\qquad \hat{n}_{21k} = n_{2.k}\,\hat{r}_{21k}$$

More formally this model can be expressed in the two equations

$$r_{11k} = \alpha + (0)p_{1.k} + e_{1k} \qquad\qquad r_{21k} = \gamma + (0)p_{1.k} + e_{2k}$$

These equations state that the lines that show the relationships of r_{11} and r_{21} to p_1. have zero slopes and different intercepts α and γ. The equation used for the estimation of the parameters was obtained by substituting these expressions for r_{11k} and r_{21k} in the basic row equation.

With only the group effect present, as illustrated in Figure 9.3, the two lines overlap. Formally, this can be expressed in the equations

$$r_{11k} = \alpha + \beta p_{1.k} + e_{1k} \qquad\qquad r_{21k} = \alpha + \beta p_{1.k} + e_{2k}$$

In order to estimate the parameters α and β we substitute the expressions above for r_{11k} and r_{21k} in the basic row equation relating the two conditional row proportions and the two marginal proportions. This substitution leads to the equation

$$p_{\cdot 1k} = \alpha + \beta p_{1\cdot k} + e_{2k} + (\alpha + \beta p_{1\cdot k} + e_{1k} - \alpha - \beta p_{1\cdot k} - e_{2k})p_{1\cdot k}$$

Rearranging this equation and cancelling terms we get

$$p_{\cdot 1k} = \alpha + \beta p_{1\cdot k} + e_k$$

where e_k again equals $e_{2k} + (e_{1k} - e_{2k})p_{1\cdot k}$. The usual least squares estimates of α and β are obtained by minimizing the sum $\Sigma\, e_k^2$ with respect to the two parameters. From these estimates we get estimates of r_{11k} and r_{21k} and thereby also estimates of the missing cell entries in each table.

With different intercepts and equal slopes for the two lines, as illustrated in Figure 9.4, the model with both individual and group effects can be expressed formally in the equations

$$r_{11k} = \alpha + \beta p_{1\cdot k} + e_{1k} \qquad\qquad r_{21k} = \gamma + \beta p_{1\cdot k} + e_{2k}$$

In order to estimate the parameters we proceed as before. By substituting the expressions for r_{11k} and r_{21k} in the basic row equation we get the equation

$$p_{\cdot 1k} = \gamma + \beta p_{1\cdot k} + e_{2k} + (\alpha + \beta p_{1\cdot k} + e_{1k} - \gamma - \beta p_{1\cdot k} - e_{2k})p_{1\cdot k}$$

Rearranging and cancelling terms the equation becomes

$$p_{\cdot 1k} = \gamma + (\alpha + \beta - \gamma)p_{1\cdot k} + e_k$$

where e_k equals $e_{2k} + (e_{1k} - e_{2k})p_{1\cdot k}$ as before.

Again we get a simple regression model for the estimation of the parameters, and this model can be used to estimate the intercept γ and the slope $(\alpha + \beta - \gamma)$. But there is no way we can get separate estimates of the three parameters α, β and γ from only two estimates, intercept and slope. Without additional information of some kind, it is therefore not possible to recover the cell entries when both individual and group effects are present. For most cases it would be realistic to assume that both types of effects are present, but we see that it is then not possible to recover the missing cell entries. In Appendix 3 we consider ways of estimating the three parameters when different kinds of additional information are available.

The final model, with group, individual, and interaction effects, is illustrated in Figure 9.5. This model, with different slopes and intercepts, can be expressed formally in the equations

$$r_{11k} = \alpha + \beta p_{1 \cdot k} + e_{1k} \qquad\qquad r_{21k} = \gamma + \delta p_{1 \cdot k} + e_{2k}$$

where r_{11} and r_{21} now have different slopes as well as different intercepts. Substituting these expressions for r_{11k} and r_{21k} in the basic row equation and rearranging the terms we get the equation

$$p_{\cdot 1k} = \gamma + (\alpha - \gamma + \delta) p_{1 \cdot k} + (\beta - \delta) p_{1 \cdot k}^2 + e_k$$

where again $e_k = e_{2k} + (e_{1k} - e_{2k}) p_{1 \cdot k}$. In order to estimate the three parameter combinations γ, $\alpha - \gamma + \delta$ and $\beta - \delta$ one can use multiple regression procedures with $p_{\cdot 1}$ as the dependent and $p_1.$ and $p_{1 \cdot}^2$ as independent variables.

APPENDIX 3

ESTIMATION OF CELL ENTRIES
WITH PARTIAL ADDITIONAL DATA

The example in the fourth section consists of 25 tables, 8 with cell entries and 17 without. Probably the simplest way of estimating the parameters in this example is to use the 8 tables with known cell percentages to estimate the four parameters α, β, γ, and δ. The equation

$$r_{11k} = \alpha + \beta p_{1 \cdot k} + e_{1k}$$

can be used for a simple regression analysis to find estimates of α and β. Similarly, the equation

$$r_{21k} = \gamma + \delta p_{1 \cdot k} + e_{2k}$$

can be used for a simple regression analysis to find estimates of γ and δ. The margins of the other 17 tables can be used in a multiple regression analysis, with the model expressed in the equation

$$p_{\cdot 1k} = \gamma + (\alpha - \gamma + \delta) p_{1 \cdot k} + (\beta - \delta) p_{1 \cdot k}^2 + e_k$$

to find estimates of γ, $\alpha - \gamma + \delta$, and $\beta - \delta$.

By now, we basically have two sets of estimates, and it may be that the two sets of estimates are not consistent with each other. Unless the two sets of estimates do diverge too much, they should be combined to form one set of estimates. For example, we have an estimate c_s from the simple regression and an estimate c_m of γ from the multiple regression analysis. One possible way to combine the two estimates is to let the final estimate c be equal to the mean $(1/2)(c_s + c_m)$. It is also possible to use a weighted mean where the weights could be proportional to the number of tables used for each estimate. That gives

$$c = (8/25)c_s + (17/25)c_m$$

But unless the number of tables in the two groups is very unequal, the two means will not differ greatly.

Similarly, for β and δ we have the estimates b_s and d_s from the two simple regression analyses and, from the multiple regression analysis, the estimate $(b-d)_m$ as an estimate of the difference between the two parameters. One way to get another estimate of β is to find the estimate b_m, where

$$b_m = (b-d)_m + d_s$$

Here we are adding the estimate of δ to the estimate of the difference $\beta-\delta$ to get an estimate of β. An overall estimate b of β can finally be obtained from the mean $b = (1/2)(b_s + b_m)$. The same can be done for the parameter δ. From the simple regression we have the estimate d_s, and another estimate can be found by taking

$$d_m = b_s - (b-d)_m.$$

The final estimate of δ can be taken as the mean $d = (1/2)(d_s + d_m)$.

Finally, for α we have the estimate a_s from the simple regression analysis. From the multiple regression analysis we have the estimate $(a-c+d)_m$ of the parameter combination $(\alpha-\gamma+\delta)$. A possible estimate of α is therefore found by considering

$$a_m = (a-c+d)_m + c - d$$

That is, to the estimate $(a-c+d)_m$ we add the estimate c and subtract the estimate d in order to get an estimate of α. The final estimate can be found as the mean $a = (1/2)(a_s + a_m)$.

The four estimates a, b, c, and d can be used to estimate the conditional row proportions according to the expressions

$$\hat{r}_{11k} = a + bp_{1.k} \qquad\qquad \hat{r}_{21k} = c + dp_{1.k}$$

For the last 8 tables we have the actual values of the r's, and to the extent that the estimated values correspond to the actual values for those tables, we have a partial check on the appropriateness of the model and estimating procedures.

Another set of estimates could be obtained by minimizing the sum $\overset{25}{\underset{}{\Sigma}} e_k^2 + \overset{8}{\underset{}{\Sigma}} e_{1k}^2 + \overset{8}{\underset{}{\Sigma}} e_{2k}^2$ with respect to the four parameters. One would get the resulting estimates by solving the four normal equations for the four estimators. For a discussion of this and other estimating procedures, see Boyd and Iversen.[22] One could also proceed in a more stepwise fashion. By assuming that there is no interaction effect, there would be only three parameters to estimate. If the resulting estimates can be used to recover the known r's, it may not be necessary to go to the model with four parameters.

APPENDIX 4

GENERALIZATIONS TO LARGER TABLES

With two nominal variables forming tables with I rows and J columns, there is a basic identity for the kth table relating the conditional row proportions denoted by r's, the marginal row proportions $p_1.$'s and the jth margin column proportion $p_{.jk}$, which can be written

$$p_{.jk} = r_{1jk}p_{1.k} + r_{2jk}p_{2.k} + \ldots + r_{Ijk}p_{I.k}.$$

In order to estimate the r's, we need to specify a model for how the r's are determined, either by the row proportions or some other variables. Perhaps the simplest such model is the one that corresponds to the model above with individual effects only. This model is characterized by having r_{ij} be almost constant from table to table. For r_{ijk} this model can be expressed in the equation

$$r_{ijk} = \alpha_{ij} + e_{ijk}$$

By substituting for all the r's in the equation above we get

$$p_{.jk} = \alpha_{1j}p_{1.k} + \alpha_{2j}p_{2.k} + \ldots + \alpha_{Ij}p_{I.k} + e_k - \alpha_{Ij}$$
$$= (\alpha_{1j} - \alpha_{Ij})p_{1.k} + \ldots + (\alpha_{I-1,j} - \alpha_{Ij})p_{\bar{I}-1,.k} + e_k$$

where e_k becomes the appropriate residual term.

Regression methods can be used to estimate the α's and thereby the r's in the jth column of all the tables. With J columns we have at least $J - 1$ of these analyses to do in order to estimate all the cell entries. The r's in the last column can be found by subtraction, since the r's are conditional row proportions and add to one in each row.

Going beyond this model and trying to bring in notions of group and interaction effects, things become somewhat more complicated. With more than two categories we need to make the r's functions of several marginal proportions in order to capture the complete group composition. With four categories, Catholic, Protestant, Jewish, and other, we should write r as a function of three categories in order to get the full group effect included in the model. But with I rows in the tables, we can only estimate $I(I + 1)/2$ parameters using regression analysis the way it has been done above. For $I = 4$ we can estimate ten parameters. One possible model would then be to have the r's expressed as functions of the p's according to the equations

$$r_{1jk} = \alpha_{0j} + \alpha_{1j}p_{1 \cdot k} + \alpha_{2j}p_{2 \cdot k} + e_{1k}$$
$$r_{2jk} = \beta_{0j} + \beta_{1j}p_{1 \cdot k} + \beta_{2j}p_{2 \cdot k} + e_{2k}$$
$$r_{3jk} = \gamma_{0j} + \gamma_{3j}p_{3 \cdot k} + e_{3k}$$
$$r_{4jk} = \delta_{0j} + \delta_{4j}p_{4 \cdot k} + e_{4k}$$

But we cannot write each r as a function of all three marginal proportions, because that would require a total of 16 parameters. It is not necessary to write the r's as functions of all four marginal proportions since the proportions always add to one for each table. But we will never be able to estimate 16 parameters, which means that we have to make a choice between competing models. Only with additional data of some kind might it be possible to estimate all 16 parameters.

APPENDIX 5

ESTIMATION OF INDIVIDUAL LEVEL RELATIONSHIPS WITHOUT HAVING BIVARIATE DISTRIBUTIONS FOR INTERVAL LEVEL VARIABLES

For the individual-level data in the kth table, we assume that the relationship between X and Y can be expressed by the equation

$$y_{ik} = a_k + b_k x_{ik} + e_{ik}$$

where i refers to the ith observation and k to the kth group. By adding over all the observations in the group and dividing by the number of observations we get the basic row equation

$$\bar{y}_k = a_k + b_k \bar{x}_k$$

relating the group means, intercept and slope. The intercept a_k corresponds to r_{21k} in the two category nominal case and the slope b_k corresponds to the difference $r_{11k} - r_{21k}$. The two means correspond to the two marginal proportions. Since a proportion is a special case of a mean when the variable is scored 0 and 1, the correspondence is complete.

In order to specify a model that will enable us to estimate the intercept and slope above, it is now natural to let the group variable be measured by the mean $\bar{x}$. Just as we had a model with the r's depending on $p_{1.k}$, we now propose a model that has a_k and b_k depending on $\bar{x}_k$. To be consistent with the earlier case, the model is expressed in the equations

$$a_k = \gamma + \delta \bar{x}_k + e_{1k}$$
$$b_k = (\alpha - \gamma) + (\beta - \delta)\bar{x}_k + e_{2k}$$

Because of the two parameter differences it may look as if the model is written out in an unnecessarily complicated way, but it has to be remembered that b_k corresponds to the difference $r_{11k} - r_{21k}$, and that is why the model is written out with differences between the parameters. Substituting for a_k and b_k from this model into the basic row equation above we get the equation

$$\bar{y}_k = \gamma + (\alpha - \gamma + \delta)\bar{x}_k + (\beta - \delta)\bar{x}_k^2 + e_k$$

where $e_k = e_{1k} + e_{2k}\bar{x}_k$. Aside from a slight and unimportant reformulation of the residual term, this is exactly the same equation as we had for the most general case in the third section with the marginal proportions replaced by the means of the marginal distributions. Thus, the whole discussion in that section on the estimation of the parameters with the presence of individual, group, and interaction effects applies directly here.

The various effects show up in the following patterns for the relationship between X and Y in the various groups. When there is only an individual effect present, we have from the third section that $\beta = \delta = 0$. That means that the intercept and slope in the kth group become

$$a_k = \gamma + e_{1k} \qquad\qquad b_k = \alpha - \gamma + e_{2k}$$

Thus, the relationship between X and Y is characterized by the same regression line in each of the groups in this case. With only the group effect present we have $\alpha = \gamma$ and $\beta = \delta$. Thus, the intercept and slope become

$$a_k = \alpha + \beta \bar{x}_k + e_{1k} \qquad\qquad b_k = e_{2k}$$

Here the intercept in each group depends on the mean of X in the group while the slope is equal to zero except for a small residual term. This corresponds to what we have in the third section where the presence of only the group effect implies that the two variables are not related within each group.

With both individual and group effects present, but no interaction effect, we have $\beta = \delta$. In that case the intercept and slope in the kth group become

$$a_k = \gamma + \beta \bar{x}_k + e_{1k} \qquad\qquad b_k = \alpha - \gamma + e_{2k}$$

This means that the regression line in each group has a nonzero slope, and that all the groups have the same slope except for the residual term. The intercepts differ from group to group and are functions of the group mean. Finally, with all three effects present, the relationship between X and Y is characterized by regression lines that have both different slopes and intercepts in the various groups. And both the slopes and intercepts depend linearly on the group means.

With only the individual effect present we can estimate the common slopes and intercepts, since the equation relating the group means and the parameters reduces to

$$\bar{y}_k = \gamma + (\alpha - \gamma)\bar{x}_k + e_k$$

Simple regression analysis with the observed means as the two variables will give us estimates of the two parameters above.

With only the group effect present the same equation reduces to

$$\bar{y}_k = \alpha + \beta\bar{x}_k + e_k$$

and again we get a linear relationship between the group means. With both the group- and individual-level effect present we get

$$\bar{y}_k = \gamma + (\alpha - \gamma + \delta)\,\bar{x}_k + e_k$$

which also specifies a linear relationship between the group means. Thus, we get the same difficulty with interval level data as with nominal level data, that one cannot distinguish between the three cases above on the basis of the group means alone. This model is discussed extensively by Boyd and Iversen.[23]

NOTES

1. W. S. Robinson, "Ecological Correlation and the Behavior of Individuals," *American Sociological Review* 15 (1950), 351-357.

2. Leo Goodman, "Ecological Regressions and the Behavior of Individuals," *American Sociological Review* 18 (1953), 663-664.

3. A. Mandansky, "Least Squares Estimation in Finite Markov Processes," *Psychometrika* 24 (1959), 137-44; L. G. Telser, "Least Squares Estimation of Transition Probabilities," in C. Christ (ed.) *Measurement in Economics* (Stanford: Stanford University Press, 1963), 270-292; T. C. Lee, G. G. Judge, and A. Zellner, "Maximum Likelihood and Bayesian Estimation of Transition Probabilities," *Journal of the American Statistical Association* 63 (1968), 1162-1179; Donald Stokes, "Ecological Regression as a Game with Nature," in J. L. Bernd (ed.) *Mathematical Applications in Political Science* (Charlottesville: University Press of Virginia, 1969), 62-83; Gudmund Iversen, *Estimation of Cell Entries in Contingency Tables When Only Margins Are Observed,* Ph.D. dissertation, Harvard University, 1969.

4. W. S. Robinson, "Ecological Correlation and the Behavior of Individuals."

5. O. D. Duncan and B. Davis, "An Alternative to Ecological Correlation," *American Sociological Review* 18 (1953), 665-666.

6. Leo Goodman, "Some Alternatives to Ecological Correlation," *American Journal of Sociology* 64 (1959), 610-625.

7. G. A. Miller, "Finite Markov Processes in Psychology," *Psychometrika* 17 (1952), 149-167.

8. Leo Goodman, "Ecological Regressions and the Behavior of Individuals," "Some Alternatives to Ecological Correlation."

9. W. S. Robinson, "Ecological Correlation and the Behavior of Individuals."

10. Gudmund Iversen, "Recovering Individual Data in the Presence of Group and Individual Effects," *American Journal of Sociology* 79 (1973), 420-434.

11. J. A. Davis, J. L. Spaeth, and C. Huson, "A Technique for Analyzing the Effects of Group Composition," *American Sociological Review* 26 (1961), 215-225.

12. *Ibid.*

13. Leo Goodman, "Some Alternatives to Ecological Correlation;" O. D. Duncan, R. P. Cuzzort, and B. Duncan, *Statistical Geography: Problems in Analyzing Areal Data* (Glencoe: The Free Press, 1961); R. Boudon, "Proprietes Individuelles et Proprietes Collectives: un Probleme d'Analyse Ecologique," *Revue Francaise de Sociologie* 4 (1963), 275-299; L. H. Boyd, Jr. and G. Iversen, *Contextual Behavior: Concepts and Statistical Techniques* (Belmont, CA: Wadsworth, 1979).

14. *Ibid.*

15. Gudmund Iversen, "Recovering Individual Data in the Presence of Group and Individual Effects," pp. 420-434.

16. L. H. Boyd and G. Iversen, *Contextual Behavior.*

17. Donald Stokes, "Ecological Regression as a Game with Nature."

18. L. H. Boyd, Jr., *Multiple Level Analysis with Complete and Incomplete Data,* Ph.D. dissertation, University of Michigan, 1971.

19. L. H. Boyd and G. Iversen, *Contextual Analysis.*

20. Gudmund Iversen, *Estimation of Cell Entries in Contingency Tables.*

21. Robinson, "Ecological Correlation and the Behavior of Individuals."

22. L. H. Boyd and G. Iversen, *Contextual Analysis.*

23. *Ibid.*

EDITORS' POSTSCRIPT

Much of the original impetus behind this volume was provided by an extended investigation of American political history carried out by the editors with the support of National Science Foundation Grants (GS-28913, GS-42717, GS-28911, GS-42730, and GS-42733). While each of us had worked more or less extensively with the source material of historical political behavior on earlier occasions, this experience brought sharply to our attention the rich opportunities for advancement of social scientific knowledge which these sources afford, opportunities which we were able to realize in only the most limited ways. The experience, moreover, forcefully reminded us of the complexities and difficulties peculiar to these sources, particularly the data provided by historical election returns, and suggested that their effective use required methodological approaches somewhat different than those employed in other areas of systematic, quantitative political inquiry.

The research opportunities and the difficulties, complexities, and methodological issues presented by these sources seemed to us of sufficient importance to merit more extended discussion. To do so effectively, however, required that we draw upon the experience and expertise of other scholars. Thus, we must begin our acknowledgments by expressing our gratitude to the other authors who generously agreed to contribute to this volume. We are also indebted to the National Science Foundation. The Foundation did not directly support this volume, but our own contributions would have been impossible without the experience gained through research conducted with its support.

It is commonplace to observe—and, indeed, we have stated in this volume—that computers have allowed the creation of enormous data archives. While it is true that computers permitted this development, computers did not make it happen. Computers are used everywhere, but relatively few areas of social science research have established high quality data archives to facilitate secondary analysis. There is an understandable desire by researchers to protect their data from further scrutiny; thus special efforts are required to bring together high quality data from a variety of sources. Two men, Angus Campbell and Warren E. Miller, deserve special recognition for their leadership in establishing this practice in political analysis.

Warren Miller founded the Inter-university Consortium for Political and Social Research, a primary mechanism for access to basic data, directed it through its formative years, and has remained a loyal supporter and source of advice and guidance. Without the data provided by the Consortium, our own research, and that of countless other social scientists, would have been impossible. We owe as well a very large personal debt to Warren. Through the years, Warren has aided and assisted us in ways too numerous to mention; he has shown us many kindnesses, and we have learned much from his scholarship.

We must end our acknowledgments on a sadder note. We cannot adequately express our deep indebtedness to the late Angus Campbell. Angus provided a model of scholarship and of personal integrity. He was always a source of wise and kind counsel. He encouraged and facilitated the establishment of the principle of data sharing from which we have all benefited. We are sure that the other contributors will join us in modestly dedicating this volume to Angus. He enriched us all; we are poorer for his passing.

INDEX

ABOUT THE AUTHORS

HOWARD W. ALLEN is Professor of History at Southern Illinois University at Carbondale. He received his Ph.D. in history from the University of Washington. He is author of several articles on American political history as well as *Poindexter of Washington: A Study of Progressive Politics.*

KAY WARREN ALLEN completed her master's degree in history at Southern Illinois University in 1977. She is presently employed in the Office of Institutional Research and Studies at Southern Illinois University at Carbondale.

ERIK W. AUSTIN is Senior Research Associate in the Center for Political Studies of the Institute for Social Research, and Director of Archival Development of the Inter-university Consortium for Political and Social Research, located at The University of Michigan. He received an A.B. degree from Dartmouth College, an M.A. from The University of Michigan (both in history) and is currently working on a Ph.D. degree in history at The University of Michigan. He is the author of several articles on electoral history and quantitative data resources for the study of historical politics.

WALTER DEAN BURNHAM is Professor of Political Science at Massachusetts Institute of Technology. He is the author of *Presidential Ballots, 1836-1892* and *Critical Elections and the Mainsprings of American Politics.* In addition, he has edited and contributed to *The American Party Systems* and *American Politics and Public Policy,* and is the author of numerous articles about American electoral politics.

JEROME M. CLUBB is Executive Director of the Inter-university Consortium for Political and Social Research, a Research Scientist in the Center for Political Studies of the Institute for Social Research, and Professor of History, The University of Michigan. He has written a number of articles on American political development and social history, and is an author or editor of several books including, most recently, *Partisan Realignment: Voters, Parties, and Government in American History* with William H. Flanigan and Nancy H. Zingale.

WILLIAM H. FLANIGAN is Professor of Political Science at the University of Minnesota. He received his Ph.D. in political science from Yale University. His previous publications include (with Nancy H. Zingale) *Political Behavior of the American Electorate*, as editor (with Joel H. Silbey and Allan G. Bogue) *The History of American Electoral Behavior*, and most recently *Partisan Realignment: Voters, Parties, and Government in American History* with Jerome M. Clubb and Nancy H. Zingale.

GUDMUND R. IVERSEN did his undergraduate work at the University of Oslo, has master's degrees in mathematics and sociology from the University of Michigan and a Ph.D. in statistics from Harvard University. He has taught at The University of Michigan, where he also directed the summer training program of the Inter-university Consortium for Political and Social Research. Currently he is Professor of Statistics and Director of the Center for Social and Policy Studies at Swarthmore College. He has written several texts on statistics for the social sciences, and he is the coauthor with Lawrence H. Boyd of *Contextual Behavior: Concepts and Statistical Techniques*.

RAY M. SHORTRIDGE is managing partner of Shortridge Farms and an Assistant Professor in the Political Science Department at the University of Louisville. He received his Ph.D. in history from The University of Michigan. He is author of a number of articles and papers concerned with American political history and with methods of historical research.

MICHAEL W. TRAUGOTT is Associate Research Scientist in the Center for Political Studies and Lecturer in the Department of Political Science at The University of Michigan. He is also Director of Resource Development at the Inter-university Consortium for Political and Social Research. He did his undergraduate work at Princeton University and received his Ph.D. in political science from The University of Michigan. He is the author of several articles on American electoral behavior and campaigning, and coauthored *Using Computers* with Jerome M. Clubb.

NANCY H. ZINGALE is Associate Professor and Chairman of the Political Science Department at the College of St. Thomas. She received her Ph.D. in political science from the University of Minnesota. She is coauthor (with William H. Flanigan) of *Political Behavior of the American Electorate* and author of "Third Party Alignments in a Two-Party System: The Case of Minnesota" in *The History of American Electoral Behavior*. Recently she coauthored (with Jerome M. Clubb and William H. Flanigan) *Partisan Realignment: Voters, Parties, and Government in American History*.